The Government Wears Prada

The Government Wears Prada

Why taxes will keep rising and what Canadians can do about it

Colin Craig

ISBN: 1505581133
ISBN 13: 9781505581133

CONTENTS

Introduction · vii

Part One: Why taxes keep rising and how it will impact you · · · · · 1

1   The Age of Denial · 3

2   Storm Clouds Raining on Your Wallet · · · · · · · · · · · · · · · · · · 24

Part Two: The taxes we pay and the role of government · · · · · · · 33

3   The Government Taketh ... and Taketh ... and Taketh · · · · · · · · · · 35

4   What's the Role of Government? · 42

Part Three: The five forces behind wasteful spending
and what you can do about it · 69

5   Special Interest Groups · 71

6   Government Employee Unions · 98

7   The Bureaucracy · 130

8   The Politicians · 170

9   The Public · 204

10   Conclusion · 219

Acknowledgements · 227

Endnotes · 229

About the Author · 249

Index · 251

INTRODUCTION

The Wilsons are like many Canadian families. They have no idea what is coming.

Like many of us they try to read the newspaper and pay attention to what's going on, but they're not the type to read academic reports and government budget documents on Friday nights.

No, they're normal people.

In many respects, they're a great example of the average Canadian family. Mitch and Katie Wilson live in a modest home in Winnipeg. The young couple's house isn't in a wealthy suburb, but it's not in the core area either; it's somewhere in between.

Like many Canadians, they have a mortgage on their bungalow and a loan for their mini-van. During the day, Mitch uses the new van as he completes his training as an electrician. Katie takes care of their children and teaches music to local kids in the family's garage during the evenings. Mitch renovated it into a comfortable classroom for teaching several years ago. To save money he did the work himself, learning along the way and leaning on relatives a bit here and there.

Between their small music lesson business and Mitch's electrician income the couple makes ends meet. They're not rich, but they're not poor either – they're actually not far off the average household income in Canada. But lately Katie has been finding it harder and harder to balance the family budget.

"Every time I open the paper there seems to be a story about a tax increase or a government fee going up," says the young mom. "What's troubling is that taxes and fees always seem to go up faster than our household income. Whether it's the electricity bill, property taxes or new fees for this, that or the other thing, we're really feeling the squeeze."

Sadly, she's right. Her family's property tax bill, hydro bill, water and sewer charges and school tax bill have all been going up faster than her household's income in recent years. Not to mention, her provincial government recently raised the sales tax and started charging it on such necessities as home insurance and haircuts. Provincial tax increases in both 2012 and 2013 were 25-year record highs.

What Katie, Mitch and many other people in Canada don't realize is we're on track for things to continue to get worse. Much worse.

The financial pain the Wilsons are experiencing due to government taxes and fees going up is actually being felt by many other Canadian families across the country right now.

If you don't believe it, try asking a senior citizen how much their Canada Pension Plan (CPP) cheques went up this year. Then ask them if their property tax bill went up by the same percentage. Any senior with good record-keeping skills will invariably show you their CPP only went up by a bit while their property taxes went up by a higher rate. Chances are they'll be able to tell you about other taxes and fees going up too.

The reality is that many government decisions around taxation and spending simply aren't sustainable for many seniors, families like the Wilsons, businesses and countless other taxpayers. Something has to change.

And that's why I decided to write this book.

I wanted to give everyday Canadians a plain-English, quick briefing on why taxes keep rising, why we're on track for them to rise substantially over time and, most importantly, what people can do about the problem.

I've spent more than a decade working in multiple governments and for a national taxpayers' watchdog organization, the Canadian Taxpayers Federation. I feel like I've had a front-row seat to observing the many inefficient ways governments spend the money we already give them.

I have also read up on the major problems facing Canada – the ones that politicians don't seem to want to talk about when they're busy announcing new spending on such nice-to-have items as new stadiums, museums and other pet projects.

In *The Government Wears Prada* I look at four major financial challenges that are contributing to tax increases right now and will cause substantial increases in the future. The four challenges include:

- *Shrinking tax base*
- *Rising health care costs*
- *The nation's infrastructure deficit*
- *Government employee pension problems*

While "shrinking tax base" may sound really dull, it's part of a problem the *Globe and Mail* has called a "ticking time bomb."

Federal government data shows that in 2010, there were about 4.9 people of working age for every person over the age of 65 in Canada. By 2030 that ratio is expected to drop to just 2.7 working-age people for every person over 65.

Imagine the impact on government revenues as our nation's share of retired people increases while our share of working age people decreases. That's not a slight against senior citizens, it's just a reality that retired people earn less and thus pay less in taxes. How will Canada cope with that cash crunch?

At the same time, more older people in Canada means more pricey health services such as triple-bypass heart surgery, hip replacements and long-term care. Throw in deferred bills for government infrastructure like roads and bridges, and costly government employee pension problems, and one doozy of a financial storm is facing our nation. Even worse, these problems aren't decades away; they're starting to impact governments now.

And then, of course, there's the reality that total government debt in Canada is over $1 trillion. Yes, there are no pennies saved for the financial storm that's brewing.

What's going on in Canada right now is akin to a 63-year-old, with an average income, no retirement savings, a $300,000 mortgage, loans on the family's two vehicles and $20,000 in credit card debt going out and buying a sports car to drive around in the summer … all the while hoping to retire in a few years. It's just not responsible.

But *The Government Wears Prada* isn't all doom and gloom … far from it.

After touching on the aforementioned four major financial challenges, I explore some good news: governments typically behave like Prada-wearing, high-end-car-driving, latte-sipping organizations that act as though money is no object.

I know that sounds odd, but given that so many tax dollars are spent lavishly or inefficiently each year, if we can correct the problems, we can use the savings to address some of the four major cost pressures. Thus, we can then prevent or mitigate some of the tax increases we're facing.

Throughout the book, I explore numerous examples of wasteful government spending, from Alberta politicians being paid an extra $1,000 per month for doing absolutely nothing to government-run Tim Hortons franchises that are losing a small fortune each year. Regina taxpayers having to pay for season tickets to Montreal's Canadian Football League team is another example that just couldn't be ignored.

Perhaps most importantly, I spend the bulk of the book looking at *why* inefficient spending happens in the first place. I examine five factors that contribute significantly to wasteful and inefficient spending:

- *Special interest groups*
- *Government employee unions*
- *The bureaucracies*
- *The politicians*
- *The public*

Yes, many people gripe about the first four categories, but few seem to realize the public is at fault too. After all, who has been letting governments waste so many of our tax dollars year after year?

Some people think there's nothing that can be done about nonsensical government spending decisions, but that's simply not true. For each problem I identify in this book, I put forward concrete solutions. At the same time, I explain what everyday Canadians can do to impact government decisions for the better.

As I promised a "quick briefing" on a complex matter, let's get on with it.

"Taxpayers of Canada unite; you have nothing to lose but a tax increase."
– Colin Craig

PART ONE

Why taxes keep rising and how it will impact you

CHAPTER 1

The Age of Denial

Governments across Canada are facing absolutely enormous expenses now and in the future. With that in mind, it's amazing so many wasteful and inefficient spending practices persist.

The whole situation reminds me of the famous quote: *"Nero fiddled while Rome burned."*

The saying is based on Roman Emperor Nero, who ruled from AD54 to AD68.[1] The tale goes that Nero played a fiddle and fooled around as fire ran rampant in Rome during the summer of AD64.

Fiddles weren't around back then and some question whether Nero really did neglect the fire, but nonetheless the saying endures. The modern day meaning is to suggest someone isn't taking a problem seriously.

And that's what most governments in Canada are doing: fiddling away, letting wasteful and inefficient spending carry on while enormous financial problems continue to grow.

I'll explore the major financial challenges facing governments in Canada in a moment, but in the meantime, here are a few examples of frivolous spending.

In May 2012 the CEO of Newfoundland and Labrador's largest hospital held a press conference and tried to explain how a government-run hospital could do the unthinkable – operate a Tim Hortons and lose a staggering $260,000 serving up double-doubles and doughnuts the year before.

"Let me tell you why that happens," Vickie Kaminski, CEO of the largest hospital in Newfoundland and Labrador, told the *CBC*. *"We charge you $1.94 for that large coffee, but we insist that the staff who are pouring that coffee are*

Eastern Health staff, and they get paid $28 an hour, and no Tim Hortons pays that.[2]

I use the word "unthinkable" because Tim Hortons is, of course, widely recognized for being a very profitable venture, a "license to print money" so to speak. Across the country the franchise is known for long drive-through lineups and a steady flow of walk-in customers who are drawn to its addictive coffee.

Not surprisingly, when the hospital decided to open its own Tim Hortons in 1995, it projected nothing but success.

During an interview with *CBC News* at the opening of the new franchise, the hospital's former administrator claimed the venture would *"make a profit of about $250,000-300,000 a year and that will help us...pay the salaries of seven nurses."*[3]

Perhaps the administrator wasn't expecting to have labour costs that were double what a Tim Hortons run by the private sector would pay. Regardless, things certainly didn't pan out.

But the Newfoundland and Labrador hospital isn't the only hospital running a Tim Hortons or public cafeteria and losing money:

- According to a May 31, 2012, *National Post* story, a government-run Tim Hortons at a hospital in Windsor, ON, lost about $265,000 annually.[4]
- In Nova Scotia, *CTV News* reported the Queen Elizabeth II Health Sciences Centre lost a mind-numbing $1.4 million at its four government-run Tim Hortons locations in 2013.[5]
- Research by the Canadian Taxpayers Federation showed health regions in Manitoba and Saskatchewan had also been losing significant sums selling chocolate bars and sandwiches in hospital cafeterias.

If those government waste stories sound ridiculous, consider how tax dollars were spent in Toronto, a city that has complained for years about not having enough money to fix the city's infrastructure.

The City of Toronto paid people to go around with clipboards and audit the amount of shade in city parks.[6] The city also paid people to dress as though they were homeless. The *Toronto Sun* noted in a March 23, 2009, article that people were paid $100 as part of an attempt to make sure real homeless people were accurately counted.[7] Many rightly suggested the funds could have been better spent helping real homeless people rather than the imposters.

But those examples pale in comparison to some revelations found in an audit of the Toronto District School Board.

According to a Dec. 6, 2012, *Toronto Star* story, the cost for school board staff to install a pencil sharpener worked out to be $143 – for putting in a whopping four screws.[8] On another occasion the installation cost was "only" $118; perhaps staff invested in a power drill after the first sharpener was installed.

The cost to install a $127 whiteboard: $2,441. A whopping $190 was spent to replace a $126 toilet seat, $312 was spent to replace a couple of smoke detectors (that cost $58 each to buy) and $1,614 was spent to paint a vice-principal's office (49 hours of work).

There were so many obscene examples that it was clear to anyone reading the news that it wasn't a case of a seemingly small job turning into something much bigger. There was a pattern emerging.

Well, to everyone except Jimmy Hazel, the employee union's boss. Hazel told the *Star*:

"We don't need to f—— prove anything to anybody about costs."[9]

At least we know where Mr. Hazel stands.

In Winnipeg, city hall and the local health region decided to spend $5,000 on a website that noted sidewalk conditions in the winter (slippery, dry, etc.).[10] The goal was to try to prevent slips and falls.

The idea probably came from the right intentions, but it ignored the fact that Winnipeggers instinctively assume sidewalks are icy in the winter. After a single season and a fair amount of mocking on Twitter, the sidewalk conditions website vanished and so did $5,000 of taxpayers' money.

One could go on and on with more questionable examples of government spending from across the country. Whether it's the City of Regina giving $450 for a "Pickleball" tournament, the City of Edmonton spending $5,000 on a Haiku poetry contest or much bigger problems such as the federal long-gun registry and the billions that were wasted on a system that hoped hardened criminals would kindly register their guns before popping someone off.[11] [12]

The notion of governments wasting taxpayers' money is nothing new. Again, I raise these anecdotes because they're great illustrations of just how recklessly many governments across the country are behaving despite facing massive financial problems.

Would you go out and buy a cruise to the Bahamas if you had two existing car loans, $300,000 owing on your mortgage, $25,000 in credit card debt and dreams of retiring in the near future? Chances are the answer would be "no." Most people would probably cut back on unnecessary household expenses so that they could start tackling debt and put aside some savings. Governments are doing the opposite.

Financial Storm Clouds On The Horizon

I believe that in 10 to 20 years, many who watch government spending closely will think of this period as "the age of denial."

I say that because the four major financial challenges facing governments in Canada are well documented. There are countless government and third-party reports on the four issues I'll discuss momentarily. Politicians foolishly spending money today can't claim for a second that the looming financial problems came out of nowhere and couldn't be foreseen.

In fact, I often think of these challenges facing governments (and obviously taxpayers) as dark storm clouds on the horizon – everyone can see them coming.

When really dark storm clouds start to appear in the distance, most sensible people take a second to think about whether or not their car windows are closed or if they have left anything outside that should be brought into the house. That of course is responsible planning.

Yet in government, there has, in most cases, been anything but responsible planning. Governments have known for years about four massive financial storm clouds coming their way, but most haven't done anything about it – such as put aside a bit of savings.

Many of our elected officials saw the storm clouds coming and proceeded to go inside the house, turn on the game and do some online shopping.

As a whole they're just not taking the situation seriously enough.

Later I'll explain why wasteful spending persists in government and demonstrate just how widespread it is, but in the meantime let's explore the four financial storm clouds.

Storm Cloud #1: The Shrinking Tax Base

"Who orders coffee for a five-year-old?" my dad asks with a chuckle.

He was referring to something his father did when the two of them went to a local diner the day after his father returned home from the Second World War. It was a pretty special occasion for my dad, as he had only met his father the day before.

You see, my dad was born in 1940, shortly after his father had left for Europe. As a result, my dad never had a chance to meet his father until 1945, when he was five years old.

The two had set out for breakfast at a local diner in downtown Winnipeg that day at the urging of my grandmother. She wanted my grandfather to immediately start making up for lost time with my dad so going out for breakfast the day after his return seemed like a good way to start some good old-fashioned male bonding.

My dad doesn't recall the waitress's reaction when his father ordered him a cup of coffee, but no doubt she witnessed similar awkward outings throughout the year. After all, there were plenty of troops who suddenly found themselves in the same situation as my grandfather: returning home from the war to young kids they hadn't seen in years or had never met.

The lack of experience ordering breakfast for children would soon change, though, as the baby boom was about to begin.

Just as my dad would soon have a sibling, so would thousands of other kids across the country. Canada, like many other countries around the world, experienced a huge spike in the number of child-births after the war. This "baby boom" generation, as they would come to be known, is defined by Statistics Canada as those born between 1946 and 1965.[13]

For perspective, the average woman in Canada gave birth to about 2.6 children as of 1936.[14] Following the war, the number of births per woman jumped, peaking at 3.9 children as of 1959.[15] Fast-forward to the 1981-2011 era and the number of childbirths per woman in Canada plummeted to about half that rate, between 1.5 and 1.7 per woman.[16]

According to the 2011 census, 9.6 million Canadians (29% or approximately three out of every 10 of us) are part of the baby boom generation.[17] Some of those people weren't born in Canada, but they're still part of that huge cohort.

For years the baby boomers were a huge economic boon to the country. The boomers hit the work force, produced enormous amounts of goods and services for the nation, paid a fortune in taxes and kept this country chugging along for decades.

But those were the good old days. Add 65 years to the beginning of the baby boom generation (1946) and you'll see that the first of that massive wave of people hit retirement age in 2011.

You might be thinking – *"But Canada's population is expected to continue growing ... why does this matter?"*

You would be correct that Canada's population continues to grow – I'm not aware of any projections showing a decrease in our population anytime soon. The problem is the number of people coming into the country through immigration, as well as the number of childbirths happening each year, just isn't keeping up with the huge wave of baby boomers that are retiring every day.

The composition of Canada's population is changing. It's becoming older and older.

Consider how the numbers are expected to play out in the future. According to the 2011 Fiscal Sustainability Report, authored by the federal's government's *Office of the Parliamentary Budget Officer,* the ratio of working-age people (ages 15-64) to those over the age of 65 is as follows:[18]

- **1971** – 7.8 working-age people for every 1 retiree
- **2010** – 4.9 working-age people for every 1 retiree
- **2030** – 2.7 working-age people for every 1 retiree

This ratio is known as the "dependency ratio" and you can see how Canada is facing a seismic shift.

Why is this a major challenge for taxpayers and governments?

It's simple. When you retire you tend to earn less money and thus you pay less in taxes. Think about someone who is 55 years old and making $60,000 or so per year. They're going to pay a lot more in income taxes and sales taxes than a 70-year old retired senior who is getting by on $25,000 per year in combined income from the Canada Pension Plan and other retirement income they may have.

According to Statistics Canada, the median income of those in the 45 to 54 age block was $41,300 in 2011. Yet, for the 65 years of age and older category the median income was only $23,700.[19]

This reality probably isn't a shock to many people – it's fairly common knowledge. The reason I bring it up is to show how, in terms of tax revenue, governments benefit a lot more from having more people working rather than retired. Think of the cash crunch governments will face as a huge segment of the population starts to retire.

And let me be clear for a second: I'm not criticizing seniors. Most seniors paid their share of taxes during their working years; now it's their turn to kick up their heels and retire. Yet, governments spent all the tax dollars the baby boomers contributed during their working years and didn't save any for this cash crunch.

You can see why the federal government has bureaucrats studying this issue and why it's called the "shrinking tax base." The implications are absolutely immense for governments financially. A February 2010 article in the *Globe and Mail* called this problem a "demographic time bomb."[20]

The bottom line of the shrinking tax base problem is that as time marches on, Canada's population is going to continue to be made up more and more of retired people relative to the number of people working. Experts predict governments are either going to have to raise taxes, cut spending or a combination of the two.

If you're trying to think of an easy way to explain this to a friend or if this issue still doesn't make sense to you, think of it this way.

Imagine you're in your 50s and you have four siblings.

Between the five of you, you do a lot for your 75-year-old mother. The five of you chip in for her pills, shovel her snow, cut her grass, take her out for dinner four times a week, help clean her house, pick up her groceries, etc. It's a bit challenging but the five of you get by.

Now imagine you're in the year 2030 and dear old mom needs more help than ever. On top of that two of your siblings are retired and can no longer chip in for mom's needs as they have their own problems to worry about. Another sibling can now only help about half as much as she once did.

Instead of five of you taking care of dear old mom, there are now just two and a half people taking care of her.

This example isn't a perfect comparison with what's happening in Canada, but you get the idea – those still taking care of mom are going to have to cut back on her perks or you and your siblings will have to start doing a lot more – it's that simple.

That's similar to what is going to be happening in Canada, but on a much larger scale.

Storm Cloud #2: Rising Health Care Costs

Try visiting a local seniors' centre with a clipboard and ask 15 random seniors what health care services they've received from the government in the past few years.

Then take your clipboard over to a nearby junior high school and ask a bunch of teens the same question.

Once you weed out the smart-aleck answers provided by the teens (and perhaps one or two from wily seniors), you would probably find the seniors tended to have more expensive health procedures such as hip replacements, cancer treatment and open-heart surgery while the local teens tended to have less expensive services such as annual check-ups or mending the odd broken bone from playing hockey or ringette.

This simple exercise demonstrates a compounding challenge with our nation's aging population: as people get older they require more, and more expensive, health care.

A 2011 report titled *National Health Expenditure Trends 1975 to 2011* by the Canadian Institute for Health Information (CIHI), a non-profit organization that is funded by government and crunches all kinds of health care numbers from waiting lists to health expenditures, illustrates the cost of health services by age group quite clearly.[21]

Table 1: Provincial/Territorial Average Per Capita Health Care Spending (2009)

Age	Average Annual Expenditure
<1	$9,121.36
1-4	$1,450.68
5-9	$1,250.32
10-14	$1,244.35
15-19	$1,498.06
20-24	$1,685.99
25-29	$1,974.00
30-34	$2,115.70
35-39	$2,102.52
40-44	$2,127.95
45-49	$2,369.70
50-54	$2,817.09
55-59	$3,408.45
60-64	$4,212.80
65-69	$6,072.71
70-74	$8,405.89
75-79	$11,482.61
80-84	$14,886.59
85-89	$22,630.99
90+	$24,729.84

Table 1 shows the average Canadian infant (under one year) costs the health care system a small fortune when they're born: $9,121. However, after someone's first birthday, his or her health care usage drops off dramatically (not that you really have any say in the matter during the early years!).

Those ranging from one year to 59 years of age "only" cost the Canadian health care system $1,244-$3,408 per year. I say "only" because once someone hits 60, his or her cost to the system really starts to take off.

People in the 60-64 bracket cost an average of $4,212 while individuals between 70 and 74 cost the system an average of $8,405. The amounts keep climbing until people hit 90 and cost a whopping $24,729 per year.

It's great that Canadians are living longer. But as a huge wave of our population moves into the more expensive age categories, experts predict the health care system's costs will go through the roof.

The CIHI itself doesn't seem to be in that camp ... at least not yet. Its 2011 report suggests the aging population is "manageable" in terms of what it will cost the health care system.[22] CIHI claims that while health spending in Canada increased by 7.4% each year on average from 1998 to 2008, an aging population only contributed to about 0.8% of the average increase.[23]

Yet, 0.8% per year compounded over a decade adds up quickly. Once a decade goes by, that's an extra 8.3% on a system that is already struggling. Considering the CIHI estimates governments in Canada spent $118.9 billion in 2009, 8.3% works out to about $10 billion.[24]

The way politicians throw around "millions" and "billions", it's easy to forget what those numbers represent. In fact, even journalists sometimes confuse the two. So here's an easy way to remember the difference.

A million minutes ago is a little less than two years ago.

A billion minutes ago was not long after Jesus was alive.

And a trillion? As in Canada's combined government debt of more than a trillion dollars? A trillion minutes ago – or 1.9 million years back – was when Homo erectus emerged.

The other notable point about the CIHI's lack of concern is that the boomers just started hitting the more expensive retirement years when the CIHI released its numbers in 2011. Thus, their 0.8% per year calculation doesn't reflect baby boomers hitting the aforementioned expensive age categories.

If the CIHI's rosy position on the cost of an aging population seems too good to be true, perhaps a report by the Fraser Institute seems more plausible.

The Vancouver-based think tank came out with a report in 2012 titled *The Unfunded Liability of Canada's Health Care System* and it attempts to calculate the difference between future revenue streams for health care and the cost of future health care services.

The study notes:

"Medicare is thought of as an insurance plan: individuals contribute to a pool of funds when they are healthy and younger, and are able to receive benefits from that pool in later years or in times of need. The reality is that this program is funded on a 'pay-as-you-go' basis. That is, rather than accumulate funds in individual or even collective accounts for future payment, current contributions (taxes) are used to pay the benefits of current recipients."[25]

In other words, governments haven't saved a penny for when the baby boomers reach ages that typically require really expensive health services. This goes back to my previous comment about the boomers paying a fortune in taxes while they worked, but governments blowing all the money and not saving any for when the boomers need expensive health procedures.

After crunching mountains of data, the think tank concluded something a bit more alarming than the CIHI's take. Ponder these snippets from the Fraser Institute's Dec. 10, 2012, news release:

"The Canadian health care system was facing a $537.7-billion shortfall at the end of 2010, an amount equal to more than $32,000 for each Canadian taxpayer ... "[26]

Nadeem Esmail, one of the Fraser Institute's senior fellows and co-author of the report noted:

"The reality of this large and growing unfunded liability is that young Canadians will likely be hit with a significantly larger tax bill in the future to pay for health care ... In the absence of reform, governments will be forced to choose between further eroding non-health care government services, further reducing available medical services, dramatically increasing taxes, or some combination."

A September 2013 study released by the Canadian Institute of Actuaries (CIA) came out with something a wee bit more catastrophic. The study concluded:

"Assuming no governmental steps to curb health care expenditures, provincial/territorial spending on health care is estimated to increase at 5.1% real growth per year, increasing from 44% today to 103% of total provincial/territorial revenues by 2037."[27]

However, under a more optimistic outlook, one that assumed health reform in order to limit spending growth to 3.5% per year, the CIA concluded:

"Even after assuming some governmental action to limit real growth rates to 3.5%—and thus to decrease 2037 health care expenditures by 30%—health care will still absorb 69% of total revenues available to provinces/territories by 2037 (86% of own-source revenues)."

No matter how you cut it, our aging population will put immense pressure on government finances and taxpayers.

This colossal challenge puts into perspective just how silly it is for hospitals across Canada to lose millions selling chocolate bars, coffee and sandwiches to the public … and how irresponsible it is for bureaucrats and politicians to sit back and watch it happen.

Storm Cloud #3: The Infrastructure Deficit

Have you ever seen one of those pictures on the Internet of a car that looks like it has been swallowed by a giant pothole? Or maybe you drive over a bridge every day that looks like it's about to fall into the river?

Municipal politicians, members of the media and other pundits refer to these problems as part of Canada's "infrastructure deficit."

The idea is that Canadian cities, towns and villages have numerous roads, bridges and other infrastructure assets that are in dire disrepair. Yet, municipal politicians claim they simply don't have the funds to fix those problems and that's why the situation gets worse each year.

You may be wondering: *why didn't municipalities repair and replace these assets all along instead of letting the situation get out of hand?*

The national organization that represents most municipalities in Canada – the Federation of Canadian Municipalities (FCM) – would likely respond with an answer along the lines of something in their 2007 report, *Danger Ahead: The Coming Collapse of Canada's Municipal Infrastructure.*

The report notes:

"...over the past 20 years municipalities have been caught in a fiscal squeeze caused by growing responsibilities and reduced revenues. As a result, they were forced to defer needed investment, and municipal infrastructure continued to deteriorate, with the cost of fixing it climbing five-fold from an estimated $12 billion in 1985 to $60 billion in 2003. This cost is the municipal infrastructure deficit, and today it has reached $123 billion."[28]

The report goes on to say:

"Across Canada, municipal infrastructure has reached the breaking point. Most was built between the 1950s and 1970s, and much of it is due for replacement. We can see the consequences in every community: potholes and crumbling bridges, water-treatment and transit systems that cannot keep up with demand, traffic gridlock, poor air quality and a lack of affordable housing. The infrastructure deficit affects all communities, from major cities to rural, remote and northern communities, where municipal governments lack essential infrastructure and do not have the tax base to develop it."

Intriguing. So politicians built a ton of infrastructure in the 1950s and 1970s, knew the assets would eventually have to be replaced or fixed, but didn't put aside any money for it? And yet somehow municipal politicians have money for a game called Pickleball and Haiku contests? Go figure.

Sure, the waste examples I just mentioned are minuscule spending examples compared to the billions municipalities claim they need. But the expenditures speak volumes about how carefree some politicians are with the money we provide them. Later on I'll show how municipal spending problems go far beyond those two small examples.

In the meantime, let's go back to that $123-billion figure for a second.

Recall how it was from a 2007 report. According to a July 2013 story by the *CBC*, the president of FCM then pegged the national infrastructure deficit at $200 billion; $77 billion higher than the 2007 estimate.[29]

To be sure, one could question the validity of FCM's $200-billion estimate. I certainly do. After all, bureaucrats and politicians are notorious for throwing 'wish list' items into budget estimates for various problems. No doubt some of the items that contribute to FCM's massive estimate could be questioned as to whether they're true necessities or 'nice to have' items.

Furthermore, the $200-billion figure represents the cost for replacement and repair of such things as bridges and roads, but some of the revenue for those items is already built into taxes you already pay your municipality.

I've felt for a long time that FCM and other municipal bodies often inflate just how large their infrastructure deficits are while exaggerating how helpless they are to do something about it. Larger municipalities especially seem to be more skilled in the art of spending public funds inefficiently than smaller municipalities. (Did I mention the City of Toronto regularly spends money to have an official poet?)

Despite my skepticism about the accuracy of infrastructure deficit figures put forward by municipalities, I do believe there is a sizable amount of neglected infrastructure across the country. Some roads I've driven on in Regina and Winnipeg look like something out of a Third World country. No doubt there are countless other examples of infrastructure in rough shape across Canada.

Storm Cloud #4: Government Employee Pension Problems

Pensions can be an extremely complex topic, so I promise to try to keep this section as straightforward as possible.

Fortunately, describing the problem from 10,000 feet is actually pretty easy.

Across the country various government bodies (federal, provincial, municipal, Crown corporations, health regions, etc.) have promised significantly more to their employees in pension benefits than what their pension funds can afford. As it stands right now, taxpayers will have to help make up the difference.

On an individual level, think about a government employee who has been promised an annual pension of $40,000. The employee is now about to retire, but the fund (to which taxpayers and the employee have contributed) can only afford to pay out, say, $30,000 per year. It seems the pension fund took a bit of a beating during the 2008 slowdown and didn't properly take into account people living longer, lower interest rates, etc.

Uh oh.

Now imagine that type of problem multiplied by millions of government employees across the country.

To "fix the problem," governments have been pouring more and more tax dollars into the plans each year to bail them out. Statistics Canada figures on annual government spending (not counting special payments) on government employee pensions is astounding:[30]

2003: $7.2 billion

2013: $18.6 billion

Without a doubt, it's the biggest bailout in Canadian history, but few people even know it's going on. I'll get into the mechanics of pensions a bit later, but in the meantime, let's explore the size of the overall problem.

According to a 2012 report by the Canadian Federation of Independent Business (CFIB), an organization that represents thousands of small and medium-sized businesses countrywide, as of 2011, governments had promised $300 billion more to government employees than the funds can afford.[31]

Yes, that's "billion" with a "b."

Within that $300-billion estimate would of course be the pension plan enjoyed by federal government employees. According to the C.D. Howe Institute, a Canadian think tank, the numbers for the federal plan aren't pretty either.

A 2011 report notes that while the federal government estimated a pension shortfall of $147 billion, the C.D. Howe Institutes calculated it's actually closer to $227 billion.[32]

Regardless, whether it's $147 billion or $227 billion, you can see it's a big number either way and will cost taxpayers dearly.

Here are a few more examples of plans across the country that are swimming in debt and relying on taxpayer bailouts to ensure government employees receive the generous entitlements they've been promised:

Table 2: Other Examples of Government Employee Pension Problems

Name	Shortfall
Ontario Municipal Employees Retirement System	$10 billion deficit[33]
Regina Civic Employees' Pension and Superannuation and Benefits Plan	$242.6 million unfunded liability[34]
Saskatchewan Teachers Superannuation Plan	$5.3 billion unfunded liability[35]
Local Authorities Pension Plan (Alberta)	$5 billion deficiency[36]
British Columbia Teachers' Plan	$855 million unfunded liability[37]
Manitoba Government	$2.3 billion unfunded liability[38]
Quebec Municipalities	$5 billion unfunded liability[39]

If all this doesn't make a lot of sense to you, here's why you should care.

If politicians continue to let government employee pension problems grow, then governments will have to bail them out with tax dollars. That will leave governments with fewer dollars to spend on services people expect (e.g. health care, fixing roads) or they'll have to raise taxes.

A Jan. 20, 2012 *CBC* story on pension problems at the City of Saint John, NB illustrates this problem.[40]

The story noted that if the New Brunswick government didn't approve changes to the city's pension plan, Saint John would have to come up with $9 million in savings right away; resulting in "100 layoffs," including firefighters.

In Montreal, pension costs grew to become such a problem that in 2012, the city asked the provincial government to step in and help them address the situation. The *Montreal Gazette* called the problem a "pension monster" and described how a whopping 13 cents of every dollar spent by the municipal government went towards pension costs.[41] Subsequent changes later led to firefighters and city staff storming city hall in 2014, throwing around papers, intimidating politicians and breaking windows.

Bill Tufts, co-author of the 2011 book *Pension Ponzi: How Public Sector Unions are Bankrupting Canada's Health Care, Education and Your Retirement*, put the coming pension bomb into perspective during an interview with Rob Breakenridge from Calgary's *630 CHED* in 2011:[42]

> **Tufts:** *"[Government employee pensions] are costing taxpayers a lot of money and it's drawing money away from those things that taxpayers expect to be getting for their tax dollars. In order to fund these pensions, and the huge costs associated with them, the politicians are left with very limited options. In order to fund the increasing costs they can perhaps cut back on services, raise taxes, increase the amount of debt either for the province or the country, and politicians across the country have done all three of these things and they're starting to get to a point where services are being risked and debt levels are getting unsustainable and most provinces across Canada are subjected to record deficit funding problems."*

Ouch.

Saving for a Rainy Day... or Not

As most of the four major problems I described have been quite predictable for a long time, you might be thinking – *"our politicians must have put some money aside to deal with those issues … right?"*

Sadly, that's not the case.

Under prime ministers Chretien, Martin and the first couple years of the Harper government, federal net debt (gross debt minus financial assets) actually went down, from $609 billion in 1996-97 to $516 billion in 2007-08.[43] That was a step in the right direction.

However, once the economic slowdown hit, the Harper government reversed all that debt repayment progress as it cranked open the spending taps; our nation's federal debt jumped substantially, surpassing $650 billion in 2011-12 and was still climbing at time of writing. The federal government's 2014-15 budget notes the government will spend approximately $29 billion this year just on interest charges, almost as much as it raises in GST revenues.[44]

Provincially, things are pretty rough as well.

Dalton McGuinty and the Ontario Liberals almost doubled the province's net debt from 2003-04 ($139 billion) to 2013-14 ($267 billion).[45] In Manitoba, the NDP doubled the province's net debt since taking office, from $9 billion in 1999-00 to $19 billion in 2014-15.[46] [47]

You can see this problem isn't limited to one particular party; politicians across the proverbial political spectrum haven't been responsible enough to put aside savings for future challenges.

Even "oil-rich" Alberta is now swimming in deficits and red ink. While Alberta's Heritage Fund – an investment fund created with resource royalties – is valued at $17.3 billion, the government's 2014 budget projects debt for capital spending to eclipse that mark when it hits $21.6 billion in 2016-17.[48] [49]

Table 3: Net Debt By Jurisdiction

Jurisdiction	Net Debt Level
Federal	-$687,478,902,913
Newfoundland and Labrador	-$9,754,671,338
Prince Edward Island	-$2,076,753,176
Nova Scotia	-$14,959,747,392
New Brunswick	-$12,138,224,480
Quebec	-$191,294,507,124
Ontario	-$287,211,994,624
Manitoba	-$18,493,707,524
Saskatchewan	-$3,805,000,000
Alberta	+$6,804,223,342
British Columbia	-$40,931,877,330
Yukon	+$127,000,000
Northwest Territories	-$537,000,000
Nunavut	+$6,137,000
Total	**-$1,261,745,025,562**

Note: Net debt figures from CFIB's debt clock as of February 22, 2015 @ 10:11PM[50]

When you combine all government debt in the country – not just federal and provincial – the picture isn't pretty. Government debt in Canada is over $1.2 trillion.

The Fraser Institute calculated that in 2012-13 net government debt worked out to $34,209 per Canadian. And here you thought you only had that mortgage and car loan to worry about![51]

One could devote an entire chapter to analyzing government debt, but what I want to stress is not that our country is going to go bankrupt tomorrow, but that our nation already has a sizable debt load. If we were debt-free it would be much easier to weather the aforementioned financial "storm clouds" that are on their way (not that it would be good public policy). But clearly that isn't the case. Politicians simply didn't save during the good times.

Don't be Scared

I hope the magnitude of the four problems I just described have put into per-spective how ludicrous it is for governments to still be losing millions while running Tim Hortons coffee stands.

Governments should have tightened their belts a long time ago. Debt should have been tackled in a meaningful way and savings should have been put aside. But clearly that hasn't happened.

If you find the first few pages of this book have made your blood boil or left you quite concerned about the future, don't worry: that's a good thing.

Apathy has ruled this country for too long; people need to be aware of these problems.

I sincerely hope you bring up some of these issues with your friends, fam-ily and coworkers and educate them about some of these matters and urge them to take action.

That's what this book is all about.

But don't bring these issues up with your contacts just yet; you don't want to present a doom and gloom scenario. Your friends, family and whomever else you decide to talk with will want a sense of hope, just as you probably do.

Thankfully, there is some.

Later I'll describe numerous examples of wasteful spending in govern-ment, why it happens, how it can be corrected and what actions taxpayers need to take. If we succeed in rooting out wasteful spending, governments can use the savings to avoid or mitigate tax hikes due to the four major financial storm clouds I described in this chapter.

But before we get to those matters, we need to make a couple quick stops. First, let's examine how these problems could impact you in a bit more detail.

CHAPTER 2

Storm Clouds Raining on Your Wallet

So far I've described four big financial problems that governments are facing right now:

- Shrinking tax base
- Rising health care costs
- The nation's infrastructure deficit
- Government employee pension problems

I've also told you governments nation-wide typically have no savings to deal with these problems. Their total debt is over $1.2 trillion.

By now you're probably wondering how all the big numbers I've thrown about will actually impact you.

The short answer to that question is: unless government behaviour changes, your taxes will keep going up. I'll give you some idea of the magnitude momentarily, but in the meantime I'll admit: it's hard to say exactly how much you'll be impacted.

You see, the problems are predominant across Canada, but not every province will be impacted equally.

For example, Statistics Canada data show that Quebec and provinces in Atlantic Canada are aging much faster than Alberta and Western Canada. Alberta in particular has been attracting young people in droves over the past couple of decades so they're likely not going to feel the squeeze from an aging population to the same extent as the rest of Canada. But even Alberta isn't out of the woods.

A "dependency ratio" released by Statistics Canada in 2012 shows the number of senior citizens (65+) as a percentage of those aged 15-64 in 2010 versus 2036. As you can see in Table 4, by 2036 even Alberta is expected to see this ratio more than double, including in the best-case scenario.[1]

Table 4: Dependency Ratio
Seniors (65+) as a Percentage of Those Aged 15-64

	2010	2036 (HIGH)	2036 (LOW)
Canada	20.4%	40.3%	37.9%
Newfoundland and Labrador	21.9%	55.1%	55.2%
Prince Edward Island	23.0%	48.4%	46.2%
Nova Scotia	23.3%	49.7%	48.8%
New Brunswick	23.0%	51.5%	50.7%
Quebec	22.2%	43.2%	40.9%
Ontario	20.0%	39.2%	36.5%
Manitoba	20.6%	36.7%	34.0%
Saskatchewan	22.3%	40.0%	38.6%
Alberta	15.0%	34.9%	33.1%
British Columbia	21.4%	40.4%	37.5%
Yukon	11.3%	31.8%	30.3%
Northwest Territories	7.7%	33.9%	32.5%
Nunavut	4.9%	18.8%	17.7%

Source: *Statistics Canada*

Another example of how provinces will feel the pain differently is reflected in government employee pension problems. I'll discuss the matter more later on, but thanks to some changes made in the late 1970s and early 1980s, Saskatchewan's provincial government doesn't have a pension headache to the same degree as other provinces.

Debt levels, development of natural resources and the politicians chosen by the public are other factors that will lead to different parts of the country being impacted differently by the four challenges in the years ahead.

Barring federal intervention, the pain will not likely be felt equally across Canada.

I bring up federal intervention as the federal government currently shares revenues between provinces through something called "equalization payments." It's sort of like an interprovincial social assistance program that takes money from provinces deemed to be "wealthy" (known as "have" provinces) and gives money to poorer provinces ("have not" provinces).

Each year the government transfers billions of dollars between provinces. According to federal department of finance figures, $16.1 billion will be transferred to "have not" provinces in 2013-14.[2]

Would the federal government step in and smooth the pain more evenly across the country if things really got out of hand? Would it increase equalization payments?

Who knows what might happen? After all, someone created equalization payments in the first place. Whether a future prime minister might make the program even more generous for such "have not" provinces (Manitoba, Ontario, Quebec and the Atlantic provinces) is anyone's guess.

Even if I had room in this book to attempt to provide tax projections for various communities across Canada, there are just too many variables involved to get the predictions right. In fact, I don't think anyone could tell you for certain how much your property taxes, income taxes, sales taxes and other fees will go up over the next 10, 20 or 30 years.

Here's a good example of why such predictions can be foolhardy.

Thomas Malthus

Ask any economics or history students about a man named Thomas Malthus and they'll probably be able to tell you why he's famous. Unfortunately for Malthus, it isn't a good thing.

In 1798, the British economist famously looked at changes in population and food production in the United States.[3] He then looked at the trend lines to develop his prediction that starvation was on the horizon. Malthus argued that because people were multiplying much faster than food production was increasing, society would hit a starvation and misery wall.

It would be a bit like if your household spending kept going up faster than your household income – eventually you would go bankrupt.

More than 200 years later Malthus's prediction has famously yet to come true. Thank goodness.

Sure, there are some people lacking access to food in the United States and different parts of the world, but that's due more to social and economic reasons than a lack of food or inability to produce it. Watch workers outside a fast food restaurant late at night or your favourite mom and pop restaurant and you'll probably see them dumping unused food into a big garbage bin behind their establishment.

Young economics students learn that Malthus failed to foresee a major decrease in birth rates and huge increases in food production capabilities. After all, the industrial revolution hadn't yet occurred and there certainly weren't any air-conditioned combines, aerial sprayers and giant grain trucks back in 1798.

Long-term Predictions Can Be Difficult

Malthus's bold, multiple-decade projection error is just one example why even the best experts can't say what exactly will happen to our tax rates 20 or 30 years from now.

One needs to keep in mind that we have no idea what advances there may be in technology, what will happen with life expectancies or the economy, to name just a few factors.

There could be a technology boom in health care, drastically curbing costs as procedures and services are automated. There could be a huge natural resource discovery in your province that significantly boosts government revenues, in turn helping to pay for future challenges. This notion will especially resonate with people in B.C., as their province is seemingly on the verge of a huge natural gas boom.

Alternatively, the public could suddenly start to vote for higher spending, and more reckless politicians who make the current situation much, much worse. For example, would the public ever be so reckless as to vote for a party promising expensive new social programs such as national subsidized day care? Who knows?

Another global economic slowdown could come along and wreak even more havoc.

For those reasons and many more it's impossible to say exactly what things will look like 20 years from now. One of the many "experts" who predicted decades ago that we would have serious oil shortages by now probably would agree that specific long-term predictions can be very difficult to get right.

But all that being said, most readers will see that the problems I've laid out will, in all likelihood, put a tremendous amount of pressure on governments to keep raising taxes. It's not going to happen overnight, but your paycheque will continue to be nibbled away at, year after year, unless things change.

Do a bit of Googling on the internet for "Canada" and "aging population," "rising health care costs," "unfunded pension liabilities," "infrastructure deficit" or "debt" and you'll find mountains of reports, articles and commentaries on the aforementioned issues. Most authors acknowledge there are several big problems out there.

While I wish these issues received a lot more attention than, say, Kim Kardashian and Justin Bieber, there are still plenty of stories out there on the four major problems I discuss in this book. The vast majority of the research and commentaries I've seen on these issues seem to recognize our nation is facing major financial problems.

Thankfully, there are several in-depth reports that can give us a rough idea as to the magnitude of the impact these issues will have on taxpayers.

The Government's Take on Things

In 2006, the federal government passed legislation to create an office known as the Office of the Parliamentary Budget Officer (PBO). Like an ombudsman or auditor, the PBO is meant to provide independent analysis of government spending and advice to the House of Commons and the Senate.

Under the leadership of Kevin Page, the country's first PBO, the office has earned respect across the political spectrum for independent, critical analysis and thought.

The PBO's *2014 Fiscal Sustainability Report* included some long-term projections on government finances. Specifically, they tried to figure out what government finances are going to look like as far out as 75 years in the future and whether or not current spending is sustainable.

The report noted, *"…the projected demographic profile of the Canadian population is one of the key drivers of PBO's long-term economic and fiscal projections."*[7]

In other words, that "aging population" issue I keep talking about is going to have a big impact, so they're watching it closely.

The report predicts the federal government's finances are looking not too bad over the long term, thanks to some recent tough decisions by the government (e.g. raising the age of Old Age Security eligibility). However, the report found provincial, territorial, municipal and aboriginal government bodies will face a whopping $34-billion (in 2014 dollars) annual shortfall in the years ahead.[8]

If you're a normal person who doesn't read through government budgets regularly, $34 billion probably doesn't mean much to you; it's just another big number. So let's put it into perspective.

The federal government's 2014 budget projected the 5% Goods and Services Tax would bring in $31 billion in tax revenue.[9] That's about $6 billion for every percentage point. So if governments have to raise another $34 billion every year, that's basically the equivalent of another 6% GST that has to be implemented.

If you live in Ontario, which currently has an HST of 13%, try adding 6% to it. Ouch! Yes, that's nearly a 20% tax on every purchase. Do the calculation for most provinces and you would see a total sales tax bill in the 18-20% range.

But let's be clear. I'm not suggesting governments would go out and collect the extra revenue they "need" strictly by raising sales taxes. They would likely do it through a number of different tax increases on individuals and businesses.

One way or another, governments will likely continue to try to suck more money out of your wallet and the tills of businesses unless something changes.

A Less Optimistic View

If you're looking for some third-party analysis on how demographic shifts will impact the nation, a good report to peruse is *Canada's Looming Fiscal Squeeze*, a research paper published by the Macdonald-Laurier Institute in 2011. Christopher Ragan, an economics professor at McGill University, wrote the paper for the Ottawa-based think tank.

In the news release for the paper, the institute noted that Ragan estimates an annual deficit of *"roughly $67 billion"* will arise unless governments change tax rates or cut spending.[10]

Clearly we're talking about a lot of money; his prediction is twice as dire as the federal government's. To put Ragan's analysis into perspective, let's take the $67 billion figure from the Macdonald-Laurier Institute's news release and again compare it with the $31 billion in revenue that Canada's 5% GST is expected to generate in 2014-15.

The $67 billion revenue gap works out to governments 'needing' an additional sales tax of about 11% *on top of* existing sales taxes. So if you're in Toronto or Vancouver that would be a 24% total sales tax. Those in Nova Scotia would pay a whopping 26% sales tax on their purchases.

But there were other issues highlighted by Ragan. Consider what he notes about the impact on government coffers that comes from an aging population and rising health care costs:

> *"Canadian governments will face a two-part fiscal challenge in the coming few decades. First, the aging of the population will lead to a slowing of national income, which is the primary tax base for governments. Second, major Canadian public spending programs will become more costly as a*

share of GDP, especially those providing health care and income support for the elderly."[11]

Finally, I would note that Ragan seems to be on the same page with something I noted in chapter one: governments are going to have to look at tax increases, reduced spending or a combination of the two to address the financial storm clouds on our horizon.

Ragan notes in his paper:

"Confronted with spending demands that rise faster than tax revenues, future Canadian governments will be faced with three broad choices. First, they can attempt to reduce the growth rate of overall spending. Second, they can attempt to increase the growth rate of revenues through increases in tax rates. Finally, they can choose to increase the scale of public borrowing. Of course, the third option is not a permanent solution since government debt eventually needs to be repaid and such repayment ultimately requires a command over resources, which in turn requires either spending reductions or increases in tax revenues."[12]

Hopefully Ragan's report and the government's own analysis have convinced you that Canadians need to pay more attention to these issues.

While it's impossible to say what exactly will happen in terms of tax changes, I feel quite safe warning that we're on a collision course for much higher taxes unless something significant changes. Further, unless things change, governments could even decide to cut back on some services we actually do care about receiving from the government.

Fortunately, there's still time for taxpayers to push governments to take action. But before we explore what can be done, let's examine the taxes we pay right now.

PART TWO

The taxes we pay and the role of government

CHAPTER 3

The Government Taketh ... and
Taketh ... and Taketh

In December 2010, *Bloomberg.com* ran a story noting how the average Canadian household had just passed the average American household's debt levels (ratio of debt to household income).[1] According to Bloomberg, it was the first time in 12 years that Canadians had exceeded our neighbours to the south in the unflattering category.

Jim Flaherty, Canada's late minister of finance, wasn't pleased with the news either. At the time, the US was still reeling from household debt problems; namely a wave of people defaulting on their mortgage payments, causing a surge in difficulty for banks and investment firms across the country. Many attributed this situation as a key catalyst for the 2008 economic slowdown.

The last thing Flaherty wanted was for Canada to experience the same type of collapse.

To address the matter, he clamped down on home mortgages, scaling back the allowable duration of loans from 35 to 30 years.[2] Flaherty also encouraged Canadians to pay off their debt more aggressively. He told Bloomberg:

> *"Our parents were more inclined to pay off that mortgage as soon as possible, and some Canadians are not as inclined to do that now ... I encourage them to do it."*

Months earlier, Flaherty had raised concerns that too many Canadians were also not saving enough for their retirement.[3]

Make no mistake, there are plenty of people who are just plain reckless with their money. But, generally speaking, are Canadians really more apathetic towards debt repayment and saving for their retirement than their parents? Or has something else changed? I would argue that in many cases it's the latter.

Tax Explosion

In the book *Tax Me, I'm Canadian!*, bestselling author Mark Milke describes some of the first taxes in Canada: an export duty of 50% on beaver pelts and a 10% duty on moose pelts. Both were implemented in 1650.[4]

Obviously, since those first duties years ago, Canada's tax system has exploded with all kinds of new taxes, from a tax on air conditioners in cars to a racetrack tax in Ontario. It's easy to see why Milke chose the book title *Tax Me, I'm Canadian!*

Take a minute and think of all the taxes various levels of government levy. It's overwhelming. There are alcohol taxes, tobacco taxes, capital gains taxes, municipal property taxes and many provinces have expensive school property taxes as well.

More and more municipalities have introduced hotel taxes and some provinces have entertainment taxes for large gatherings such as professional sporting events.

In many cases the federal and provincial governments even tax the same thing; federal *and* provincial gas taxes, sales taxes and corporate income taxes, to name a few.

Incredibly, four provinces even tax businesses for hiring people. For example, in Ontario, businesses have to pay a tax of 1.95% on every dollar they spend on their payroll above $450,000 (2013 threshold). However, if a business's payroll is $5 million or higher, they don't even benefit from the $450,000 tax-free threshold; the government charges them a lower tax rate on their entire payroll, rising as the firm's total payroll increases.[5]

Manitoba, Quebec and Newfoundland and Labrador also charge similar payroll taxes. These taxes discourage businesses from hiring more people or giving their employees raises. Each additional dollar spent on employee pay just means the business will have to pay more tax.

Beyond all these examples, there are of course the "temporary" personal income taxes we all pay.

I say "temporary" because that's exactly what the federal government promised the public in 1917 when income taxes were introduced. The new tax was sold to Canadians as a temporary measure to help pay for the nation's involvement in the First World War. Yet here we are almost 100 years later and income taxes don't appear to be going away anytime soon.

But that wasn't the only "temporary" tax forced upon Canadians. In 1995, when the federal government was battling a huge deficit, the Chretien administration came up with an additional tax on gasoline, a 1.5-cent-per-litre tax called the "excise tax."[6] The government introduced the tax to help fight the federal deficit, promising to remove the tax once the deficit was eliminated.

To the Chretien government's credit, they eliminated the deficit in their 1997-98 budget ... but they don't deserve credit for keeping the "temporary" excise tax. Prime ministers Martin and Harper didn't eliminate the tax either; in fact, it existed long enough for the federal government to return to running deficits in 2008-09. As the saying goes, there's nothing so permanent as a temporary tax.

Not only have the number of taxes increased in Canada over the years, so have the rates. For example, in most provinces, if you research your provincial sales tax you'll probably find it started out as something like "just a 5% sales tax on goods sold."

Manitoba raised its 5% sales tax to 7% in the 1980s and to 8% in 2013. But not only has the rate gone up, the government started charging it on a number of additional services over the years; including necessities such as home insurance.

Nova Scotia and Quebec have also raised their provincial sales taxes, including recent increases to 15% and 14.975% respectively. (Note: both are harmonized tax rates and include the 5% GST.)

Returning to personal income taxes, we find a similar story. When income taxes were introduced, people only paid the tax on earnings above $1,500 per year (this is known as the "basic personal amount"). $1,500 doesn't sound like much of a threshold, but back in the day that was a fairly high amount.

According to the Bank of Canada's inflation calculator, $1,500 in 1917 dollars works out to $22,500 in 2014. Wouldn't it be great to be able to earn $22,500 before paying income taxes?

In 2015, the federal government starts taxing people's earnings once they hit just $11,327. (The $11,327 threshold actually would have been lower, but in the early 2000s the Canadian Taxpayers Federation successfully lobbied the federal government to protect taxpayers by starting to automatically increase the threshold each year for inflation.)

At the provincial level, as of 2015, basic personal amount thresholds range from a low of $7,708 in PEI to a high of $18,214 in Alberta. The national average is close to $11,000.

Several provinces have also been busy increasing actual personal income tax rates in recent years. For example, the Ontario government raised personal income taxes in its 2012 budget and again in 2014. Similarly, the Alberta government's 2015 budget proposed personal income tax hikes and a myriad of other tax hikes.

Many municipalities have also been busy raising taxes; property taxes in particular. But perhaps what's most troubling is that many have been raising taxes faster than people's paycheques have increased. When that happens, people either have to cut household spending on things that matter to them, find a way to earn extra money (e.g. part-time job) or go into debt. All three options are usually not too popular with taxpayers.

Here is some data on tax increases in select major cities versus average earnings increases:

Table 5: 2013 Property Tax Increase vs Earnings

City	Actual Rate Increase	Average Income Up
Ottawa	2.09%	1.55%
Toronto	2.00%	1.55%
Winnipeg	3.87%	0.59%
Saskatoon	5.00%	3.08%
Regina	4.45%	3.08%
Edmonton	3.30%	3.50%
Calgary	5.50%	3.50%
Vancouver	2.00%	1.03%

Source: *Respective municipal government budgets, Statistics Canada average weekly earnings data (CANSIM 281-0027)*

I should also point out another money grab; many governments have also been busy creating and increasing fees of all sorts; environmental fees, death certificate fees, garbage cart fees, alarm permit fees and dog license fees to name a few examples.

One could go on and on about all the different taxes and fees in Canada, but you can see the government's tax system has grown immensely since the good old days when just animal pelts were taxed.

The Big Picture

Given all these new taxes, and tax increases, it should come as no surprise that a 2013 Fraser Institute Study calculated the average Canadian household spent 33.5% of its household budget on taxes in 1961, compared to a whopping 42.7% of income in 2012.[7]

In dollar terms, that means a household earning $74,113 per year in 2012, paid an extra $6,818 on their tax bill annually.

Now recall Mr. Flaherty's comments about older generations paying back debt more aggressively and it's easy to see how they could afford to do so – they paid far less in taxes!

In this light, Mr. Flaherty's other comment – many Canadians aren't saving enough for their retirement years – is ironic. Had the government left more money in people's pockets in the first place, responsible Canadians would have more money to put away for retirement.

Given high household debt loads, a lack of savings for retirement years and the tax increases we've already seen, higher tax rates – to pay for the four major financial problems described in chapter one – clearly won't help the situation.

Raising taxes significantly will also lead to more stories like one I heard in 2012.

A gentleman called my office at the Canadian Taxpayers Federation and described how his elderly mother in Saskatchewan simply couldn't afford to keep her home anymore. He told me his mother had lived in her home for decades, worked hard to pay off her mortgage and hoped to stay there for many years to come.

Unfortunately, her income in her retirement years wasn't going up as fast as her municipal property taxes; something had to give. In the end she was forced out of her home, not because she couldn't keep up with yard mainte-nance or cleaning a home that was now larger than she needed.

No, she couldn't keep up with the taxman.

Sadly, the situation reminds me of the punch line from the old joke, "I'm from the government, and I'm here to help."

Are We Feeling the Edges of the Financial Storm Clouds?

If someone kept track of which Canadian has taken the all-time most calls and emails from frustrated taxpayers, Shannon Morrison would probably be a top contender.

Nearly two decades ago, Shannon was hired as an administrative assistant for the Canadian Taxpayers Federation, a still relatively new taxpayers' watch-dog organization that had opened up its first office in Regina a few years prior.

The CTF formed after separate taxpayer organizations in Alberta and Saskatchewan heard about each other, met and eventually decided to merge. For the two groups it was love at first mutual complaint about federal taxes (or something like that).

Talk to Shannon about the early years at the CTF and she'll tell you how the phones rang constantly with taxpayers venting their frustrations about various issues.

"During the early years we were inundated with calls from people upset about the creation of the GST, the federal debt and other taxes going up," said Morrison, now the vice-president of the organization's administrative wing.

Since then a lot has changed. Today the CTF has offices in B.C., Alberta, Saskatchewan, Manitoba, Ontario and Nova Scotia and the organization has more than 84,000 supporters.

According to Morrison, "by the late 1990s and early 2000s, complaints dropped off a bit. Governments started to focus on cutting taxes and balanc-ing their budgets, so we received fewer angry calls," she adds.

While the CTF has matured and grown significantly, the fiscal mood among governments has once again changed. Almost all provincial governments, and the federal government, started running deficits in 2008. As described earlier, many have also started to raise taxes.

"Recently we're getting more and more calls from people expressing frustration with taxes going up again ... particularly in Ontario and Manitoba," says Morrison. "We've especially gotten a lot of calls from seniors on fixed incomes who are having a hard time making ends meet and paying the tax man."

So what's the alternative to the doom and gloom of tax hikes?

Well, more often than not, governments are bloated organizations that waste a lot of money. They're kind of like your friend's portly dog that is too slow to even get up and greet you at the door when you pop by. Like the lethargic pet, the government has plenty of extra fat to shed.

If governments could divert wasteful spending towards addressing the four major financial challenges I described in chapter one, tax increases could be avoided or mitigated.

I'll describe how governments are inefficient in the chapters ahead, but first it's important to discuss why we pay taxes in the first place.

CHAPTER 4

What's the Role of Government?

If we're going to discuss how tax increases can be avoided or mitigated by cutting wasteful and inefficient spending, we first need to identify the role of government.

Why do we pay taxes? What services should the government provide? What services should be priorities for governments? How should governments deliver services?

Those are some of the questions we're going to look at in this chapter. But before we address those big picture topics, let's explore a few examples of questionable spending.

In 2010, the Saskatchewan Roughriders and Montreal Alouettes earned a berth in the Canadian Football League's Grey Cup. Not surprisingly, Regina Mayor Pat Fiacco made a public bet with Montreal Mayor Gerald Tremblay over who would win the annual Canadian Football League championship game.

It wasn't surprising that two politicians made a bet; mayors of cities with teams participating in major sporting events do so all the time. They do it because they know they can receive a lot of good, free media attention without having to do much work.

Usually such political wagers involve the losing team's mayor having to wear the winning team's jersey at a council meeting or some other trivial task. Sure it's a bit uncomfortable for the losing team's mayor to wear the enemy's uniform, but the politician usually comes across as looking like a good sport in media coverage, so it's still a win for them.

What Regina's mayor did in 2010, however, was over the top. In addition to committing to wear a Montreal jersey at a council meeting, and raise the

Alouettes' team flag at city hall if his team lost, he committed to buy a pair of season tickets for the Alouettes.

Unfortunately, Regina taxpayers were saddled with the $1,055 bill for Montreal Alouettes season tickets after the Saskatchewan Roughriders lost.[1]

While the tickets were to be given to a charity in Montreal, rather than to Mayor Tremblay for personal use, that's beside the point. The greater question is: should the public have to pay their property taxes so that a politician can take some of that money and gamble it away while receiving free publicity?

Isn't the point of betting to put some of your *own* skin in the game? Before most people make a bet they'll hum and haw about the consequences: 'Do I really want to risk $50?' 'Could I handle having to clean my buddy's toilet if my team loses?' Clearly, Mayor Fiacco didn't have to worry about the possibility of losing; the taxpayer had his back covered.

At least one news story didn't mention taxpayers were picking up the tab for the loss. Mr. Fiacco came across looking like quite a generous guy in a Nov. 30, 2009, *CBC* story:

> *"…Fiacco also promised to honour the second part of the wager. He'll be buying two pairs of Alouettes tickets that will be given to a charity of Tremblay's choice."*[2]

For the record, no corrections appeared in the online version of the story.

I'm guessing many readers probably feel the same way I do – Mayor Fiacco should have used his own money to bet – while others might agree with his decision. Regardless, it's a great example for what we're going to talk about – is this the role of government?

Here is another example to ponder. In July 2011, city council in St. Albert, Alberta, decided to buy a Starbucks franchise. According to the *National Post*, after a restaurant moved from one spot in the city's Servus Credit Union Place (the municipality's recreation complex) to another, council decided to fill the vacant space by buying a Starbucks franchise. It then staffed the venture with government employees.[3]

How would you feel if you owned the Booster Juice fast food franchise in the same complex, or a little coffee shop nearby? How would you feel knowing the government took some of your own tax dollars and used them to open up a competitor to your business? Again – is this the role of government?

If the Starbucks example has you scratching your head, consider this next one. In late 2012, the *Winnipeg Free Press* noted how the federal government's "Canadian Economic Action Plan" had provided $5 million to a hemp-processing company called Farm Genesis in Waskada, Manitoba, a town of about 200 in the southwest part of the province.[6] The government, of course, claimed the move would help create jobs.

Yet according to the *Winnipeg Free Press*, the 25,000-square-foot plant was built but it was never used. It seems the business plan just didn't add up after all. Rightly so, the newspaper also noted the grant *"annoyed companies already involved in hemp processing who had succeeded more or less on their own."*

$5 million of taxpayers' money – poof! Gone, just like that. Again, is this the role of government?

Core Services

I'm guessing most people probably have a rough idea of what "core" government services are; the necessary government services that society needs to function. But how often do you really think hard about why you're forced to pay taxes and which services are core services?

I'm guessing, not too often.

When I applied for a position with the Canadian Taxpayers Federation in 2008, I had to do just that. Part of the taxpayer watchdog's interview process included a written test and one of the questions was *"what is the proper role of government?"*

I had an idea of what I thought the government should be involved in, things like policing, health care, education, fixing roads, etc. However, I suspected the organization wasn't looking for a list of services, but rather a more philosophical description.

It took me a bit to articulate the role of government more generally, but in the end I noted the government's role should be limited, and it should protect people and private property from criminal activity while providing services that help facilitate the creation of wealth and jobs by entrepreneurs.

To understand that description in practical terms, let's build an imaginary government for Canada from the ground up. For simplicity, let's assume that we have just one layer of government instead of multiple levels – federal, provincial, municipal, school boards, etc. (Note: we'll discuss *how* services are delivered later on. E.g. contracted out versus in-house).

To start off, think of a country that has resources, but struggles to attract investment or achieve a decent quality of life for its citizens. Perhaps you might think of a corrupt or lawless nation in Africa or a dictatorship like North Korea.

Now imagine that someone asked you to invest in one of those countries or even to go live there. You'd probably think twice before pulling out your chequebook or packing up the family to move. After all, there's a higher probability in corrupt nations that a government figure or warlord or could come along and seize your property, kidnap your employees or pop you off and get away with it.

Conversely, that type of activity is far less likely in most developed nations. If someone stole your building crane or kidnapped your workers in a country like Canada, the US, France, Sweden, or Japan there would probably be a pretty swift police response.

Having a police service and court system, plus jails and prisons for detaining and deterring criminals, helps bring order to society. With increased security comes the ability to increase foreign investment, something that helps create jobs and opportunities for the masses. Not to mention, maintaining order helps make people feel safe and they'll be more likely to stick around.

I believe the government needs to be involved in organizing the delivery of these services due to what economists call "non-excludability." In short, it refers to purchasing a good or service from which others will benefit without sharing the cost. For example, if you personally hired someone to track down a criminal and paid to have him or her kept in a private jail for a year, all of society would benefit from a safer community, but you would be the only one footing the bill. As the service clearly benefits everyone, there is an argument for the government to levy taxes and provide the service.

The alternative would be a society without police or perhaps gated communities and private police forces all over the place. But let's face it, even if you wanted one of those two scenarios, it simply isn't politically realistic.

With that in mind, let's add policing, a court system and corrections facilities to our list of services that our new government will provide. Let's also add an independent body to run elections to help ensure the nation functions as a democracy; few like to do business with, or live under, dictators.

Next, countries obviously need money to help facilitate personal and commercial transactions. You can't allow private individuals or businesses to print up as much money as they want, so it makes sense for governments to have an arms-length agency to handle such matters.

A basic military and border control are also worth adding to the list. After all, we have to protect our nation from foreign invasion or undesirables sneaking into the country. Just like policing, these services are also non-exclusive so there's a role for government in handling these services. Decide for yourself how robust you want our military to be and how active you want it to be in the affairs of countries outside our borders.

As any civilized country is going to have to keep track of who owns what land, we'll add a "property registry" to the list of things the government manages in some capacity. Similarly, most people would also probably agree with the idea of having the government handle zoning and the planning of roads between communities, so that goods and people can move efficiently from one place to the next. No one wants a noisy factory going in next door to his or her house so a bit of community planning makes sense. Let's add those services to our list as well.

Next, when you hit the local beach you probably wouldn't want to dive in the water and find someone had dumped in nuclear waste or chemicals.

Let's add basic environmental protection services and some public parks to the mix.

While there can be some debate about health care, education and social assistance, I think most would agree no major political party in Canada is likely to suggest gutting them anytime soon. Even if one wanted to eliminate those programs, it just won't happen politically.

Let's put the word "basic" before each of those services and add them to our list. Just like the military, some will want more robust roles for government in these areas than others.

However, beyond the political necessity of adding those three services, I would note that I think there is merit in the government offering some degree of health care, education and social assistance (to provide a "hand up, not a handout") to the masses. Each service can help ensure the nation has a skilled and healthy workforce to help create wealth, either as entrepreneurs or as employees in businesses.

One could also raise the moral argument of providing K-12 education, so that even the poorest of kids have a fair start in life. Having the government involved in health care can also help ensure families aren't set back with massive medical bills from catastrophic events. Again, that's more food for thought.

Thinking of all the services we've added to our list, I think we've developed a pretty good outline of what a core government looks like: the most essential services a majority of us would probably expect.

Have I covered off every single service that most people would consider "core" or "necessary" from the government?

No. Creating a thorough listing of all potentially necessary services would probably take half a chapter to debate and flush out.

What I've tried to do is describe a basic government structure that most people (I hope) would accept as a rough framework. (Later on, when we discuss what individuals can do to shape government, you can figure out what services you might work towards enhancing or perhaps de-funding.)

The government we've just described is one that protects its citizens and private investment by running a police force, a court system and jails and prisons. The government is democratically chosen and it manages the nation's currency. It makes sure everyone has access to basic education, health care and a hand up through social assistance. Environmental protection is provided and roads are built to facilitate the mobility of people and commercial goods. Oversight in terms of a property registry and zoning help organize society a bit better too.

The government that we've just described doesn't compete with private businesses by opening up restaurants or other commercial ventures and there are no funds for covering politicians' bets on sporting events. Those types of spending decisions are left up to the public to make.

The government we have constructed also isn't cutting cheques to businesses in the form of loans or grants. Similarly, special interest groups that regularly line up at the trough for funding for their art exhibits or trips to who-knows-where in the name of who-knows-what are also not funded. No, they'll have to find voluntary donors or investors.

By not funding all those non-essential services, this leaner, more focused government will achieve some savings. Those dollars can then be used to address the four major financial challenges facing our nation instead of raising taxes.

You might be asking just how much smaller it is compared to what we see right now in Canada? 20% smaller? 25%? 30%?

The percentage is going to differ, depending on where you live and what your municipal and provincial governments are spending money on right now, but it may not be as much as people think. If you stripped away all the government programs that give loans and grants to businesses or fund special interest groups and bankroll politicians' bets, I would guess it would still probably only amount to only a few percentage points of total government spending.

To sit down and crunch the numbers would be a pretty complex task, so I thought I would ask an expert on public policy for his opinion. I approached Peter Holle, the president and founder of the Frontier Centre for Public Policy, a Winnipeg-based think tank. Holle's view was much the same as mine; shedding the aforementioned spending wouldn't amount to much at all.

According to Peter:

"The amounts spent on subsidies for business, arts and other special interest groups are really a rounding error in the big picture. Smarter, more focused and customer-oriented public services that maximize consumer choice and are provided through competitive delivery models are the key."
– Peter Holle, President of the Frontier Centre for Public Policy

One has to remember, if you crack open the spine of most provincial government budgets, you'd find spending on health care and education alone take up the majority of the budget. Throw in interest costs on the debt, social assistance expenses, running jails, fixing highways and some of the other programs we included in our new model of government and there's not a lot left over.

Look at city governments and the federal government and you'd find a similar story; the "core" services we have described take up most of the spending.

So how do we find more savings?

Well, I think the real fat actually lies in those "core" services. Governments often leave plenty of room for improvement when it comes to running those programs efficiently. Just as Holle noted, competitive delivery models and customer-oriented services are the key.

The Yellow Pages Test

In 1991, Stephen Goldsmith was elected as mayor of Indianapolis, IN.

As he describes in his book, the *21st Century City*, Indianapolis was considered by many to be a fairly well run city when he took over. From the outside looking in, Indianapolis didn't look anything like a bloated organization just begging for someone to come along and trim the fat.

Goldsmith noted in his book:

"When I came into office in 1992, Indianapolis's finances were sound: taxes were relatively low, our public workforce seemed lean, and the city boasted a healthy bond rating."[7]

Yet Goldsmith's book also notes reform initiatives he enacted from 1992 to 1997 saved taxpayers a whopping $230 million. During that period Goldsmith notes his government reduced spending every year, eventually tabling a budget in 1997 that spent 7% less than the one tabled in 1992.

To put his 7% spending cut into perspective, it's extremely rare to find a major government body in Canada – at any level – that has frozen spending over a two-year period, let alone one that has cut overall spending over a five-year period.

Goldsmith also proudly notes –

"At the same time, we made the largest infrastructure investment in the city's history – more than three-quarters of a billion dollars – and put one hundred more police officers on city streets, while reducing taxes slightly."[8]

One might think that Goldsmith simply went out and slashed services, leaving public parks full of weeds and putting the burden on citizens to literally put out fires themselves in their neighborhoods. But that wasn't the case: many service levels actually improved while Goldsmith achieved all the aforementioned savings.

So how did Goldsmith do this?

Well, the answer lies in the fact that governments are much more inefficient than many think.

When bureaucrats came along requesting more funding (or outright asked for tax increases), Goldsmith pushed back. He conducted what he called "the Yellow Pages test."

The new mayor recognized that if you opened up the Yellow Pages, you could see private businesses performing many of the same services as city workers.

For example, the city had employees to fix potholes, but so did private businesses. While city workers would fix potholes on the streets, companies would fix potholes in private parking lots and elsewhere.

Similarly, while the City of Indianapolis had employees running golf courses, collecting money for water bill payments and towing illegally parked cars on city streets, private businesses performed similar functions. There were all kinds of services that businesses could potentially provide for the city.

The problem was, no one ever seemed to check whether city services could be performed at a lower cost by hiring businesses to do the work.

Instead of simply rubberstamping higher spending and tax increases, Goldsmith's administration did something you and I do all the time: he decided to shop around to see if he could find a better deal.

His team looked at different services the city provided and essentially checked to see if there were any companies in the Yellow Pages that could do the same work. If there were, he would consider doing something called "managed competition."

Rather than go out and simply hire businesses to provide various services for a lower price, the mayor took a different approach, one that was more than fair to existing city employees.

When his team identified a city service that could be tendered out, Goldsmith encouraged city employees to put in their own bid and have a chance at preserving their jobs. The city even provided the unionized government employees with assistance in drafting their bids.

After all, the guy cleaning up a city park may know how to cut grass and pick up trash, but he probably isn't familiar with the finer points of filling out paperwork for government bid opportunities.

During Goldsmith's term in office, many private businesses won bids to provide City of Indianapolis services (for a lower price). For example, the city hired companies to print city reports and manage the city's fleet of printers. A private business started to handle bill collection at the city's water utility and another started to tow illegally parked cars. Taxpayers ultimately saw the same level of service – or better – in those areas for a lower price. In many cases, businesses were just plain much more efficient than the city could ever hope to be.

That shouldn't come as a surprise, though. After all, a company that spends all day focusing on how to be the best in its industry would likely be more efficient than a city government that focuses on delivering several dozen different services. The latter couldn't possibly spend the time and money necessary to figure out how to be the most efficient at each service it provided. Nor does it have the profit motive to do so.

However, there were several services where city workers stepped up to the plate and actually beat out private enterprise.

For example, Goldsmith noted how city pothole repair crews suddenly became very competitive when they submitted their bids. Many of the employees had done the same jobs for decades but never had the incentive to work harder or speak up and suggest changes to save taxpayers money. Once their jobs were on the line, everything changed.

The pothole repair guys decided to restructure their crews from two trucks and eight guys to just one truck and five guys. This required some remounting of pothole repair equipment in the back of one truck to fit it all in.

The move may have made things a bit more cramped in the work trucks, but the "money is no object" days were behind them; these guys now had to be competitive and mindful of costs. The pothole repair crews also cut a layer of management staff out of their bids and committed to higher levels of productivity.

When all was said and done, Goldsmith noted the city's pothole repair crews reduced their costs from $425 per ton to $307 per ton, a 25% drop. At the same time, their productivity increased by 68%: from 3.1 lane-miles per day to 5.2 lane-miles per day. Again, the city workers knew all along what had to be done, they just never had the incentive to improve.

Table 6: Indianapolis Pot Hole Repair Reform

	Before City Workers Subjected to Competition	After City Workers Subjected to Competition
Pothole Repair Cost	$425/ton	$307/ton
Productivity	3.1 lane miles/day	5.2 lane miles/day

Goldsmith turned the incentive model on its head, from focusing on how much to spend each year to what results were needed annually. From there he could figure out who could do the work for the best price.

Most importantly, Goldsmith's reforms meant Indianapolis taxpayers received a better service at a lower cost – a win-win!

But Indianapolis certainly isn't the only city to save taxpayers money by reforming services. In 2005, the City of Winnipeg hired a private business to collect garbage from people's homes in a section of the city that was still serviced by city workers. The rest of the city already had private companies doing the work.

According to city documents, the company hired for that final portion of garbage collection reduced annual costs by 36%.[9] At the same time, complaints for that area dropped by 20% to 25% annually. Yes, even though the private company had to include a profit margin in its bid, it was still able to reduce costs significantly; the city was *that* inefficient when it handled the service!

Again, this is another example of a better service at a lower price – another win-win for taxpayers.

As you may know, many governments currently hire private businesses for various services; building and repairing roads and highways, providing snow removal services and garbage pickup. Hospitals often have private security companies watching over their premises and government buildings often use private cleaning companies.

But there are still plenty of governments that don't explore such partnerships and that is a problem. Many government bodies continue to provide services in-house without ever bothering to conduct the "Yellow Pages Test" to see if they could reduce costs by hiring an outside firm or challenge employees to do better.

Before any government decides to raise taxes it should follow Goldsmith's lead and explore managed competition.

The Rest

So far we have identified entire services the government shouldn't be involved in, such as handing out money to businesses and starting up Starbucks restaurants and other businesses to compete with the private sector.

We've also determined that governments can pursue managed competition to unlock the potential of government employees or achieve savings by hiring a private company.

But what can you do with services such as policing, writing curriculum for schools or firefighting? After all, they can't be easily contracted out.

One wouldn't expect the government to hire a private security firm to replace a city's police force. (Even if you do like that idea, no government would likely entertain that notion anytime soon.)

So if there are certain services that governments are going to have to handle, what should be the goals and guiding principles in terms of how they're delivered?

I would break things down into three goals and guidelines from a cost perspective:

1. Price and Service: The government should put taxpayers first and aim to deliver a combination of the best service at the best price. While some unions think the role of government is to employ people, I would argue the point of government is actually to serve the public in the most cost-effective manner possible.

However, providing the "best" service doesn't mean the sky is the limit in terms of cost. That brings us to point number two.

2. Affordable: Government spending needs to be affordable. Politicians need to take into account what taxpayers can actually afford.

Some people might feel safer having a police officer on every block, but obviously taxpayers couldn't afford such a high level of service. Governments need to find the right balance.

3. Reasonable Pay and Benefits: Given government employee pay and benefits represent a majority of government spending, it's an issue that is too big to ignore.

I would argue that government employees should be paid a competitive salary and benefits package, one that is on par with similar work provided in the private sector. For example, if the average mid-level accountant in business makes $60,000 annually, then accountants in government performing similar duties should be paid about the same.

After all, if governments pay their employees peanuts, they're going to attract pretty crummy candidates. Conversely, if governments pay their employees a fortune, it's not really fair to the taxpayer who is footing the bill.

So is the government meeting the three aforementioned objectives? Well, let's go back and check.

Is the Government Efficient?

My trip to the Parliament Buildings in Ottawa in 2010 was quite different from any previous visits I had made to the nation's capital.

This time I found myself walking up to the Parliament Buildings wearing a tuxedo and accompanied by a guy in a pig costume and a blonde-haired model in an evening gown.

I was hosting "The Teddies."

If you've never heard of the Teddies, they're an event the Canadian Taxpayers Federation holds during awards season each year, usually in March just after the Oscars.

The event consists of a 20-minute press conference inside the Parliament Buildings, during which a spokesman for the organization highlights numerous examples of wasteful government spending that occurred throughout the previous year. "Winners" are announced for the most ridiculous municipal, provincial and federal spending initiatives. A lifetime achievement award is also handed out annually.

The "awards" ceremony is a lighthearted event that pokes fun at government waste. The model helps with presenting the "award" and handing the envelopes to the spokesperson while the person in the pig costume helps class things up even further.

Even the award itself is tongue in cheek. It's a pig statue named after Ted Weatherill, a former federal bureaucrat who was fired for racking up inappropriate expenses way back in 1999.

A quick review of all nominees and recipients over the years (see *Taxpayer.com*) will show that governments have given the CTF plenty to work with.

While the competition makes for good head-shaking and a bit of amusement, the large volume of "worthy" nominees is not good news for the taxpayer because these are your tax dollars foolishly being spent.

The reality is governments often have a poor track record when it comes to spending public funds; they're just not efficient. Too often governments behave like Prada-wearing, high-end-car-driving, latte-sipping organizations that act as though money is no object. While you would probably think twice before buying a chic but expensive pair of $1,000 Prada shoes, in government, luxurious decisions are often made haphazardly.

After all, politicians and bureaucrats are spending someone else's money – yours!

Unlike private companies that have to work hard to earn business from customers, the government's revenue stream – taxation – comes in with ease.

Taxes, of course, aren't an option for the public. Throw in the fact there's no profit incentive in government and it's easy to see why such careless spending decisions persist. It's always easier to spend other people's money.

That shouldn't be surprising though. Just ask yourself how many times you've taken a rental car for a car wash?

You probably never have. It's not your car so why bother?

You might try to avoid accidents because you might face a penalty. However, there's no surcharge for bringing it back with mud or road salt on the sides, so most people don't worry too much about it. It's the same with money. People are often more careful with their own money than they are with other people's.

Consider what my former colleague Jordan Bateman, the B.C. director for the Canadian Taxpayers Federation, uncovered in 2012. Translink, the government's transit body that runs its "SkyTrain" service, had spent a whopping $532,444 on 13 big-screen TVs for use at five train stations in 2009. (Don't do the math or the cost per TV will make your stomach groan.)[10]

The goal behind purchasing the new TVs was to mount them in stations so that riders could learn of any emergency closings of Translink gates or other important news. Yet a walk-around investigation by Bateman to each of the stations found that only four of the 13 TV panels were actually in use. So much for the emergency warning system.

Another great example of government mismanagement involves a northern research station in Churchill, Manitoba. In 2009, the Churchill Northern Studies Centre received a grant for $11 million from the federal government to expand its facility.

No doubt the centre was ecstatic to hear the news; few organizations wouldn't cheer at the thought of expanding. However, around the same time the organization saw a different department in Ottawa cut its operating grant by $80,000 per year.

It seemed to be a classic case of the left hand not talking to the right hand, or in this case one department not communicating with another.

Senator James Cowan noted:

"The $80,000 goes toward the operating funds of the technical staff and the day-to-day operations of the centre. Here is the government handing money out to make welcome infrastructure improvements while taking away the money required to operate the facility."[11]

A valid point: why fund an organization to expand if you're not sure they can keep the lights on in the new section?

Given these two examples, the government-run Tim Hortons and Toronto District School Board anecdotes from chapter one, and other examples of government folly that I've recounted so far, hopefully you can see the government isn't as careful with your money as you would be.

Is the Government Affordable?

The question of whether or not government is affordable is obviously a highly subjective one. Whether or not you think the government is taking too much of your income or just enough is going to depend on your needs and values.

If you have four children and a job that doesn't pay well, you're probably going to feel the pinch a lot more from government tax increases than a multi-millionaire with no kids.

Similarly, if you asked two or three neighbours what percentage of their income would be reasonable for the government to take, you're probably going to hear different answers. One might say 30%, another 40%, and if you live by an anarchist or a communist, you might hear figures like 0% or 100%.

So how do we determine if the government is affordable or not? I'm going to leave that up to you to ponder.

Given your current situation, do you think the government is taking too much? Would you rather pay less in taxes and see the government spend less money on some of the more questionable things I've already discussed?

Another way to analyze the situation is to ask whether you can keep up with recent tax increases. In chapter three I showed how many city governments have been raising taxes faster than most people's paycheques are going up. How do politicians in those cities think taxpayers can keep up?

I think the whole question of affordability of government spending is one worth asking. When I looked into that topic a couple years ago I discovered a very broken relationship between government and taxpayers.

In 2013, I filed a number of Freedom of Information requests with various government bodies in Manitoba. (For those who aren't familiar with the process, it allows citizens, journalists, watchdog groups and others to apply for copies of government documents. There are a number of documents that are out of bounds but the process can be useful for holding governments accountable.)

I asked school divisions and city governments in both Winnipeg and Brandon (Manitoba's second-largest city) what analysis they did to take into account changes to taxpayers' incomes when deciding recent tax hikes. I also asked the province's power utility, Manitoba Hydro, what analysis it undertook to determine whether ratepayers could afford the Crown corporation's ambitious and highly risky plan to raise hydro rates by 3.95% every year for 20 years.

I filed similar requests with the City of Regina, Saskatoon and Moose Jaw.

All five Manitoba government bodies either responded bluntly that changes to taxpayers' incomes isn't a consideration or they used flowery language to hide the embarrassing reality.

I thought at least one of the five government bodies would have produced analysis demonstrating they reviewed Statistics Canada data to learn what was happening to the average Manitoban's income. Surely a bureaucrat or politicians would have noted something like *taxpayers incomes are only going up by 2% so we should keep tax increases at 2% or lower.*

Nope. None of them seemed to take income changes into account.

Regina and Moose Jaw provided similar responses. Saskatoon at least provided some survey data and claimed its citizens were behind tax and fee increases.

Overall, I observed government bodies out spending money on new projects, all the while just assuming taxpayers could afford the expenditures by paying higher taxes. If you live outside of Manitoba or Saskatchewan, try asking your municipal and provincial governments the same question: what analysis did they conduct prior to their last tax increase? You'll probably find the same result; ability to pay just isn't taken into consideration by the government.

Fundamentally, I believe the relationship between taxpayers and government bodies in Canada is broken. Governments not only need to start considering what taxpayers can actually afford, governments need to consider what taxes and fees other levels of government are charging.

For a lot of people, the government is already unaffordable. For those squeaking by right now, imagine what will happen if taxes jump substantially.

Are Government Employees' Salaries and Benefits Competitive?

I've worked for three different governments and have interacted with a lot of government staff over the years while working for the Canadian Taxpayers Federation.

I can tell you that there are some really great people who work in government and care deeply about how tax dollars are spent. There are also those who are just there to collect a paycheque.

My observation shouldn't come as a surprise though. There are literally millions of people working for the government across the country in one form or another, be it a department, a hospital, a school, a university, a Crown corporation, etc. Whenever you talk about any large group of people, you're probably going to find some good apples and some who aren't so good. For that reason, I really don't care for sweeping statements like "*all government employees are overpaid and underworked*" or "*people who work for the government are all honest and hard working.*"

No doubt there are some who fit both moulds. While working as a watchdog for the CTF, I would regularly get calls and emails from whistleblowers working for the government in various capacities. Each would usually describe seeing something that was wasteful or inappropriate, and then speak out.

In one case, a government employee scanned a couple of big group photos that one of their colleagues had received during "work trips" to Disneyland and Las Vegas. The whistleblower then mailed the pictures to me with a few notes about the wasteful trips. The whistleblower would email once in a while from a fake account and keep me up to date as I started to investigate the trips by filing requests for information with the government.

At one point I received a rather amusing email back:

"I just wanted to let you know that your information request isn't going anywhere. It's sitting in the CFO's drawer collecting dust. He thinks that you are going to forget about your request. You might want to shake the tree over there."

Needless to say, I shook the tree. Information was brought to light, future trips were cancelled and the CFO was placed on leave. None of that would have happened without the whistleblower's concern for tax dollars.

I raise these points because when one questions government pay and benefit levels, government employee union bosses will often respond, *"you're just against people that work for the government."* Another classic I chuckle at is *"you want everyone to work for minimum wage."*

Governments need to offer a competitive pay and benefits package or they're not going to entice very good candidates. But when you look at Statistics Canada numbers comparing government and non-government employees, the situation is pretty one-sided. In fact, it's not even close.

On average, those working for the government are paid more money, are more likely to have workplace pension plans (usually the most expensive type) and tend to take more sick time than everyone else. Hockey fans could call it "the government employee hat trick."

Government employees also have better job security too.

That's not to say there aren't exceptions, we're just talking big picture numbers.

Let's start with pay. Statistics Canada data from June 2012 show people in government earned an average of $1,040.36 per week, or $54,098.72 per year.

If you look at the same data for those working outside of government, the average weekly pay was only $806.59 or $41,942.68 per year.

Union bosses and socialist think-tank advocates would likely suggest that the private sector's numbers are lower because they include lower skilled jobs such as fast food employees, retail outlets and gas station workers making minimum wage.

But that argument ignores all the low-skilled jobs in government. Is cutting grass in a city park really a high-skilled task? What about a cashier at a government-run golf course? Or, say, what about the employee selling doughnuts at one of the government-run Tim Hortons outlets we discussed in chapter one?

Conversely, shouldn't all the millionaire hockey players and highly paid CEOs be inflating the private sector numbers? Those numbers would have an impact, but even with them in the mix, the biggest names in hockey can't close the pay gap.

While comparing overall average pay numbers in government and the private sector is interesting, I would argue the best way to look at the situation is by comparing similar positions in each sector.

Government employees serving up double-doubles at the hospital in Newfoundland and Labrador received about $28 per hour. That figure included benefit costs, but it's pretty well known that private sector workers employed at Tim Hortons don't see much in the way of benefits (e.g. pensions, dental plans, etc.) nor does their pay stray far above minimum wage.

Another good example is a comparison between YMCA lifeguards and lifeguards at City of Winnipeg pools.

In 2007, while working for Winnipeg's Economic Opportunity Commission, I spoke with the YMCA and was told their lifeguards made $9-10 per hour. At the time, lifeguards working in City of Winnipeg-run pools were making $17-22 per hour, plus benefits. In other words, roughly double.[12]

So that's two examples of nearly identical positions in the public and private sector and in each case the compensation gap is immense; government employees are paid far more.

However, I've usually found the compensation gap between government employees and the private sector to be more excessive on the pension and benefits side, at least when it comes to office work.

Looking at government pay reports, I would often come across positions where someone was making a salary of $55,000 or so when similar private-sector positions would earn around $45,000 or $50,000. That gap doesn't look too large (especially when compared to the lifeguard example), but the salary numbers fail to account for the generous pension typically offered to the government employee. Throw that in the mix and it changes everything.

A 2015 report by the Canadian Federation of Independent Business (CFIB) came to a similar conclusion.[13]

Using 2011 census data, the CFIB looked at different professional classifications in the private sector and compared the information to similar work in the public sector. What the organization found was startling.

CFIB reported that federal government employees earned about 13.0% more in wages than those working outside of government in similar classifications. However, once benefits were accounted for, particularly pension costs, federal workers enjoyed *33.2%* more in compensation than those in the private sector. Those golden government pensions strike again!

At the provincial level, the report found government employees were paid about 5.5% more than those outside government; but with benefits, provincial government employees made about *21.2%* more.

Finally, those working for municipal governments in Canada enjoyed an 8.9% wage premium over those working outside government. The compensation gap grew to *22.3%* once you included benefits. Overall, the CFIB calculates the compensation gap between government employees and everyone else comes out to $20 billion each year.

Things don't seem very fair to the taxpayer do they? (And to think some people just want the government to go out and raise taxes!)

Let's move on to the biggest part of benefit costs: pensions.

In 2012, the Canadian Taxpayers Federation issued a press release exposing a huge gap between government employees and everyone else when it came to pensions.[14]

The CTF highlighted Statistics Canada data that showed 87% of government employees had workplace pensions compared with just 24% for everyone else. The numbers weren't a blip on the radar either; they were part of long-term trends. Over the previous 30 years, more and more government employees enjoyed workplace pensions while more and more private sector workers did not.

But it's not so much that government employees have a workplace pension that's the problem, it's that most government employees (82% versus 13% in the private sector) have the most expensive plan out there – a defined-benefit plan.

Pensions can be really complicated, so I'll simplify this as much as possible.

First, let's talk about how most people – the 76% of us in the private sector who don't have employer-funded pensions – save for retirement.

Each month private sector employees take some money from their paycheque and invest in an RRSP or some other kind of investment such as a mutual fund. For example, they may decide to invest $300 each month.

Then they cross their fingers and hope their investment grows enough so that they have a little nest egg to rely on when they retire. Ultimately the average non-government employee is on their own. If their RRSPs lose value due to a recession or for a multitude of other reasons, that's it. The choice is either work longer and save up more money or retire with less money. No one will intercede to bail them out.

Government employees have an entirely different reality.

Most government employees have some money deducted from each paycheque and the funds are deposited into their workplace pension plan. At the same time, the government matches that contribution. So if you're a bureaucrat putting $300 into your pension plan per month, the government puts in another $300 … plus you receive the interest on the extra $300!

But it gets better – for government employees, that is.

Most government employee pension plans guarantee their members a certain payout upon retirement based on a set formula. It's often based on their best, final few years of pay.

So let's say a government employee reaches retirement age and has been promised $30,000 per year from their pension plan (note: whatever annual amount is promised usually rises over time for inflation). The government employee could even live to a hundred and draw significantly more from the fund than he or she ever put in. In fact, it's not uncommon for government employees to draw on their pensions for more years than they paid into the plan while working for the government.

Who covers the shortfall if the fund can't afford the payments? You guessed it; the taxpayer has to help out. The pension fund manager will regularly check whether there's enough money to meet pension plan's promises. If the number crunchers determine there isn't, both the government (taxpayers) and the employee end up contributing more money each month; perhaps both might have to increase their contributions from $300 to $350 per month.

I've made up the numbers in the aforementioned example to keep it simple, but you can see how the arrangement typically works. The plan requires lots of guesswork: how long will plan members live? How much interest will the pension fund earn over time? What will happen with inflation and employee wages in the future?

The high level of risk involved with getting all these questions right is why the private sector has largely moved away from these plans over the last 30 years. It's also why governments are seeing huge shortfalls (the "unfunded pension liabilities" I mentioned in chapter one) across Canada.

The bottom line is pension benefits enjoyed by government employees are typically far more expensive than those enjoyed by people outside of government.

In a nutshell: three-quarters of non-government employees are scrambling to save for our own retirement while also paying ever-higher taxes to bail out cushy government pension plans. These bailouts are one reason why most government employees are able to continue to retire in their 50s.

We've talked about pay and pensions, now let's touch upon sick time and job security.

It's well-known that it's pretty hard to get fired or laid off from a government job. Everyone seems to know a friend, neighbour or relative who has pushed the limits of government patience when it comes to poor work ethic.

Take for example, Franklin Andrews, a federal bureaucrat with the Department of Citizenship and Immigration.

According to a Sept. 9, 2011, *Toronto Sun* article, Andrews acknowledged spending between 50-100% of his work hours between September and November 2008 and May and August 2009 visiting *"adult sites, sports sites or doing online banking"* while his colleagues were busy logging overtime.[15]

Andrews was fired for his bad behaviour, but lucky for him, his union contract provided an appeal process and he was eventually hired back by the government.

While Andrews pointed out during the appeal process that he still finished his work, it doesn't excuse the fact that his colleagues were so busy that they logged overtime and he clearly didn't step in to help them.

If you can literally waste months fooling around on your computer looking at inappropriate material – and get away with it – it gives you a bit of insight into how lax it can be to work for the federal government.

Beyond stories of people not losing their jobs for bad behaviour, the government also doesn't react the same way when times are tough.

During the economic slowdown, the private sector suffered. People lost their jobs, faced pay cuts, wage freezes and many other not-so-pleasant consequences.

In government, the economic slowdown was largely like water off a duck's back.

Take a look at Statistics Canada's employment numbers from 2007 to 2012. During the economic slowdown, as the private sector was suffering a huge employment loss, the public sector saw a net *increase* in the number of people working for the government *every year*.

In the private sector, there was a reduction of about 340,000 jobs from June 2008 to June 2009. Employment inched up in 2010, but it wasn't until 2011 that things returned to where they were pre-recession. Hands down, government employees are also clear winners when it comes to job security.

Table 7: Employment Numbers (millions)

	June 2007	June 2008	June 2009	June 2010	June 2011	June 2012
Public Sector	3.25	3.39	3.41	3.49	3.58	3.67
Private Sector	13.54	13.69	13.35	13.59	13.74	13.74

Source: Statistics Canada Table 282-0089
Note: Private sector figures include the self-employed

Turning to sick leave, the Canadian Taxpayers Federation obtained data in 2013 that showed government employees in Canada took an average of 10.5 sick and disability days in 2012 versus 6.7 days for everyone working outside government.[16]

An extra four days per year may not sound like much, but multiply that by millions of government employees countrywide and that's quite the price tag. Put another way, government employees taking an extra 3.8 days is 57% higher than those working outside government. Clearly we're not talking about a minor tweaking that needs to occur when it comes to sick leave usage in government. Hands down, government employees 'win' the sick leave category as well.

Summary

Hopefully you can see government bodies in Canada are often a long way away from being cost-effective organizations.

In many cases, governments have tried to become all things to all people. Many governments aren't sticking to core services and a lot of opportunities still exist for governments to reduce costs by partnering with the private sector. In terms of services the government delivers in-house, there is often much room for improvement.

Finally, while not all government employees are overpaid compared to their counterparts in the private sector, the overall situation is quite lopsided. It's especially unfair to those working outside government and footing the bill.

So if all these problems are so clear, why on earth do they persist?

PART THREE

The five forces behind wasteful spending and what you can do about it

CHAPTER 5

Special Interest Groups

Throughout chapter four I described what a cost-effective government could look like. I also described how governments are inefficient and often wasteful with tax dollars. I concluded the chapter by asking *"if all these problems are so clear, why on earth do they persist?"*

Over the next five chapters I'm going to discuss how five "forces" contribute to wasteful and inefficient government spending. At the end of each chapter I'll describe possible solutions for addressing each force.

The first of those five forces are special interest groups. For the purposes of this chapter, one can think of a special interest group as a business, formal organization or loose-knit group of people who seek handouts, loans or other financial gifts from the government. (Note: although government employee unions are considered by many to be a special interest group, chapter six is entirely devoted to them.)

To understand why special interest groups often approach the government for funding, think of a common expression that people often use when trying to make sense of an odd government spending decision: *"it's easy to spend someone else's money."*

The expression is fitting as politicians and bureaucrats both wake up each day and spend someone else's money – the public's – and both are known for often being loose with the public purse.

Unlike in business, politicians and bureaucrats don't have to work as hard to keep costs down because they don't have competitors; tax dollars roll in almost by default.

Special interest groups know that bureaucrats and politicians are often carefree with the public purse. That's why special interest groups walk into government offices across Canada every day, year after year and ask for money.

They know that if they ask you to invest in their project or donate to their cause that you might say 'no.' It's easier for them to convince politicians and bureaucrats about spurious "job creation" numbers and "spinoff effects" that could come from throwing tax dollars at their project. Politicians often parrot those claims when smiling for the cameras and handing over big cheques to various groups.

In other cases, special interest groups merely take advantage of funding programs that politicians create. Either way, special interest groups are successful at obtaining billions of tax dollars each year. Not all special interest groups 'waste' the public funds they receive, but too many receive public funds that should not.

Let's take a look at the different types of special interest groups that seek your money, why government handouts aren't advisable and what can be done about the problem.

Broken Window Fallacy

A key argument used by special interest groups, and politicians, is that by spending tax dollars on select projects, the government is helping to "create jobs." However, that's just not true.

John Stossel, a U.S. journalist, does a great job dispelling the "government creates jobs" myth to rest in a YouTube clip called *"John Stossel's Broken Window Fallacy."*[1]

In the clip, Stossel describe how governments often claim that spending money on things like new roads and military aircraft will create jobs, as people will need to be hired for each project.

While Stossel approaches the issue from an American perspective, Canadian politicians use the same rhetoric, making the lesson valid north of the border.

In the clip, Stossel is seen walking down the sidewalk of an old area that looks like Manhattan and he begins to throw baseballs at the second floor windows of an apartment building. Stossel jokingly claims that by breaking the windows, he too was creating jobs. He explains that someone would have to be paid to clean up the broken window, deliver the new glass and install it.

He also notes that people would be required to build the truck that transports the glass, put a decal on the truck and all the other supporting services as well.

His ridiculous example of throwing baseballs through windows includes the same rhetoric used by politicians behind their examples of jobs they "create."

He explains that if someone didn't have to use their money to pay to clean up and replace the broken glass in their home, they could have used their money for something else – like buying things they wanted from local businesses.

Similarly, when the government spends *your* money to "create jobs," then there's less money in your pocket to "create jobs" by buying a teapot or a newspaper from a local store or dining at a local restaurant.

Stossel closes his segment by noting that government spending really just shuffles money around, it doesn't create any jobs. Instead of using your own money to buy something you want, the government spends your money on what it wants.

You may actually support the government's decision to take some of your tax dollars and build a new road or buy a new fighter jet, but don't be mistaken: the government isn't "creating jobs."

When governments spend money on social programs or give corporate welfare to businesses and other special groups, they're reducing the amount of money you have to spend on things that are important to you. It's not a question of 'job creation,' but a question of control – who spends your money, you or the government?

Lessons from the *"Broken Window Fallacy"* will be useful throughout this chapter.

Corporate Welfare

Cliff Oldridge is a former 17-year employee with the federal government's Industry Canada department.

During his time with the federal government, he was responsible for carefully reviewing applications for funding by various businesses. Once a grant or loan was approved, it was Cliff's job to monitor how well each recipient spent the funds and met certain goals. He was then expected to report back regularly to higher-ups.

Cliff described to me how he would receive Christmas cards and lunch invitations from businesses that received grants and loans from the government during his early years in the department. He never accepted any gifts from funding recipients and was always mindful of why they treated him like their new best friend.

Not surprisingly, when Cliff was transferred to the division that asked businesses to repay their loans, the Christmas cards dried up and Cliff was no longer Mr. Popular in the eyes of recipients.

Toward the end of Cliff's time with the federal government, he grew jaded about the whole 'corporate welfare' system. Year after year he would see the same companies walking in with their annual funding requests like addicts seeking drugs. For many companies, the government became a crutch; their businesses just didn't have a solid foundation and would perish without the handouts.

As for the politicians, Cliff was dismayed at the annual rubber-stamping of his division's annual budget. Seldom was there much in the way of scrutiny. He kept expecting politicians to dig into the results and focus on the number of actual jobs supposedly created and ask tough questions such as, *"how long did those jobs actually last?"* But the tough questions seldom came. The politicians almost always focused on the claims they could make publicly and the news coverage they would receive from cheque presentations rather than making sure that government loans were actually repaid or tracking job numbers over time.

Cliff described how he eventually grew so frustrated with the system that one day he found himself walking to a tall office tower in downtown Ottawa. The whole way there he carefully watched over his shoulder and once inside, he purposely got off the elevator on the wrong floor, just in case there were any followers. Cliff then found a stairwell and popped down to his destination.

Once he was sure he wasn't being tailed, Cliff located the Canadian Taxpayers Federation's office, walked inside and spilled the beans on what he knew from working in the department.

Cliff was careful not to share anything commercially sensitive or a business's private details with the taxpayers' watchdog, but he did explain just how backwards and reckless his department was with millions of dollars each year. He also carefully described what information the CTF should ask for in order to expose the problems to the public.

Cliff could have tried speaking to his superiors inside government, but he knew it would have been fruitless; the politicians were too pleased with the ribbon-cutting opportunities and the bureaucracy was too committed to the status quo. He knew the only way to change things was to expose through the media just how bad the system really was: he felt the public needed to know the truth.

The CTF lapped up what Cliff shared and within no time at all they went to work on filing information requests with Industry Canada, just as Cliff had directed.

"During one meeting with my colleagues, my boss actually walked in and talked about an information request filed by the CTF," Cliff recalls with a laugh.

"The boss actually said 'boy, these guys have great advisors.' While it felt like somewhat of a compliment, I probably sweated a bit more in that meeting than usual!"

Oddly enough, Cliff has almost spent as many years analyzing business subsidy programs during his retirement years as he did while working for the department.

In fact, one of the studies he helped the CTF with was one of the first reports I worked on, a 2009 report titled *"Western Economic Diversification: 22 Years of Pork Barrel Spending."*

As I started to go through the data that Cliff and a former colleague had gathered, I could see quite quickly why Cliff was so critical of corporate welfare and departments such as Western Economic Diversification (WED).

It was clearly a political slush fund if ever there was one.

Established in 1987, WED was tasked with trying to drive economic development in Western Canada by handing out cash and loans. Yet, after going through the list of the 21,340 recipients that had received funding as of 2009, I started to wonder: what *wouldn't* qualify for funding?

Given the program was set-up to "diversify the economy", one probably wouldn't be surprised to see that bicycle manufacturers, aerospace companies and golf tee manufacturers all received funding. (Governments often give funds to businesses and claim such recipients are "job creators.")

However, WED had also been busy handing out funds for everything from mural-painting projects in Moose Jaw, to municipal golf courses. Baseball diamonds, hockey rinks and signs that greet people to small towns were also funded.

How a well-raked batter's box on a baseball diamond diversifies an economy has me baffled to this day. It's one thing to claim you're "diversifying" an economy by giving money to businesses, but it's another to fund virtually everything under the sun, seemingly to curry votes for politicians.

We created in the report a chart that plotted funding by year and then overlaid dates for federal elections. Interestingly enough, funding often peaked during an election year or leading up to it.

In terms of sheer numbers, the department had handed out 21,340 grants or loans over the 22-year period for a total of $3.9 billion. Of the $801 million in loans that were dispersed, as of 2009, only $415 million had been paid back, an abysmal repayment rate of just 51.8%.

Could you run a bank while customers only repaid half the money loaned out? In the private sector such an arrangement would never work, but in government taxpayers end up footing the bill.

Not all the money was a waste. In fact, the report notes:

"...few Canadians would disagree with taxpayer dollars being used to fund cancer research projects. However, appropriate departments, in that

instance the department of health, should be the ones funding such projects, not through WED's 'catch all' approach."

And that's just it – using public funds to fix up baseball diamonds and hockey rinks is hardly the type of spending that would get most people's backs up. But it surely doesn't make sense to have WED, and numerous other departments, involving multiple levels of government, studying the same projects and each cutting cheques – think of the duplication!

But perhaps the icing on the cake in the WED report was the number of jobs created. Ah yes, the very reason why the department exists in the first place. The report notes:

"Although the department was created to drive economic development in Western Canada, it does not track the number of jobs it has created nor the number that have been sustained. In other words, it uses a fingers-crossed, shotgun approach to spending."

The report also notes:

"CTF requests for job numbers always get the same response: 'Western Economic Diversification does not track estimated jobs created or estimated jobs maintained.'

Go figure. One might think that after 22 years of funding, politicians would have demanded that the number of jobs created by the department be measured each year. I guess not.

The CTF's conclusions about Western Economic Diversification were not surprising. They were actually similar to numbers found in a May 2000 CTF report titled *ACOA: The Lost Decade: A 10-Year Quantitative Analysis*. The Atlantic Canada Opportunities Agency is similar to WED, except it hands out pork barrel funds in Atlantic Canada.

According to the report, from 1989-90 to 1998-99, ACOA had dispersed funding to 22,867 different recipients for a total of $2.6 billion.

Included in the list of recipients were some pretty big names: Bombardier, the Royal Bank, Pratt & Whitney as well as IBM Canada and Domtar. I guess this is what you might call "reverse Robin Hood."

Big unions such as the Canadian Auto Workers also received cash; so did teachers' associations and various Chambers of Commerce.

As with WED, one had to ask what *wouldn't* qualify for funding from ACOA? Golf courses, snowmobile clubs and other recreational activities were given cash as well.

Just as we saw in the WED report, ACOA also didn't do too well when it came to loan repayments: of the $591 million that was loaned out, more than 34% had to be written off.

One thing that hasn't been written off is the penchant many politicians have for funding such corporate welfare programs. While the amount of tax dollars spent on such schemes sure has added up over the years, positive results certainly have not. It's one of many forms of special interest group funding that should be brought to a halt.

Bailouts

Just as governments claim they're creating jobs by handing out money to growing businesses, governments also claim they're "protecting jobs" by giving money to businesses that are about to go under.

One classic case where we heard this claim was the enormous auto bailout in 2009.

General Motors and Chrysler both claimed they needed a loan from the federal government and Ontario's provincial government or they would go out of business and send the world into chaos ... or something like that. Proponents of the bailouts suggested there would be economic upheaval due to the significant role the auto sector plays in the province's economy.

While it's true the auto sector is a significant industry in Ontario, and a shutdown of one or two of the aforementioned automakers would have a sizable impact in the short term, a bailout wasn't the only option.

Both firms could have filed for bankruptcy protection, giving them a chance to restructure while warding off creditors. Perhaps the firms could have addressed a couple of the root causes of their financial problems, such as not selling enough products or paying employees a small fortune to do low-skilled work on an assembly line.

Consider what a Dec. 18, 2008, *Maclean's* magazine article had to say about the situation:

> *"On average, Canadian auto-sector workers make about $35 an hour – $72,000 a year – plus benefits. The average wage of a Canadian manufacturing-sector employee, by comparison, is $20.75 an hour, or $41,500 a year."*[2]

Or perhaps, as the U.S. Congress pointed out, the firms could have sold off the private jets they owned. A Nov. 19, 2008, *CNN.com* article described a rather amusing exchange in Washington between lawmakers and the cap-in-hand auto executives:

> *"There is a delicious irony in seeing private luxury jets flying into Washington, D.C., and people coming off of them with tin cups in their hand, saying that they're going to be trimming down and streamlining their businesses,"* Rep. Gary Ackerman, D-New York, told the chief executive officers of Ford, Chrysler and General Motors at a hearing of the House Financial Services Committee.
>
> *"It's almost like seeing a guy show up at the soup kitchen in high hat and tuxedo. It kind of makes you a little bit suspicious."*
>
> He added, *"couldn't you all have downgraded to first class or jet-pooled or something to get here? It would have at least sent a message that you do get it."*[3]

While we might scoff at the union greed that contributed to putting the car companies in a vulnerable position or the extravagance of the auto company executives, a business's private failings are just that: a business's private failings. It should be up to each business to figure out how it's going to stay afloat, not taxpayers.

If bailouts were in the interest of taxpayers, VHS and Betamax would still be around as would roller skates, Atari 2600 game systems and Pogo Balls.

But perhaps one of the worst "slap in the face" aspects of the $13.7-billion auto bailout was the 2012 announcement of a cancellation of the production of the Chevy Camaro at a plant in Oshawa, Ontario, and the shipment of jobs to Michigan. Years prior, the government had "helped" lure the production of the Camaro to Ontario with all kinds of assistance.

Talk about a strange way of saying "thanks for the bailout."

Thomas Walkom described the situation in the *Toronto Star*:

"Yet as Canadian autoworkers found out last month when GM announced plans to cancel Camaro production at its Oshawa plant, bailouts and subsidies don't guarantee jobs. That's because governments that make these deals rarely require ironclad employment commitments from corporate recipients.

"And because subsidies usually take the form of low-interest rate loans or outright gifts rather than shareholder equity, donor governments rarely have any say over a company's future hiring plans."[4]

I'm not suggesting the solution is for governments to have some say over the operations of companies to which they give tax dollars; the solution is for governments to not engage in subsidies in the first place. Instead, taxpayers should be the ones deciding which businesses receive their money: either through buying a business's product or perhaps through an investment.

If you think the government bailout to auto companies was an exception, you're incorrect. Walkom highlighted another great example back on Dec.11, 2013. He wrote about the recent news that Kellogg, the big cereal maker, was shutting down an old plant in London, Ontario. At the time, it employed 565 workers.[5]

Just a few years prior, the Ontario government gave Kellogg a $9.7-million low-interest loan to build a new plant in Belleville, Ontario, one that employs 100 people. In addition, the generous Ontario government also gave the firm $2.7 million in 2007 for buying processing and manufacturing equipment.

If you're keeping score at home, as subsidies to Kellogg increased, the numbers of people it employed decreased.

Incredibly, Walkom notes that up until the announcement of the London Kellogg plant closure, the Ontario government *was prepared to give Kellogg another grant, this one worth $4.5 million, to support its Belleville operation.*

While bailouts may seem to provide temporarily relief on the surface, far too often they fail because the recipients have structural problems that can't be fixed with a financial Band-Aid from the government.

Pro-Sports Subsidies

As a sports fan (a die-hard baseball fan) and someone who enjoys studying public policy, one of the sections I loved the most in Mark Milke's first edition of *Tax Me, I'm Canadian!* is the section on pro sports subsidies.

Milke's 2002 bestseller explores several arguments put forward by pro sports teams as to why governments should provide them with public funds … Milke then dispels those myths one by one.

One of the parts I enjoyed most in Milke's chapter on pro sports subsidies was some research he dug up by Raymond J. Keating from the Cato Institute. It addresses something we're going to examine first: who should foot the bill for building pro sports facilities?

Keating noted that a number of Major League Baseball stadiums were built before the depression and entirely with private funds. His list included Yankee Stadium in New York, Fenway Park in Boston, Tiger Stadium in Detroit and Wrigley Field in Chicago.

He also noted that Maple Leaf Gardens in Toronto, the former home of the Maple Leafs built in 1931, was 100% privately funded.

So if teams used to be able to pay for their own facilities – even during the Great Depression – why are taxpayers now so often called upon to help foot the bill?

Milke's chapter puts the absurdity of the situation into perspective.

Back in the day, professional sports team owners would foot the bill for their stadiums and arenas, sell tickets to the games and use the money to pay for player salaries. The owners would make money, the players would get paid to travel around and play a game for a living and the taxpayer didn't have to worry about subsidizing the whole process like they do today.

Fast-forward 100 years and everything has changed. Pro-sports salaries have skyrocketed and taxpayers are often forced to pick up the tab for the construction of stadiums and arenas (while many can't afford to attend the games).

According to *Ballparks.com*, the new Yankee Stadium in New York received over $200 million in government assistance.[6] The new baseball stadiums in Minneapolis and Detroit received $392 million and $115 million respectively.[7] AT&T Stadium, the new home for the NFL's Dallas Cowboys, was built with $325 million from taxpayers.[8]

In Canada, our pro sports scene is more limited, consisting primarily of seven NHL teams, a Major League Baseball team (Toronto Blue Jays) and an NBA team (Toronto Raptors). But we have our share of pro sports subsidy examples as well; the Rogers Centre in Toronto, the MTS Centre in Winnipeg, Rexall Place in Edmonton, Scotiabank Saddledome in Calgary and Canadian Tire Centre in Ottawa all received public funds.

Beyond outright grants for construction, there are other revenue streams to sports teams courtesy of governments. For example, a March 2012 article by the *Winnipeg Free Press* noted the Jets' owners receive about $11 million per year in tax breaks, tax rebates and lottery funds.[9]

A bit of caution: don't read the aforementioned article on subsidies and financial support to the Winnipeg Jets the same day you read more recent stories that show the value of the privately-owned Jets has doubled from $170 million in 2011 (when they were bought and moved to Winnipeg) to $340 million in 2013, it might make your blood boil.[10]

Governments allowing the cost of sports tickets and luxury boxes to be written off as business expenses also support pro sports teams. The Ontario government estimated in 2013 that it lost $15 million a year in revenue by allowing such write-offs.[11] Further, while it's not a subsidy per se, governments also spend millions each year on advertising at pro sports facilities.

I hope the big picture seems clear. We've gone from an era when players made decent pay, owners built their respective sporting facilities and taxpayers could choose to support a local team if they so desired, to an era when players are making a fortune, owners are getting rich and taxpayers are forced to subsidize teams and their facilities.

Talk about a tough pill to swallow.

So what's the alternative? Think about a couple of facts.

First, not every new NHL arena in Canada is paid for with public funds. Three current NHL arenas were actually paid for completely with private funds: the Air Canada Centre in Toronto, the Molson Centre in Montreal and GM Place in Vancouver.

Clearly it's *still* possible, even in this age of high salaries, for owners to build a pro sports facility themselves and make a buck. I would argue even smaller market franchises like the current Winnipeg Jets could operate without a subsidy from taxpayers.

The second point to note is that we all know there is a lot of room on the expense side of the ledger for NHL teams and other franchises to cut back.

If the Blue Jays or Flames want a new stadium or arena, they could easily fund either if they didn't pay their players obscene amounts of money each year.

If a team suddenly dropped its salaries in order to pay for a new arena or stadium, the team might suffer on the ice or field in terms of the quality of players signed. There's a tendency for teams to perform better as payrolls increase. However, one possible solution is something Milke has suggested: restrict governments from subsidizing businesses through the North American Free Trade Agreement.

In other words, if every team owner had no choice but to pay for their own facilities, then player salaries would have to come back down to earth.

Now let's visit the owners' arguments that pro sports teams create jobs and other economic activity and so they're entitled to at least some tax dollars. The story goes that some fans will visit from other cities to take in sporting events and jobs will be "created" in the process.

But couldn't that argument also be used by other businesses?

Picture a big law firm in downtown Vancouver with 50 employees who regularly commute from Surrey, Burnaby, Richmond and other municipalities.

Like the sports teams, the law firm is also attracting people from outside the municipality, in this case its own employees. And when those employees head to Vancouver each day for work, no doubt many will also spend money on things like parking and perhaps lunch or dinner at a local restaurant. The employees may also go shopping at a Vancouver store on their lunch break or before they head home from work.

But unlike the NHL team that only attracts people to the city for 41 home games, the Vancouver law firm is actually attracting the employees to the Municipality of Vancouver about 240 days per year or so (after you subtract weekends, holiday time, sick leave, etc.).

No doubt several other types of businesses could make the same argument, but obviously we could never develop (nor should we) a bureaucracy to evaluate how many people each business attracts and then provide them with a tax break or subsidy to help them out.

Team owners also point to increased foot traffic in restaurants on game night and increased merchandise sales at local retailers.

Yet those arguments also fall apart when you consider the alternative. If people didn't buy a Calgary Flames jersey or head to a local pub on game night to watch the Flames, they're not just going to sit at home and stare at the wall. No, they're going to spend the money on something else. Perhaps they may spend it on a ticket to a minor league game or maybe put the savings towards building a new deck. Who knows what people would do with the money? But it is clear it will return to the economy one way or another.

If you can't fathom how your city would survive without your favourite team, recall that Winnipeg was without an NHL team for 15 years, from 1996 until the 2011 season. Yet the city's economy still grew, the city's population still increased and the sun still came up each day. Sure, the loss of the Jets crushed the hearts of many in the city, but life went on.

The problem of sports teams holding taxpayers ransom isn't exclusive to the NHL and MLB in Canada; the Canadian Football League (CFL) has its own set of unique issues that ultimately result in taxpayers footing the bill.

It's difficult to compare the CFL to the NHL, NFL or Major League Baseball, because its salaries are far lower. The CFL also doesn't have lucrative TV contracts that exist for the NFL or high merchandise sales for CFL goods and apparel. Finally, naming rights deals for CFL stadiums pale in comparison to similar contracts in the NFL.

So how can CFL teams continue without big taxpayer subsidies for new stadiums? Well, two ways.

First, instead of looking at great new stadium drawings, falling in love with them and then building a palace on the backs of taxpayers, teams should consider a less sexy option, but more fiscally responsible option; repairing their old digs.

In 2008, while politicians in Winnipeg were falling over themselves to use tax dollars to build a new stadium for the Blue Bombers, they claimed fixing up the old stadium would cost $52.5 million, so building a new one for $115 million (the estimate before project ballooned to over $200 million) made a lot of sense.

Thankfully, *Winnipeg Sun* columnist Tom Brodbeck obtained the engineering report the politicians kept quoting from and exposed that their own report said repairing the stadium would cost only $14.4 million.[12] The politicians chose to quote a larger number that not only included a repair job, but also a grand renovation scheme.

Sure, $14.4 million would only have extended the life expectancy of the Bombers' stadium by another 10-20 years, but the club probably could have paid that bill themselves, unlike the $210 million stadium they ended up receiving, largely thanks to the taxpayer.

An engineering report on Mosaic Stadium in Regina came to a similar conclusion: a relatively small repair bill to fix up the ol' football stadium. But like we saw in Winnipeg, the politicians chose the more expensive option of building a new facility. In both cases, public input through a referendum just wasn't part of the process. Taxpayers were just given the bill.

Another option is for cities to choose new stadium designs that don't come with all the bells and whistles. The reality is, most CFL facilities are only used a dozen or so times a year. Teams could easily cut back on luxuries, and fans could accept that they're only at the stadium a few times a year, for a few hours each time.

If you're looking for some academic research on the subject of sports economics, I recommend an article in the September 2008 edition of *Econ Journal Watch* by economics professors Brad Humphreys from the University of Alberta and Dennis Coates from the University of Maryland. [13]

Of particular interest, Humphreys and Coates note:

"Both academic economists and consultants reach a conclusion about the economic impact of professional sports franchises and facilities, but these two groups reach opposite conclusions. The clear consensus among academic economists is that professional sports franchises and facilities generate no 'tangible' economic impacts in terms of income or job creation and are not, therefore, powerful instruments for fostering local economic development. The clear consensus among consultants who produce 'economic impact studies' is that professional sports franchises and facilities generate sizable job creation, incremental income increases, and additional tax revenues for state and local governments."

So there you have it. Independent economists give a thumbs-down to the claims of economic development arising from sports facilities while consultants – hired by proponents of the project – give a big thumbs-up to funding pro-sports teams and their facilities.

Take your pick.

Film Subsidies

Sports teams aren't alone in playing governments off against each other in order to milk as much money as they can from taxpayers. Hollywood is another billion-dollar industry that is in on the action.

Most provinces in Canada, as well as the federal government, have what are known as film tax credits. But don't let the name fool you; the program is more like a big subsidy program for movie productions than it is any kind of tax credit.

What happens is a provincial government, or the federal government, will reimburse a film for either a percentage of its labour costs or the cost of its production. For example, the provincial government in British Columbia offers a 35% refundable tax credit on labour costs related to filming within the province.[14]

So if you're a big Hollywood production and spend $100,000 on labour costs on a shoot in downtown Vancouver, you'd receive $35,000 back from the government. In addition, the federal government offers a 25% refundable tax credit on labour costs provided they meet certain criteria.[15]

Defenders of the subsidies argue that the tax credits attract Hollywood film productions to town, and the subsequent hiring of local labour is good for the economy as it helps employ people who in turn pay taxes. Proponents also like to talk about local businesses that benefit as well, such as those who may provide catering or perhaps materials for building movie sets. Sound familiar? It should because it is the same argument proponents of pro-sports subsidies use.

Like the pro-sports subsidy arguments, the film subsidy rhetoric unravels under scrutiny.

Think about the corner grocery store near your house. It also employs people and no doubt it pays for services from other local businesses; perhaps it might hire a local doormat cleaning service or an ad firm to help with drafting up flyers. Little grocery stores often sell local products as well, such as buns from a local bakery.

The rhetoric put forward by film tax credit proponents could also be used by the little factory or car repair garage you pass by on the way to work. In fact, most businesses could probably come up with the same arguments. But the reality is that there isn't a tax credit for every type of business out there. So why does the film industry have its own special subsidy? It shouldn't.

The film industry actually uses a subsidy established in one jurisdiction to push for higher subsidies in another. The loser, of course, is the taxpayer footing the bill.

Consider a June 17, 2013, article in the *Globe and Mail* titled: *"B.C. Wants Truce With Ontario, Quebec On Film Tax Credits."*[16] The article begins:

> *"B.C.'s Finance Minister is challenging his counterparts in Ontario and Quebec to stop allowing Hollywood studios to pit the three provinces against each other for 'unaffordable' film tax credits.*
>
> *"'As a country, and individual provinces within the country, we are better off to stop competing to see who can send the biggest cheque to Hollywood,' Mike de Jong said Monday."*

In 2013 alone, B.C. taxpayers coughed up approximately $300 million towards film production subsidies.[17]

The situation is a bit like what has happened in pro sports. Taxpayers are coughing up more and more while players' salaries have increased; in this case, it's Hollywood actors and actresses. Think about these subsidies the next time you hear a Hollywood celebrity making $20 million per film.

Unfortunately for American taxpayers, Canada isn't the only one in on the subsidy game. Most states south of the border have tax credits in one form or another as well ... and their spending on the subsidies isn't cheap either.

According to a "back-of-the-envelope" calculation by the Tax Foundation, a *conservative* think tank in the U.S., between 2005 and 2010 taxpayers shelled out at least $3.5 billion in subsidies to film companies.

After studying the claims and numbers behind film tax credits, the think tank concluded in a January 2010 Special Report, *Movie Production Incentives: Blockbuster Support For Lackluster Policy:*

"Movie production incentives are costly and fail to live up to their promises. Nonetheless, they remain popular with state officials and many of their constituents. Some of the MPIs' negative results may eventually cause this support to wither, particularly in tough economic times. Among these failures, the two most important are their failure to encourage economic growth overall and their failure to raise tax revenue."[18]

If you think that sounds critical of the film industry's claims, note what the Center on Budget and Policy Priorities, a *liberal* think tank in Washington, had to say about film tax credits. In a 2010 report titled *State Film Subsidies: Not Much Bang for Too Many Bucks* they noted:

"Like a Hollywood fantasy, claims that tax subsidies for film and TV productions – which nearly every state has adopted in recent years – are cost-effective tools of job and income creation are more fiction than fact. In the harsh light of reality, film subsidies offer little bang for the buck."

"The revenue generated by economic activity induced by film subsidies falls far short of the subsidies' direct costs to the state. To balance its budget, the state must therefore cut spending or raise revenues elsewhere, dampening the subsidies' positive economic impact."[19]

So there you have it, liberal *and* conservative think tanks in the U.S. both came to the same conclusion about film subsidies: they don't work. It's time to scrap film subsidies in Canada.

Arts Groups Funding

Would you be outraged if you heard that your tax dollars helped lure a Belgian machine to Canada that mimics the process by which humans make … poop? Because they did.

The Belgian poop machine was an "art" installation that the Canadian Council for the Arts, a federally funded arts body, spent $15,000 to bring to Canada.

The expenditure made national headlines in 2008 when the Canadian Taxpayers Federation awarded the Canada Council for the Arts one of the annual government waste awards described in chapter four.

The CTF recognized the Council that year not just for its poop machine, but also for an $80,000 grant it gave to Cesar Saez, an artist living in the Montreal area to help him with a rather ambitious project: build a giant floating banana to fly it over the state of Texas. Why Texas? Well, it was part of his political agenda, to mock George W. Bush, the former president of the United States, who had a ranch in the state.

Saez told *CTV News* in Montreal, *"The banana has a lot of symbolism: phallic, humour, and political, too."*[20]

For what it's worth, if you look up the artist's name online, you'll come across a Wikipedia entry that suggests he is actually an Argentinian and fled the country before the project got off the ground. The word "hoax" comes up quite a bit too. Not that either tidbit should surprise anyone.

The poop machine and flying banana are low-hanging fruit for those who question such spending, but perhaps not as odd as a dead rabbit exhibit that received funding in 1999 in Winnipeg.

An artist created an exhibit called *Monstrance*, which featured skinned rabbits that were hung from trees outside a "cultural centre."[21] Each rabbit had been cut open, stuffed with a picture then sewn back up. One of the "features" of the exhibit was that as the rabbits decayed, the photos would become evident to visitors. It certainly sounds like it would have made a lovely stop for a first date doesn't it?

At this point you may be wondering how I could discuss questionable art exhibit funding without mentioning the piece de resistance, *"Voice of Fire."*

If the name doesn't ring a bell, perhaps a description by former MP Felix Holtmann, will help you recall the exhibit. Holtmann, then chair of the House of Commons standing committee on communications and culture, had this to say about the piece:

"It looks like two cans of paint and two rollers and about ten minutes would do the trick."

The piece of art, as you might gather from Holtmann's description, is extremely simple. It's an 18-foot vertical, rectangular canvas covered with just three vertical stripes, two blue stripes on the outside and a single red stripe up the middle.

The artwork was obtained in 1990 by the National Gallery of Canada, a government subsidized art gallery, and made national news for its price tag. Just as the Canadian economy slid into a recession, the Gallery purchased the piece for a whopping $1.8 million (around $2.8 million in 2013 dollars).

Understandably, the news didn't sit well with Canadians. The book *Voices of Fire: Art, Rage, Power and the State* described the public's reaction:

"Objections came from all quarters. The general public voiced its disapproval in on-the-street interviews with the broadcast media and in letters to the editors of daily newspapers; Canadian artists condemned the gallery through a statement issued by a national artists' lobby group; and members of the Conservative party, the political party in power, threatened to rescind the purchase ... The public uproar over Voice of Fire lasted for two months before subsiding."[22]

I could go on and on with example after example of outlandish art exhibits receiving funding. Sure, I've highlighted some of the more absurd examples, but that's just it with art; it's a highly subjective form of expression. No doubt there were some people who actually liked the dead rabbit exhibit.

The question is, should the government be funding art in the first place? Is that really the role of government? Should taxpayers really be forced to fork over millions, if not billions, to the government each year that in turn is spent by bureaucrats on art *they* decide is worthy?

Even if you answered "yes," given the many serious financial storm clouds that are gathering on our horizon, we simply can't afford to keep funding such activities. Surely most people would put health care, roads and policing ahead of some of the aforementioned art examples.

We need to remember that if someone creates inspiring art they shouldn't have a problem selling it for a profit. People buy art all the time in stores, community fairs, etc. from artists who aren't subsidized. Why do they buy the art? Because it provides a value to them so they have no problem reaching into their pocket to support it.

You may hear arguments that public art simply wouldn't exist without public funds. Yet, the "art can't survive without subsidies" crowd always seems to forget about all the artists who don't accept government handouts for their work.

Search for "U2 Out of Control Slane Castle live" on YouTube and you'll come across a music video by the famous Irish rock band. During the video clip of a live performance, the band's lead singer Bono tells the inspiring story of how the band got its start.

Bono tells how, decades ago, he went to his father and asked for a loan of 500 pounds. He told his dad he wanted the money to put towards trying to score a record deal in London. The singer goes on to describe how each band member asked the same of their parents.

The band has gone on to become one of the most successful music acts of all time. If U2, a small band from Ireland, can scrape together funds from people who believed in them, why can't other artists?

If you like that heart-warming story about family coming together to help someone's artistic dream, you'll probably like the story of a giant banana statue in Melita, a small town in southern Manitoba. Melita is jokingly referred to as being part of the province's "banana belt" (because temperatures are often a couple of degrees warmer there than the rest of southern Manitoba). The people of Melita decided to play to their nickname, by erecting a large banana statue.

Instead of going to the government and seeking a big cheque courtesy of taxpayers, proponents reached into their own pockets and worked hard to raise $106,000 in donations to pay for the statue.

Greg Leader, who headed up the banana project, told the Winnipeg Free Press:

"No government money, no nothing. Just pure donations. I wouldn't want government money for something like this."[23]

If you think the public is only capable of raising $100,000 or so for an art project, consider Crazy Horse, the large memorial that is being carved into the side of a mountain near Mount Rushmore. The immense carving depicts a former Sioux Chief, Crazy Horse, riding a horse and pointing straight ahead.

Once completed, the memorial in South Dakota will be the largest mountain carving in the world. However, as it began in 1948, it certainly is one of the more time-consuming art projects taken on in recent years. The project would have been completed years ago but those involved have always refused government funding. They wanted full artistic control.

Over the years, proponents have worked hard to raise voluntary donations for the project, including one in December 2013 for $10 million from South Dakota philanthropist T. Denny Sanford.[24]

So if a little town like Melita and the people of South Dakota can see the merit in retaining integrity and refusing government subsidies, why couldn't people in Vancouver have raised voluntary donations for a giant poodle statue that went up in 2012?

Weighing in at a cost of $97,000, the seven-foot aluminum-cast poodle sits on top of a 25-foot pole, presumably to keep it away from cats.[25] The federal government, the City of Vancouver and Translink (government-funded transit body) took care of the bill for the installation in a residential area of Vancouver. Just like other forms of art, the poodle also has its critics and fans.

But again, couldn't the project's fans have reached into their own pockets to foot the bill? That would have told you whether people really wanted it or not.

The bottom line with art is that it's highly subjective. Bureaucrats and politicians shouldn't be the ones deciding which art is funded; those decisions should be left up to taxpayers. Canada's many talented artists, who regularly produce popular pieces of art, won't have a problem continuing to sell their work on its own merit.

Others

It's not just businesses, pro sports and artists that are at the trough seeking public funds for their pet projects. There are many other organizations and individuals seeking *your* money for *their* projects as well.

Some are less controversial than others. For example, Habitat for Humanity is a charity that assists low-income people with home ownership. Beneficiaries are not only required to work on the home they purchase, they must also pitch in and help build homes for others in the program. The organization was given free land courtesy of the B.C. government in 2013.[26]

Is anyone really going to get upset about such support? Probably not. Several non-profits help save the government money as their activities help keep people off government services like social assistance and government housing.

However, there are plenty of other groups and projects that are gobbling up cash for more questionable purposes. For example, the Canadian Centre for Policy Alternatives, a left-wing think tank based in Ottawa, has eaten up thousands of tax dollars over the years. In short, the organization pushes for higher taxes and a larger role for government in our lives.

Obviously those who disagree with the think tank's ideological views will probably be disappointed to learn it receives lots of public money through "membership fees" to the government or by selling its research. From 2009-10 to 2011-12, the organization received over $123,000 from Manitoba taxpayers alone.[27]

A couple of other good examples come from a Jan. 7, 2013, *Maclean's* article on 99 "stupid" things the government spent tax dollars on:

"Tear down the haul: The federal government subsidized Quebec City's summer festival to the tune of $1 million, in part to help pay for a show by former Pink Floyd band member Roger Waters. The Plains of Abraham was the last stop on the aging rocker's Wall Tour, which earned a total of $158 million from worldwide ticket sales."[28]

Not to be outdone, Halifax was in on the concert bailout action as well:

"A black eye: In May, Halifax councillors voted to cut a cheque for $360,000 to cover bad debts stemming from a money-losing Black Eyed Peas concert two years earlier."

If you visit the federal government's web site and look in the "disclosure of grants and contributions over $25,000" section of each department's "proactive disclosure" area, you can find all kinds of other groups snatching up tax dollars.

Here are a few examples of big cheques provided by the Canadian Heritage department:[29]

- *$26,202 - Manitoba Metis Federation Southwest Region Inc.*
- *$3,193,840 - Canadian Canoe Association*
- *$57,500 Gaspesian British Heritage Village*
- *$1,410,000 - Association Canadienne-Francaise de l'Alberta*
- *$138,100 - K-W Oktoberfest Inc.*

With all due disrespect to the aforementioned groups and ethnicities, why are taxpayers having to foot the bill for their private interests?

If you're French and living in Alberta, aren't you capable of deciding if you want to donate to the "Association Canadienne-Francaise de l'Alberta" or not? Obviously the answer is "yes." So why is the government stepping in?

Aside from various special interest groups, there are all kinds of universities, students and professors receiving research grants for questionable topics. Not to demean their studies – to each one's own – but given the big-picture problems our country is facing, do these topics really help the government or broader society prepare for what's coming?

- *$11,034 - For studying parody and humour in early Japanese Buddhism*
- *$72,593 - Study on linking gender, climate change, adaptive capacity and forest-based communities in Canada*
- *$56,243 - German-speaking Emigre-Neuroscientists in CDA & US 1930s-1970s*
- *$74,918 - Mobilizing Lesbian Knowledge: Building the Archives of Lesbian Oral Testimony*
- *$36,921 - "Scottish Agriculture and the Fictions of Improvement"*[30]

Sadly, one could go on and on with similar questionable grants.

Solutions

When it comes to dealing with special interest groups, the policy solution is pretty easy: just don't fund them. Sure, there may be the odd group that is worthy and could perhaps provide a service (e.g. a shelter giving a hand up to the homeless) in a more cost effective manner than if the government provided it (social assistance and government housing programs). But on the whole, funding to special interest groups is an area for governments to cut back. The public is more than capable of deciding for themselves which projects to support financially.

I like Mark Milke's idea to amend the North American Free Trade Agreement (NAFTA) to restrict governments from subsidizing businesses. Achieving an agreement would make it hard for any political party to simply opt out. However, convincing both the U.S. and Canadian governments to sign on to such an agreement is likely easier said than done.

Instead of asking what can legally stop political parties and politicians from being able to engage in such spending, I think we need to ask what will make political parties not want to fund such activities in the first place? The answer lies in educating voters in order to change their preferences.

If politicians know that voters are fed up with funding special interest groups, you'll see politicians make promises during elections like opposing grants to businesses or perhaps requiring a referendum before public funds are used for a new stadium.

For example, during the 1995 election in Ontario, Progressive Conservative leader Mike Harris held a press conference on top of a downtown Toronto office tower and announced his party would cut the hundreds of millions of dollars spent on "corporate welfare" each year.

So how do we educate voters and change their preferences? How do we create the ripe conditions so that more politicians like Harris come forward with the courage to commit to tackling the problems we've explored? I'll discuss that challenge more in depth in chapter nine.

But before we get there, we need to tackle one of the biggest forms of special interest groups, a group so large that it gets a chapter all to itself: government employee unions.

CHAPTER 6

Government Employee Unions

Government employee unions are the second major force that contributes to wasteful and inefficient government spending.

Recall, government employees tend to earn more than their counterparts in the private sector, they generally have far more generous pensions and benefits, and take more sick time as well. Plus government employees often enjoy job security that is second to none.

Why are so many politicians scared to do anything about the problem? How can governments afford to be so generous with their employees? What can be done?

Those are some of the issues I'm going to discuss in-depth in this chapter.

But before we delve into those matters, let's explore a few examples of government employee unions gone wild ... just to get your blood pumping.

In April 2007, a couple of city workers were driving around Yorkton, Saskatchewan, in a water truck and doing some spring cleaning when they noticed smoke coming from a nearby home.

The duo decided to drive over and take a look.

When the pair arrived on scene they found a home on fire and the city's fire chief, but no firefighters had arrived yet. The chief asked the city workers if they could start dousing the fire with water from their city truck until fire crews arrived. The pair happily obliged.

Firefighters eventually showed up to finish the job, but what unfolded afterwards was, in short, appalling.

The public works crew received an award from the RCMP for their efforts, but according to a *CBC* story on the incident, the firefighters' union actually filed a grievance against the fire chief over what happened.[1]

The union claimed the chief's actions resulted in "contracting out" and violated their collective agreement. In other words, the union felt the home should have continued to burn until firefighters arrived on the scene. According to the union, the progress the public works employees achieved in containing the fire should have been discarded in the name of union job preservation!

If that anecdote makes you shake your head, consider this next one about the Canadian Union of Public Employees (CUPE) strike in 2009 in Windsor, Ontario.

At the time, Windsor was like many cities in that city employees still handled garbage collection. When CUPE decided to strike, garbage collection was put on hold, including at city parks.

If you've never lived through a garbage strike, I can tell you it isn't fun; I lived through one in Toronto back in 2002. It was surprising how it didn't take too long before garbage really started to pile up on the streets. The smell was especially offensive for pedestrians, even worse during hot summer days and when you would pass by the odd home that had put out dirty baby diapers … but I digress.

Public parks also deteriorate quickly during such strikes. I can remember walking by one during the Toronto strike and seeing garbage cans overflowing with waste.

Windsor's garbage strike also saw overflowing bins and litter-filled parks. But what made the situation even more newsworthy was that some striking city employees decided to make the problem worse.

During the strike a couple of grandparents wanted to teach their grand-daughter about keeping the community clean, so they popped by a local park to volunteer and pick up litter.

According to an *A-Channel* news report, the trio was busy picking up garbage in the park when some striking city workers came along and started emptying garbage bags full of rubbish right in front of them. Thankfully, the grandfather captured the incident on a cell phone camera.[2]

The clip that ran on the news shows a rather portly striker dumping a bag of garbage on the ground and then kicking it around like an angry bull rampaging in a china shop.

According to the news report, the striking city worker said to the trio: *"Here's some more garbage … since you think you should be doing our jobs."*

That's quite the sense of entitlement isn't it? The government employees decided to walk off the job because they didn't like their pay and benefits yet they also figured everyone else should just sit idly by and suffer as park conditions deteriorated.

This is an attitude that I've seen expressed subtly or explicitly in one way or another by many of the elite in government employee unions over the years. They seem to think the taxpayer is there to serve them, rather than the other way around.

Sure, the typical teacher or nurse you know probably doesn't share these extremist views, but those that rise to the top of the union movement often seem to be more radical or unreasonable.

Remember the quote in chapter one from Toronto School Board union Boss Jimmy Hazel about not having to *"f—— prove anything to anybody"* about the outrageous costs for screwing in a pencil sharpener?

Or perhaps you remember an incident from 2003 involving the Ontario English Catholic Teachers Association (a union) and a former teacher, then-education minister Elizabeth Witmer. According to the *St. Petersburg Times Online*:

> *"Ontario Education Minister Elizabeth Witmer was punched, jostled and heckled by an angry mob of teachers as she left their convention in Toronto. Shouting protesters, some wearing paper bags over their heads, rushed after her. One man pushed her, one punched her and someone threw a glass of water at her. The Ontario English Catholic Teachers' Association has apologized. Teachers are upset over education cuts."[3]*

And these people are entrusted with teaching children? One has to wonder, what would the Pope say?

Certainly these radicals didn't do any favours for the many rational teachers out there who weren't at the convention and don't engage in such behaviour. Not to mention union bosses and activists who are more reasonable.

So why do some government union activists behave like spoiled, entitled children? I think it's simply because governments often treat them like spoiled children. All the pay and perks have gone to their heads.

No doubt that contributes to the entitlement attitude shared by some union radicals, the same way a kid with every toy he or she ever wanted might act a little spoiled too.

No Market Forces At Work

The pimply teen who stocks the shelves at your local grocery store could probably help explain how the relationship between taxpayers and government employees has become so lopsided.

Ask him what happens if his union goes on strike and holds out for something outrageous like an immediate $5 hourly wage increase for all employees; perhaps a jump from $16 per hour to $21 per hour for the typical store worker.

Even the teen could probably recognize that such a demand could potentially drive the company he works for out of business. After all, wage increases have to get passed on to the consumer through higher prices. A big jump in prices could lead customers to shop somewhere else, potentially never coming back.

The pimply teen might also tell you a similar effect occurs in factories as well. If factory workers push for too much in terms of wages and benefits, the factory's cost structure could get too high and increase the cost of goods it produces, ultimately reducing sales and causing a drop in production. This is one reason why we often see factory owners pack up shop and move to jurisdictions with lower cost structures.

And it's not always a move to low-wage countries like China or Vietnam. As I noted in chapter five, General Motors packed up shop and moved Ontario jobs to Michigan, a state with slightly lower wage costs and labour laws that are becoming more balanced.

The bottom line is most unions in the private sector know that businesses have to be competitive. If union members make it too difficult for the business to operate, they know it could actually put their own jobs at risk.

At the same time, businesses know they can't offer their employees peanuts. If businesses don't offer competitive wages and benefits they'll lose good workers to other companies and will then have to spend time and money hiring and training replacements.

Thus, there's a delicate balancing act that goes on between business managers and labour. In government, the same check and balance doesn't exist.

For example, if a municipality gives its firefighters a generous pay increase, the extra cost is passed on to taxpayers through higher property taxes. You obviously can't shop around for lower-priced firefighting services; it's a government service that you must pay for.

Either you pay the property tax increase or you have to pack up your things and move.

Similarly, when a teachers' union or nurses' union receives a big pay increase, you get stuck with the bill. Sure, you could put your kids in private schools or buy your health care in the U.S., but as long as you still live in the province you still have to pay for the union's salary increases through your income taxes, sales taxes, and other provincial taxes that fund those services.

There is virtually no force keeping government employee pay and benefits in line. Taxpayers cannot choose a more competitive service in the same way that a consumer can simply go to another store if prices rise.

And because firefighters, nurses, police officers and many other government employee groups are often considered an "essential service" they are typically forbidden from striking. Because they can't strike, an arbitrator is often brought in during labour negotiations to hear the government's side, the union's side and then determine a pay increase.

Unfortunately for taxpayers, arbitrators usually decide pay increases that are above inflation and higher than what everyone else is receiving. This is one reason why the gap has grown in Canada between government employees and everyone else; all those 3% increases for certain government employee unions add up while everyone else is receiving 2%. I've simplified the numbers, but it's not difficult to see how the trend becomes a problem over time.

While some people might move to friendlier tax regimes, unsustainable government employee pay increases are becoming a problem nationwide. Government unions in one city or province often use gains in another jurisdiction as justification for demanding a similar wage and benefit increase.

For example, when a firefighters' union bargains with a municipal government, they will point to recent contracts in other cities and argue *"we deserve the same or more to stay competitive."*

Once the union inevitably receives the generous increase, firefighters unions across the country will then point to that increase and push for the same. And so goes the cycle of increases, a problem I often refer to as "public sector leapfrog." Unions leapfrog each other continually, always landing on higher pay levels with no force keeping their pay in line like we see in business. All the while the taxpayer loses.

In an April 15, 2013, article on government pay, *Maclean's* describes this phenomenon, noting:

> *"A few years ago, Saskatoon's firefighters were given an 18% raise. They got the raise because Regina's firefighters were making 12% more. On that basis, an arbitrator awarded firefighters in nearby Moose Jaw a 17% raise. By then, firefighters in Regina had become the provincial paupers. So last September, an arbitrator bumped up their pay by 14%."*[4]

Interestingly, and quite possibly around the time Regina's firefighters received a pay increase, Alex Forrest, president of the firefighters' union in Winnipeg, posted the following on Facebook:

"Alex Forrest is traveling to Regina for their contract arbitration involving wages and benefits. We all need to work together in western Canada. Good luck Regina!"

On another occasion he tweeted:

"Just arrived in Edmonton to assist and observe the Arbitration for wages for all Edmonton Firefighters. Great work by the EFFU!"

Alex Forrest and the firefighters union clearly demonstrates cooperation among unions to push for higher and higher pay. I have little doubt that Forrest and firefighters are the only ones engaging in this behavior.

Over the years I've encouraged governments to follow the union lead: work together on the other side of the bargaining table, on behalf of taxpayers, to get the system under control. Otherwise the consequences could be dire. Clearly, even if you move to another province, it's hard to avoid this game.

The big-picture point I'm making is that the government's relationship with its employees is completely different from the relationship between businesses and their workers.

Some might balk at that suggestion and point to Detroit.

In 2013, after decades of financial and social problems, the Motor City filed for bankruptcy. The city's massive government employee pension debt was a significant factor. Some might try to call that the "check and balance" in government.

Sure, Detroit filed for bankruptcy, and its pension and labour costs were a major part of the problem … but who wants to end up like Detroit?

During the decades-long path to bankruptcy, Detroit experienced a long, slow erosion of people moving out of the city, crime increased, the poor were left behind and the community collectively saw a massive drop in real estate values. Drive around Detroit today and it's quite depressing. No one in their right mind wants to repeat the Detroit experience.

We also need to recall that the Detroit example was anything but a swift move like you see in the private sector. If a business's labour costs get way out of control, it'll collapse in relatively short order. There's seldom a long, slow 30- or 40-year decline like we saw in Detroit.

Different Incentive Structure

Another key difference in government is that those negotiating labour contracts on behalf of the government don't have the same incentive structure as private businesses.

Private businesses are incentivized to roll up their sleeves and bargain hard with employees. After all, higher costs reduce profits for owners or shareholders. In government, bureaucrats and politicians negotiate with other people's money. If a government employee union receives a 3.2% increase instead of a 3.1% increase, it's often no skin off the back of the government's negotiator. But for a business owner that tiny 0.1% difference could reduce profits by thousands or even millions of dollars.

If that same business is bidding on a major project, and if margins are tight, a 0.1% difference could literally make or break the firm's ability to win the contract. Businesses are more likely to bargain harder to get that extra 0.1% as there's more at stake.

Now think about a top government manager in a hospital or health region negotiating with the nurses' union. The government manager may think nothing of preserving or enhancing the nurses' pension. To the manager, having a golden government pension probably just seems normal; the manager probably has one too! But what seems normal to the government manager is quite different in the private sector.

In 2009, I had a meeting with a few staff working on the federal government's new Canadian Museum for Human Rights, the massive new facility that opened in Winnipeg in 2014.

I was invited in for a meeting as I had been chirping in the media about the huge cost overruns with building the museum (then "only" about $45 million over budget, it eventually went more than $90 million over budget).

During our meeting, I inquired about the pension plan for employees. A staff person in the meeting indicated that the museum decided to join the federal government's employee pension plan (a golden plan if ever there was one). I then asked:

"Was there was any thought to not having a pension plan for staff?"

Given the massive cost overruns, I hoped that the generous government pension might have been on the chopping block. At the time, Statistics Canada data had showed approximately three-quarters of people working outside government in Canada didn't have a workplace pension. Thus, by eliminating the golden pension plan, employees at the museum would have been like most Canadians working outside government.

But judging by the reaction on the employees' faces I may as well have suggested they work 20-hour shifts and get paid $5 a day or some other radical idea. The notion of not having a workplace pension was clearly a foreign concept to them. They just couldn't seem to wrap their heads around not having a golden retirement awaiting them.

Political Interference

Another key difference in union negotiations between businesses and governments is political involvement. Namely, politicians are involved in government union negotiations but not in private sector union discussions.

Politicians often determine whether or not they're willing to see a strike happen and even how long they are willing to put up with such a strike. If politicians don't want the headache that comes with striking employees, they may decide to cave in and provide, say, a 3% increase rather than holding out for a 2.7% increase. This obviously costs the taxpayer more money.

One has to remember, increases in pay are always passed on to tax-payers and they impact budgets determined by politicians. This leads to perhaps the biggest distortion of the whole process: politicians' concern for votes.

Politicians are keenly aware that rolling up their sleeves and bargaining hard with government employees, especially just before an election, could cost (or gain) votes. Politicians know that it's not just the votes of, say, the union's 10,000 members that are on the line. Union members will often try to sway the votes of their spouses, family members and the public too.

This same dynamic doesn't happen outside government because union workers employed by a business don't vote for or against their bosses.

According to 2010 Statistics Canada figures, of the 3.5 million govern-ment employees in the country, 2.5 million were unionized.[5] That works out to 71%, which is much higher than the 16% of private sector workers who are unionized (1.7 million that year). Now imagine if each of those 2.5 million unionized government employees has the ability to impact just one other voter. That means we're potentially talking about five mil-lion votes on the line, a calculation that politicians have no doubt already considered.

Not only do those union members vote, many will get involved dur-ing elections. Unlike those working outside government (who merely foot the bill), unionized government employees are much more motivated to get involved because they're impacted by politicians in a much bigger way.

If you were a government employee, which politician would you want running your workplace?

Politician A – Promises to reduce the size of the bureaucracy (potentially cutting your job)
Politician B – Is content to keep on growing the bureaucracy and spending as if money is no object, guaranteeing your job and all of its perks

The answer is clear.

If you're an education minister who upsets a teachers' union by ordering your staff to bargain harder, or by introducing semi-regular tests of teachers, good luck to you. Don't be surprised if the union comes at you like a ton of bricks during the election with an army of motivated teacher volunteers who deliver flyers or knock on doors for your opponents. Certainly other politicians know they can face the same type of wrath from other government employee unions.

Government employee unions have also been known to run big ad campaigns to scare the public into voting against a particular party. In the 2007 election in Manitoba, the nurses union did just that.[6] The ads featured nurses talking about 'how bad things were' when the Progressive Conservatives were in power in the 1990s. The ads zoomed in on nurses' hands and showed them fidgeting nervously to drive home their point. If there were an Oscar award for Manitoba political attack ads, the nurses' union ad would be tough to beat.

The creators of the union's ads clearly knew which emotional buttons to push with the public in order to help their friends in the NDP get re-elected and keep the gravy train barreling down the track.

And that's not a partisan jab; the NDP is recognized across the country as the party most closely connected to unions. In fact, if you review the party's federal constitution, you'll see it even sets aside delegate positions for union leaders at the party's conferences.[7]

So why does that matter?

Well, when the NDP holds a policy convention to determine its position on various policies, including those that impact unions specifically, the aforementioned union groups are guaranteed a set number of votes on each decision.

Meanwhile, the average Joe working in a factory, who supports the NDP and would like to go to the convention, would have to be elected as a representative from their local NDP riding association. The latter could be a difficult task if the riding has a lot of grassroots supporters vying for the same delegate spot. Clearly, it's much more difficult for average members in the NDP to influence party policies than it is for the union elite.

To see just how powerful unions can be in the NDP's affairs, reflect on the role they had in the Manitoba NDP's 2015 leadership vote. After rebel MLAs and cabinet ministers in the NDP caucus tried to oust Premier Greg Selinger, a leadership vote was called. Of the 2,217 delegate positions up for grabs, the Canadian Press reported that up to a whopping 691 spots were set aside for unions in the province.[8]

If the federal Conservatives or Liberals set aside delegate positions for the CEO of Ford Canada or local Chamber of Commerce presidents, the NDP would be incensed and scream from the rooftops. It's amazing the NDP's enormous conflict of interest doesn't receive more media attention.

Another example of union support for (and influence over) the NDP comes in the form of cold hard cash.

The "party donations" section of Elections Saskatchewan's web site shows donations to both the Saskatchewan Party (made up primarily of liberals and conservatives) and NDP during 2011-12. The reports show 30 trade unions donated a whopping $325,552 to the NDP that year while only five unions coughed up a mere $10,752 to the Saskatchewan Party.[9] [10]

Looking to British Columbia, *Global News* crunched the numbers behind donations to political parties in the 2013 B.C. election and found that the NDP received $2,491,191 from unions versus only $6,010 in union donations to the B.C. Liberal party.[11]

While the federal government outlawed union and business donations to political parties in 2006, the ban wasn't too effective in stopping the NDP from receiving union funds.[12] Instead of accepting direct donations, the party was caught accepting large sums of money from unions for "advertising" at its conventions. The only reason the NDP was caught is because the Conservative Party filed a complaint with Elections Canada. An investigation took place and the NDP was eventually forced to repay $344,468 to various unions and outside organizations.[13]

But that's not all. Unions have funded front groups, such as one calling itself "Working Families." Ultimately Working Families is a shell organization, largely funded by unions, that tries to pass itself off as an organization of average families that have come together to speak out. In reality, Working Families inevitably attacks any candidate deemed to be unfavourable to the union elite.

For example, in the 2011 Ontario election, the organization ran tons of ads specifically attacking Progressive Conservative party leader Tim Hudak. They spent more than $1 million on ads suggesting he was a puppet of big business and would cut health care, amongst other allegations.

You may be thinking: *"ah yes, but what about business groups that spent money attacking Hudak's opponents?"*

Well, consider some numbers from Elections Ontario, the government body that runs the province's elections.[14] According to its 2011-12 annual report, third parties spent almost $6.1 million running ads; $5.6 million of which was spent by just two unions and the aforementioned *Working Families* group:

Elementary Teachers' Federation of Ontario - $2.7 million
Ontario English Catholic Teachers Association - $1.9 million
Working Families - $1 million

To put those figures in perspective, here are numbers from the same report on how much the Progressive Conservative Party of Ontario, the Ontario Liberals and Ontario NDP spent during the 2011 Ontario election on all forms of campaign expenses (signs, office rental, ads, etc.):

Progressive Conservative Party of Ontario - $9.6 million
Liberal Party of Ontario - $9.3 million
New Democratic Party of Ontario - $4.2 million

In other words, the business community largely stayed silent while the Liberals and NDP benefitted from nearly $6 million in union ads that either attacked their mutual opponent (Hudak and the Progressive Conservatives) or promoted big government spending.

It's true that conservative-minded and liberal-minded parties across the country tend to receive more financial support from businesses than the NDP does (that is, in provinces that still allow union and business donations), but even if you assumed all the grants and loans governments give to businesses are somehow a payback, the spending is minuscule when compared to the billions spent by governments on salaries and benefits for unionized government employees.

Just imagine a politician capitulating to a union that helped out during his or her campaign; perhaps by caving and agreeing to a 3.5% pay increase instead of holding out for 3.0%. That extra half percentage point may not seem like much, but multiply it by thousands of employees across the union and then consider how that's a permanent increase. Taxpayers will not just pay for the payback once, but likely every year in the future. After all, union compensation contracts almost always go up, not down.

Clearly, unions are powerful at shaping elections, influencing politicians' decisions and obtaining what they want. Nothing I've presented is really that earth-shattering; the relationship between unions and the NDP is fairly well known. Most people know unions can aggressively spend (mandatory) membership dues on election ads to support parties that reward their members. Further, union endorsements of NDP candidates are often fairly public.

But perhaps this tidbit will illustrate the need to rethink the relationship.

Former U.S. president Franklin Roosevelt (Democrat) actually opposed both collective bargaining with government employee unions and strikes by government employees. The otherwise union-friendly president noted in an Aug. 16, 1937, letter to the Federation of Federal Employees:

"All government employees should realize that the process of collective bargaining, as usually understood, cannot be transplanted into the public service. It has its distinct and insurmountable limitations when applied to public personnel management."[15]

In other words, even Roosevelt, an otherwise labour-friendly politician, recognized that governments operate under a completely different environment when they negotiate with employee unions from what we see in the private sector.

So why don't we treat the situation differently and address problems that have arisen? We should. Later on, I'll discuss some ideas for reform.

Costly Clone Pay

"It really burns me up that I can put in a ton of extra time working on my lesson plans, helping coach school teams and support other school activities, but yet I get paid the same as colleagues who don't lift a finger to help out and they leave right after school."

Carol, a friend of mine who is a teacher, and is the type of person who gives 110% to her job, said that a few years ago when discussing how teachers are paid.

Like virtually all other teachers and most government employees, Carol is stuck in an outdated compensation system that pays people based on years served, not performance. Not only is the system detrimental to go-getters like Carol, it's costly for taxpayers as well.

I'll explain the problem using teacher contracts as an example, but the problem extends to other unions in government.

Across Canada, when a teacher accepts a job at a local school division, they are forced to join the local teachers' union. Unlike some states south of the border, teachers in Canada don't have the option of not joining a union when they start work in unionized workplaces (provided that particular job classification is covered by the union).

Once a teacher accepts a job in the public school system, pay is determined by something called a "salary grid," also known as a "pay grid."

Basically, it's a table with columns that indicate different classifications of teachers (often the number of years spent in university to complete their degree) as well as rows that indicate how many years of experience the teacher has.

One then cross-references the two pieces of information to determine a teacher's pay. For example, if you were a "Category 5" teacher (Bachelor of Arts degree and teaching degree) in the Greater Victoria School Division with three full years of experience, you would have made $53,271 in the 2008-09 school year (at the start of your fourth year).[16]

Table 8: Greater Victoria School Division
Teacher Salary Grid as at July 1, 2008

Step	Category 4	Category 5	Category 5+	Category 6
0	$42,508	$46,510	$50,084	$51,340
1	$44,505	$48,763	$52,513	$53,830
2	$46,502	$51,017	$54,942	$56,321
3	$48,499	**$53,271**	$57,371	$58,811
4	$50,496	$55,524	$59,800	$61,302
5	$52,493	$57,778	$62,229	$63,792
6	$54,490	$60,031	$64,657	$66,283
7	$56,487	$62,285	$67,086	$68,773
8	$58,484	$64,539	$69,515	$71,264
9	$60,481	$66,792	$71,944	$73,754
10	$64,040	$71,117	$76,322	$78,151

Source: Greater Victoria School Division Contract

As you can see, the system doesn't account for performance within the classroom or the additional efforts expended by the teacher on extra-curricular activities. The pay grid essentially treats teachers like clones.

When the Greater Victoria contract was announced, it was noted that the teachers in that division would receive a 2.5% pay increase in 2009 and 2.0% pay increase in 2010. The increase doesn't sound like a big increase, but is it?

Recall the teacher we previously discussed. Once they finish the 2008-09 school year, they'll have four years of experience, moving them into the next pay grade. This is known as a "step" increase.

But not only does the teacher receive the step increase, all the numbers on the salary grid also go up by an average of the negotiated 2.5% increase. The salary grid for the 2009-10 school year looked like this:

Table 9: Greater Victoria School Division Teacher Salary Grid as at July 1, 2009

Step	Category 4	Category 5	Category 5+	Category 6
0	$43,571	$47,673	$51,336	$52,623
1	$45,618	$49,983	$53,826	$55,176
2	$47,665	$52,292	$56,315	$57,729
3	$49,712	$54,602	$58,805	$60,282
4	$51,758	**$56,912**	$61,295	$62,834
5	$53,805	$59,222	$63,784	$65,387
6	$55,852	$61,532	$66,274	$67,940
7	$57,899	$63,842	$68,764	$70,493
8	$59,946	$66,152	$71,253	$73,045
9	$61,993	$68,462	$73,743	$75,598
10	$65,641	$72,895	$78,230	$80,105

The teacher in our example – moving from Step 3, Category 5, to Step 4, Category 5 – would have seen a pay increase from $53,271 to $56,912 – a 6.8% increase in just one year. These pay numbers are a bit stale now, but you can see how the system works.

The following year, the teacher would have seen another pay increase automatically due to another year of experience, plus an additional 2.0% increase based on the contract stipulation. According to the contract with the union, the pay table for the 2010-11 school year looked like this:

Table 10: Greater Victoria School Division
Teacher Salary Grid as at July 1, 2010

Step	Category 4	Category 5	Category 5+	Category 6
0	$44,442	$48,626	$52,363	$53,676
1	$46,530	$50,982	$54,902	$56,279
2	$48,618	$53,338	$57,442	$58,883
3	$50,706	$55,694	$59,981	$61,487
4	$52,794	$58,051	$62,521	$64,091
5	$54,881	**$60,407**	$65,060	$66,695
6	$56,969	$62,763	$67,599	$69,299
7	$59,057	$65,119	$70,139	$71,903
8	$61,145	$67,475	$72,678	$74,506
9	$63,233	$69,831	$75,218	$77,110
10	$66,954	$74,353	$79,795	$81,707

The teacher who was paid $53,271 in 2008 ended up making $60,407 in 2010. That's a 13.4% increase in just two years.

Of course anyone reading the newspaper would have heard that teachers were "only" receiving a 2.5% raise in year one and 2.0% in the second year; a far cry from the 13.4% some teachers actually received. Clearly, if you look closely there's a lot more to the increases than meets the eye.

Teachers automatically receive step increases each year until they max out at 10 years' experience (although some provinces have additional top-ups after 15 years).

Now you can see why my friend Carol was upset. In her opinion, she works a lot harder than some other teachers who have worked the same number of years, yet she's paid the same. As for taxpayers, we have to pay for such generous increases to all teachers, regardless of performance.

The grid system comes from "collective bargaining," the practice whereby unions hire someone to negotiate pay on behalf of their members rather than sending every member in to meet with a manager and negotiate his or her pay individually. Union negotiators seek pay levels based on years served rather than performance. This type of approach is the backbone of the union movement, as the union elite place "equality" and "seniority" well above aspects such as "merit" or "performance."

Look for teacher contracts anywhere in the country and you'll find the same type of salary grid system. You'll also find a similar structure for nurses, police, firefighters and various other government unions. The grids may have fewer steps and the information may not be presented the same way, but the "treat everyone the same regardless of performance" and "pay based on years served" approach is the norm.

Of course unions have many arguments in favour of the status quo, but sadly, their system is to the detriment of their best and brightest members. Not to mention students.

Note what *StateImpact* (a partnership of public radio stations in Ohio) and Cleveland's *Plain Dealer* newspaper had to say about teacher evaluations and pay in Ohio, a state where teachers are paid on a similar salary grid system (that is, based on years of experience and academic credentials).

The 2013 report by the two organizations noted:

> *"There is little connection between how much money Ohio teachers make and how much knowledge they impart to students over the course of a single year … "*[17]

In other words, teachers who have been around for ages and make a lot more money don't necessarily produce better results in the classroom. In terms of "value-added" data – students learning *more* than expected – the study noted:

> *"… Older teachers in Ohio are paid significantly more than their younger colleagues but did not outperform them in the 2011-12 school year on value-added. The findings on the relationship between value-added and teacher pay echo what researchers have found in other states, including Florida, New York, North Carolina and Washington."*[18]

But the real kicker was this conclusion:

"…The 34 Cleveland teachers who received the state's highest rating earn about $68,600 on average, compared with about $71,500 for the 112 teachers who received the state's lowest rating."

The results shouldn't surprise anyone. The "pay all teachers like clones" argument falls flat when one considers:

1. Most of us have been through the public school system and know that some teachers are just plain better at their jobs than others. Teachers aren't clones and shouldn't be treated as such.
2. Many of us know at least one teacher personally and have heard them speak quite frankly about the fact that some of their colleagues are ineffective.

Indeed, I've talked to many teachers about this subject and have often heard them express: *"oh yes, we can tell who the good teachers are in the school and the ones who aren't so good."*

The reality is, in any profession you're going to have people who are ineffective, people who meet expectations and over-achievers. And just like those teachers who can sort the good from the bad, professionals from other sectors can figure out who is really good at a particular job and who isn't. If we can put a man on the moon, surely we can figure out a way to identify and reward the best teachers, police, firefighters and other government employees.

The reason I bring up the whole pay grade system is that it's important to see how a news story reporting a 2% pay increase for government employees often isn't the full story. For newer employees, who are still climbing those "steps" in their contacts, the "2% increase" often works out to a whole lot more.

Taxpayers need to be mindful of the complete story behind the pay grid system as well as the shortcomings of this model, especially as they relate to performance. When politicians face a problem in terms of poor results – whether it be a high crime rate, low student test scores or anything else – they often resort to throwing more money at the problem. Low student test scores?

"We're committing $15 million to improve test scores." Crime inches up a point or two? *"We're investing in 50 more police officers."*

Sometimes, there's a much better alternative: tweak the pay model to improve productivity.

If governments really want to stand up for taxpayers, while still being a good employer for the top teachers, firefighters, cops and desk jockeys out there, they'll look seriously at changing the status quo.

Big Pay Picture

Government salaries are a runaway train. In particular, select unions – ones that governments often block from going on strike – have seen their pay grow by leaps and bounds courtesy of the taxpayer. Well, here's some evidence from Statistics Canada to back up that assertion.

Table 11: Average Canadian Income Comparison 2000 vs 2010

	2000	2010	% Increase	Old Premium	New Premium
Government Managers	$59,739	$89,275	49.4%	88.1%	113.6%
Police Officers	$55,380	$82,189	48.4%	74.4%	96.6%
Firefighters	$52,664	$77,105	46.4%	65.8%	84.5%
Registered Nurses	$39,257	$57,451	46.3%	23.6%	37.5%
Police Officers (Mgmt)	$67,828	$98,009	44.5%	113.6%	134.5%
Secondary Teachers	$42,503	$58,413	37.4%	33.8%	39.8%
Elementary Teachers	$39,723	$53,198	33.9%	25.1%	27.3%
Average Canadian Worker	$31,757	$41,795	31.6%	-	-

Source: *Statistics Canada*

According to the Statistics Canada table (above) you can see the average manager in government saw a 49.4% pay increase between and 2000-2010.[19] [20] Meanwhile, the average Canadian (which includes government employees, so the number is inflated) only received a 31.6% pay increase. In fact, police, firefighters and nurses all saw much higher pay increases than the average Canadian worker.

So much for the rhetoric from unions about *"staying competitive"* and *"keeping up."* The reality is they've been blowing the taxpayer away for years.

If we turn to the "premium" columns in the table, it shows how the average government employee's pay (in respective categories) compared to the average worker in Canada during 2000 and 2010.

In 2000, you can see the average manager in government made 88.1% more than the average Canadian worker. Fast-forward to 2010 and the average government manager now makes 113.6% more than the average Canadian.

Similarly, firefighters made 65.8% more than the average Canadian in 2000, yet they now make 84.5% more.

You can see why government employees are sometimes referred to as "the new rich" … the gap is growing between government employees and everyone else.

Golden Pensions

When financial markets crashed in 2008, people working outside the government likely cringed every time they opened up their RRSP and investment statements each month. Retirement nest eggs that took people decades to build had plummeted in value in no time at all.

Across the country, thousands of people who worked outside the government, and were about to retire, suddenly had to cancel their retirement parties or postpone their plan to head off to the lake for good. They would have to work a few more years to save and rebuild their retirement nest eggs.

But as those private sector workers cancelled their retirement party plans, many of their silver-haired counterparts in government retired as if nothing happened.

How could they do it? The answer is two-fold.

In chapter four I explained how most government employees in Canada enjoy a golden, expensive type of pension plan ("defined-benefit") that puts a lot of risk on the backs of taxpayers. The plans are structured so that government employees are guaranteed payouts for the rest of their lives regardless of market performance or how long they live.

When government employee pension funds tanked, governments simply poured in more money to make sure employees could retire on time and with the same benefits. And boy did governments ever pour in more money! Here are the Statistics Canada numbers on combined government spending in Canada on government employee pensions:

2003: $7.2 billion
2013: $18.6 billion[21]

Not to mention, the increase in spending on government employee pensions is on top of all the pay increases government employees received over the same period. You may have read about a group of government employees receiving a 2 or 3% pay increase, but chances are there was a sizable increase in government spending on their pensions as well!

Union bosses often claim government employee pensions wouldn't have needed these huge bailouts if it weren't for governments spending pension surpluses in the past or deferring contributions to the plans. But that's not true. The figures I've noted don't include special payments governments are making to make up for years when they didn't put in their share.

In 2003, not including special payments, total government spending on employee pensions worked out to about $2,800 per government employee enrolled in a plan. By 2013 that figure had skyrocketed to about $5,800 per employee; more than a 100% increase in just a decade. Just imagine someone putting $5,800 into your RRSPs each year!

The second reason why government employees have been able to keep such a lavish perk is due to the fact pensions are a very complex topic and the general public simply doesn't understand just how good government employees have it. Had the average taxpayer understood just how golden these plans are they probably would have demanded reform a long time ago.

For some big picture analysis on the subject, consider what pension expert Bill Tufts, co-author of the bestselling book *Pension Ponzi*, had to say about the government employee pension plans that are common in Canada:

"The typical government worker in Canada can retire and receive 70% of their final salary for the rest of their life after just 30 or 35 years of work. That's after contributing 8 or 9% of their pay each year. If this math seems too good to be true, that's because it is. It explains why these plans are in trouble across the country and requiring taxpayer bailouts."

Clearly this is an area where governments need to scale back spending. It's just not fair for taxpayers to keep working well into their 60s – and pay higher taxes – so that government employees can continue to retire in their 50s, and with golden benefits.

Sick Leave

In June 2013, the *Toronto Star* ran an article titled: *"Teacher Sick Days Rising as End of School Year Nears."* The article described an influx of teachers calling in sick following the provincial government's decision to halt the practice of allowing teachers to store up unused sick days year after year.[22] Under the old model teachers could use any banked sick days to complement long-term disability leave.

The *Star* noted:

"Under the controversial new contract imposed this year by Queen's Park, Ontario teachers had their sick days cut from 20 to 11 per year, and lost the right to bank unused sick days."

At the time of the story, an associate director with the Peel District School Board (Mississauga, Brampton and Caledon area) noted how a whopping 1,664 of the division's 10,000 teachers called in sick on a recent Friday. It was such a spike in sick days that the division had to scramble to find staff to cover for the absent teachers.

The *Star* called the decision to cut the sick time "controversial," but the real controversy should have been the fact that teachers had access to 20 sick days a year in the first place (or the ability to roll them over year after year).

Statistics Canada data obtained by the Canadian Taxpayers Federation showed Ontario private sector workers only took 5.8 sick and disability days in 2012, while the average public sector employee took 8.8 days.[23]

So why would teachers need three times the number of sick days as private sector workers and nearly two and a half times their public sector counterparts?

The oft-repeated claim that *"kids are little germ bugs and teachers are more susceptible to getting sick"* only goes so far. That might account for a few extra sick days per year, but access to three times what the private sector could take? What about private sector employees who also work around children, such as those in kids' museums, toy stores or daycares?

This is just another example of benefits gone wild in the public sector. Unfortunately, it's not just teachers, and it's not just in Ontario.

In table 12 you will find the average number of sick or disability days taken by public sector employees in 2012, by province, versus those in the private sector. As you can see, those in government take more than those working outside government in every province in Canada.

Table 12: 2012 Sick/Disability Leave By Province

	Public Sector	Private Sector
Quebec	12.2	8.5
Manitoba	12.1	7.1
Nova Scotia	12.0	8.4
British Columbia	12.0	7.4
Prince Edward Island	11.3	6.3
Saskatchewan	11.0	6.9
Newfoundland and Labrador	10.7	7.9
New Brunswick	10.7	7.1
Canadian Average	10.5	6.7
Alberta	9.1	5.6
Ontario	8.8	5.8

Source: Canadian Taxpayers Federation custom purchase of Statistics Canada data

Clearly, high levels of sick leave in government is a contagious situation that politicians to need to address nation-wide. The antidote of course is a reduction in the number of days offered in the first place.

Territorial Rights

There are all kinds of other perks and costly clauses in government employee union contracts across the country, but perhaps one of the more debilitating measures is the "territorial rights" unions have to various workplace tasks.

In multiple government settings I've worked in, I've heard of white-collar employees essentially being handcuffed when it came to doing simple tasks like moving a desk or hanging a picture. They could easily do such simple tasks themselves, but if they did, the union would complain.

Union bosses would argue that moving a desk five feet was actually the responsibility of some government maintenance guy who worked deep in the bowels of the building somewhere. By allowing a white-collar employee to do the work, he or she would be reducing the need for another employee's job.

This, of course, was the nub of the firefighters' argument at the beginning of the chapter. They were concerned that the fire chief's decision to have public works department staff put out the fire was somehow reducing their workload. Eventually, they saw how ridiculous the argument looked, and withdrew their labour board complaint. But nonetheless it showed the radical mindset of some in the labour movement.

While the firefighters gave up their case, other "territorial rights" issues persist and the rigid environments restrict the ability of governments to become more efficient and flexible.

"Labor-Electoral Complex"

In 1961, U.S. President Eisenhower referred to a "military-industrial complex" during his farewell address to the nation.[24]

Eisenhower noted how after the Second World War there were several companies that had become permanent producers of military weapons and machinery. Without wars and high military spending, their sales would suffer. Eisenhower warned lawmakers to be careful about how closely they associated with lobbyists from that industry. The latter of course having a huge incentive to support wars and military spending.

While the military-industrial complex term and concept is fairly well known among those that follow politics, and young economics and political studies students, a similar phrase was coined in late 2013 by Michael Bloomberg, then outgoing mayor of New York City.

In his final address, a speech to the Economic Club of New York in late 2013, Bloomberg warned of what he referred to as a "labor-electoral complex."[25]

Specifically, Bloomberg touched on the huge financial noose that government employee unions had placed not only on New York City, but also on cities across the United States. At the same time he discussed the problem of shortsighted politicians worrying about their own electoral success rather than tackling the unsustainable nature of some labour contracts and their gorging on tax dollars.

Bloomberg noted how his city offered: *"benefits that are over and above what the market offers, and what other governments offer. And those costs continue to grow, and as they do it limits our ability to increase base salaries."*

He went on to note:

"Since 2010, 38 local governments have filed for bankruptcy, largely because of out-of-control pension costs. And more are now flirting with it. But even if struggling cities escape bankruptcy, the funds that must be diverted to cover skyrocketing pension bills are funds that cannot be invested in the future, which can set off a downward spiral that, as New York found out in the 70s, is deeply painful and takes decades to recover from.

"As a country, we must confront this crisis before that happens. It is one of the biggest threats facing cities — because it is forcing government into a

fiscal straitjacket that severely limits its ability to provide an effective social safety net and to invest in the next generation.

"The costs of today's benefits cannot be sustained for another generation – not without inflicting real harm on our citizens, on our children and our grandchildren."

The Bloomberg example is from the United States, but the lesson can be applied in Canada as well.

Across our country, the pension plans for government employees are struggling, and we too have a huge wage gap between those working and paying for government services versus those regularly receiving a government paycheque … not to mention the costly pensions and all the other perks.

However, unlike the United States, Canada doesn't seem to have too many senior politicians even willing to talk about the problem so frankly. Perhaps you can help educate your local politicians about these issues and some of the following solutions.

Solutions

I've outlined a number of problems that government employee unions create for governments and taxpayers; bullying politicians with attack ads and union pay models that ignore performance to name a couple. So what are the solutions? How can governments get public sector pay and benefits under control while combating the immense influence unions have over politicians?

Here are a few solutions worth considering:

1) Ability to Pay Acts: In 2012, Jim Wilson, a member of Ontario's provincial parliament, tabled a piece of legislation called the *Ability to Pay Act*.

What the bill proposed is something governments should have enshrined as a practice years ago: a requirement to take into account what the taxpayer can afford when deciding pay for government employees.

A Sept. 27, 2012 *National Post* article on the proposed legislation noted:

"Mr. Wilson's bill would require arbitrators to take into account a number of criteria, including unemployment rates, personal income levels, comparable private-sector wages, the fiscal situation of the employer..."[26]

Wilson's proposed legislation would make it more difficult for arbitrators to do things like give firefighters (and other unions that cannot strike) a 3% or 3.5% pay increase when the average taxpayer only saw an increase of 1% or 2%. And that's the point. No one has a problem with giving a government employee a good pay package, or reasonable pay increases, but the compensation decisions need to be affordable for the taxpayer and take into account how much the average taxpayer's paycheque is going up.

On its own, the *Ability to Pay* legislation wouldn't get at one of the main problems with the pay grid system – paying people based on years served rather than performance – but it would be a step in the right direction.

2) Performance Pay: In 2011, the State of Indiana passed legislation that now requires teacher pay to be determined by performance measures.[27] Under the new law, teachers are rated and classified under four categories each year: "highly effective," "effective," "improvement necessary" and "ineffective." Those found to be in the latter two categories are not allowed to receive a pay increase until they improve.

While the Indiana legislation is focused on teacher pay, the approach could probably be applied to other fields. Perhaps government bodies in Canada could do something like implement a more straightforward pay system for police, providing base pay, plus a top up based on performance measurements, peer review and supervisors' assessments. Maybe there could even be additional pay for working in a rougher neighborhood while lower pay for less risky police work.

Nurses could be evaluated in a similar manner. While you wouldn't want criminals evaluating how well police treat them, it would be appropriate to take into account how well patients feel they're being treated by nurses.

One thing seems clear: if there's a will to move to a more innovative and fair model for public sector compensation, there's a way.

3) Pension Reform: Part of the answer to Canada's government employee pension problems comes from the province of Saskatchewan where, back in the late 1970s and early 1980s, Saskatchewan's NDP began putting almost all new employees in a less costly (and less risky) type of pension plan known as a "defined-contribution" plan. Existing employees were given the option of being grandfathered into the old plans or moving into the new, less costly plans.

In other words, the government helped stop the bleeding. The government recognized the problems associated with the expensive and risky defined-benefit pension plans enjoyed by most provincial government employees and largely addressed the situation.

Defined-contribution plans still involve governments matching employee contributions into their pension fund, but that's where it stops. There's no requirement for governments to bail the plans out if a recession comes along or to guarantee employees payments for life.

Today, Saskatchewan still has pension woes at the provincial level, largely from the old plans, but the problems aren't as dire as what other provinces are facing ... provinces that did nothing to address the problem decades ago.

Other governments should follow suit, putting new employees in defined-contribution plans and even considering the conversion of existing employees over to such plans as well. The latter option would mean existing employees could keep the benefits they've already earned, but from here on they would no longer be able to accrue additional golden benefits.

4) Right to Work Legislation: *The Charter of Rights and Freedoms* protects freedom of association in Canada. That means you have the right to decide if you want to join a recreational hockey league, a Ukrainian dance troupe, a left-handed stamp collectors club or whatever other group may tickle your fancy.

So shouldn't you also have the right to decide if you want to join a union when you accept a job with a business or government?

I would argue "yes," but that currently isn't the case in Canada. People have no choice but to join a union if the job they've accepted is covered under a collective agreement. Meanwhile, many teachers, police, nurses, firefighters and other workers might tell you they don't want to join the union but they have no choice. Additionally, you might hear them gripe about their union's political ads and activities: *"they certainly don't speak for me."*

Regardless, those not-so-keen union members do have to pay a small fortune in union dues each year, some of which is often used to help fund political attack ads and other political activities (subsidizing people to go to conventions, donations to political parties, etc.).

South of the border things are different. About half of all states have legislation that allows workers to decide if they want to join a union or not; it's known as "right to work" legislation.

Allowing workers the freedom to decide if they want to join a union or not might be the last thing the elite in Canada's union movement want to see happen, but it makes sense.

Giving workers freedom to join the union would mean they would no longer be forced to fund unions and pay for political activities they may not agree with.

Not only would such a move reduce the immense influence unions have over politicians, it could also be great for Canada's economy.

A 2013 study by the Mackinac Centre for Public Policy, a Michigan-based think tank, compared the economic outcomes of states that adopted right to work legislation and those that hadn't between the period 1947-2011. The study found those states that had passed right to work legislation benefitted from *"increased employment, higher pay and expanding population."*[28]

Ultimately, if this move helps the economy, that's good for taxpayers too. More people working, and businesses doing better ultimately means more sharing of the tax burden.

5) Restrict Dues to Bargaining: Another option that has been floated from time to time is to restrict union dues to bargaining activities. This idea would put a stop to unions using a large portion of members' dues on partisan ads (that grassroots members might not agree with).

Unions would be allowed to raise voluntary donations for such advertisements, but gone would be the days of the union elite spending dues as they pleased.

This proposal is easier for politicians to consider implementing than something as "controversial" as letting workers decide if they want to decide to join a union or not. Regardless, it could still improve our democratic process.

Under this proposal politicians would of course still have to be mindful of the votes of those in the public sector, but many could sleep better at night knowing they wouldn't face a barrage of union ads attacking them if they decided to promise changes that unions may dislike. Just ask former Ontario PC leader Tim Hudak how he would have felt about not having $6 million worth of union attack ads working against him during the 2011 election.

CHAPTER 7

The Bureaucracy

Government bureaucracies are the third major force behind inefficient spending. Billions of dollars are squandered each year because most government bureaucracies operate under broken incentive models. In this chapter we'll explore why bureaucratic systems in Canada are broken and possible solutions.

To get our feet wet, let's first start off by exploring something called "March Madness."

For many sports fans, the words "March Madness" bring to mind a massive college basketball tournament that occurs each year in the United States. The tournament features hundreds of young sweaty players who give it their best to win the 64-team "March Madness" tournament.

Of course, players are also concerned about attracting the eyes of professional scouts, but either way, it's an extremely competitive contest.

In government terms, the words "March Madness" mean something totally different.

The phrase still involves sweaty people, but instead of tall, young, male 20-somethings, we are talking bureaucrats of all ages and sizes and both men and women. And instead of trying to shine and get attention, they're all nervously doing what they can to fly under the radar.

You see, for most government departments, Crown corporations and agencies, their budget year runs from April 1 to March 31 of the following year.

Bureaucrats know that if their division finishes the year with a big surplus, next year's funding could get slashed by senior managers. Run a large surplus two years in a row and you may as well be walking around with a giant target on your back; cuts could even imperil your job. It's a survival instinct for bureaucrats to ensure all funds are spent each year to give the impression their division needs all the resources it is provided.

This ultimately leads to a different kind of March Madness; bureaucrats furiously spending whatever they have left in their budgets at the end of their fiscal year in March.

In business, owners and shareholders exert pressure on managers to ensure money isn't spent merely for the sake of spending money at the end of the year. That doesn't mean that private sector companies don't ever waste money, but there are people involved in the process – owners and shareholders – who have a much stronger interest to ensure money isn't wasted.

In government, that's not the case. You have bureaucrats and politicians spending other people's money and there are no owners or shareholders cracking the whip.

While the politicians are ultimately supposed to be the watchdogs of the whole system, many realize that grilling bureaucrats over potential misspending doesn't get them too far. Politicians don't earn any bonuses for stopping wasteful spending, and any savings they do help create usually just go back into a black hole.

That's not to say that there aren't politicians who carefully try to scrutinize spending, the problem is the incentives aren't in place to encourage more of such behaviour.

So how do we know bureaucrats often blow money frivolously during the month of March?

A lot of big purchases governments make have to go out for tender and those bid opportunities are posted publicly.

Greg Weston, one of the taxpayers' top friends in the journalism world, wrote a good column about this phenomenon in March 2010 while working for the *Toronto Sun*.[1]

Government tenders are usually posted for at least a month or two to ensure a lot of potential bidders see the opportunities, but Weston was able o highlight several that were posted with immediate closing dates.

He referred to what he saw as a *"sudden blizzard of urgent calls to contractors for stuff that isn't exactly an emergency."* Some of the examples included:

- The RCMP only giving suppliers a mere week to provide a bid for *"a firm quantity of 3,500 unisex athletic shorts."*
- The Defence Department giving suppliers just two weeks to bid on *"the rental and servicing of portable toilets on an as and when requested basis"*
- The *CBC* issuing a $1.5-million tender that opened on March 9 and closed on March 17 for a PR firm to assist with *"500 press releases a year."*

But don't just take Weston's word for it. Consider a snippet from a letter sent by Federal Treasury Board Minister Tony Clement to all ministers, deputy ministers and Crown corporation heads in 2012:

"In the past, we have heard stories about what is known in Ottawa circles as 'March Madness' when organizations spend unused operational funds on things such as new furniture, promotional items, stockpiling of IT hardware, and other purchases that fall outside of existing contractual obligations in order to expend their budgets prior to the end of the fiscal year. This type of expenditure – dictated by the fiscal calendar rather than real departmental needs – is something that our government strongly opposes.

"As you know, spending authority for operational matters is often delegated to various officials within federal departments. I would encourage you to speak to your deputy head and remind him or her that operational spending decisions must be based on value-for-money and address real, immediate needs now and in the future. I have already directed officials at the Treasury Board Secretariat to continue their work scrutinizing public expenditures and to pay specific attention to operational spending proposals."[2]

March Madness shows one weakness in the way governments spend money, but wasteful spending happens throughout the year and in many different forms. Let's take a look at other ways that bureaucracies are wasteful and don't have the right incentive structure to spend public funds in a cost-effective manner.

More Examples of Bureaucratic Bungling

In 2012, the Prairie Valley School Division in Saskatchewan had been complaining for quite some time to the Ministry of Education over the provincial government's new proposed funding formula. Eventually, the school division secured a meeting with the minister to discuss its concerns over what it claimed would be millions in cutbacks if the new funding formula proceeded.

To bolster its concerns, the board sent letters to other provincial politicians and parent councils urging them to speak out as well. They were hoping to create a strong united front of citizens and elected officials putting pressure on the minister to not cut back funding.

Oddly enough, citizens raised questions over something in a school board meeting note posted online. It seemed that right after the Prairie Valley School Division's upcoming "plead poverty" meeting with the minister of education in Regina, the division's board was off to Moose Jaw for a two- or three-day spa retreat.[3] Yes, nothing says *"don't cut our funding because we're cut to the bone"* like *"we're off to the spa for a few days after this meeting."*

The same board had actually attended a retreat and golf junket just eight months prior. In a bizarre move, the school board decided to hold a public board meeting while on the road at the golf retreat; a location outside of the school division. If you were a taxpayer in the Prairie Valley School Division and wanted to speak at the meeting or if you just wanted to hear what was being discussed, you would have had to have driven for an hour outside of your division to get there.

That would be like Edmonton's city council deciding to hold a public council meeting in Calgary. Bizarre idea indeed.

As you might have guessed the Prairie Valley School Division isn't too frugal with public funds. On another occasion, the division passed back-to-back motions to accept the resignation of Ben Grebinski, its education director, and then to hire him back. Why would the board do such a thing? The move was orchestrated to allow the director to be able to technically retire, begin drawing on his government employee pension and then be hired back, drawing a salary at the same time.

Perhaps perks like the $1,200 office chairs he purchased for his office made the job all that more attractive to stick around for a few more years?

While the Prairie Valley School Division and March Madness examples show inefficient spending practices by governments, there are often examples of inefficiency on the revenue side as well; and I don't mean when it comes to taxing as much as they can!

A few years ago I was speaking with a city councillor's assistant in Winnipeg who mentioned in passing how difficult it was to order an ad at a city-owned arena. The councillor she worked for at the time was hoping to put up a big sign with his picture and contact information inside the arena. It wasn't like he was the first to make the request either; the arena already had plenty of other advertisements from local businesses around the rink.

The money would flow from one division of the city to another, so it wasn't new money for the city overall. But for the bureaucrat at the arena processing the order, it still counted as revenue for their operation.

The councillor's assistant told me that she called and left several messages and had been waiting for months to hear back from the bureaucrats running the arena.

At the time, I wondered how poor the customer service must be for the public if even a city councillor's office was ignored. I also wondered how much money the city was missing out on from customers who simply gave up.

The situation reminded me of something similar I experienced in 1999. At the time, I wanted to hire Canada Post to deliver flyers to a specific part of Winnipeg. I popped down to the local mail distribution building and was invited into the back area where the head postal worker had his office. During our discussion he brought out some maps and showed me "the routes."

I was told that each postal carrier was assigned a route or two each day for mail delivery. One route could include something like all of Apple Street between Blueberry Avenue and Cabbage Avenue, one side of Banana Street and all of Carrot Street between Blueberry Avenue and Peach Avenue. It's probably easier to visualize, but the point I'm making is the routes were often comprised of streets that weren't located beside each other; some routes included streets that were located blocks away from each other.

The non-sequential system of delivery was likely set up to ensure each route had roughly the same number of doors for each postal carrier to hit each day.

Given the odd layouts of some of the routes, flyer delivery to certain neighbourhoods was particularly difficult. I inquired as to whether flyers could be delivered to only certain parts of the route but was told by the head postal worker "sorry, we can't break up the routes."

I was only 19 at the time but even then I could see how bureaucratic the Crown corporation behaved. I couldn't believe they would turn me away over a simple request such as *"for this route, please don't deliver flyers to Apple Street."*

If I had requested something complicated like *"do every second house on this side of Apple Street only"* I could see why the head postal bureaucrat would refuse. If you're a mail carrier and have a ton of unaddressed mail with all kinds of complicated instructions for each flyer it could become a bit of a nightmare.

But my request was pretty straightforward. I wasn't even asking for a mailman to do more work, but less. After the postal bureaucrat told me *"we can't break up the routes,"* I responded with something like *"so I should take my business to someone else because you don't want to give a mail carrier a simple note telling him or her to not do a street?"*

I was actually more diplomatic, but the response was the same: *"yes."* Canada Post ended up missing out on a fair amount of business that day. Think about how much other business they've missed over the years by refusing to "break up the routes," and other reasonable customer requests.

The bottom line with all of these examples is that government bureaucracies often don't have the right incentives to keep costs down or increase revenue by offering better customer service.

A lack of competition nipping at the government's heels, and politicians failing to crack the whip hard enough (and a seemingly endless supply of money), leads to a lethargic system continuing on in the same direction much like a steamroller with its steering wheel locked in position.

Let's explore a few more reasons why bureaucracies contribute to the hemorrhaging of tax dollars and some things that can be done to address the problems.

"Award-Winning" Government Programs

A big problem in government is that there often isn't enough of a focus on results. And when there is, results in one government body are frequently compared with other government bodies, which are also inefficient.

I wouldn't be surprised if senior city managers looked at the advertising revenues from the aforementioned city arena that was apathetic about the councillor's advertising request and compared the revenues with another city arena that provided equally poor service. Thus, the manager could have concluded that the revenue figures from the arena were in line with its peers, so all was well.

The problem with comparing government results with other governments is it's a bit like a race between obese dogs. One of the little chubbers will eventually be crowned the fastest in the pack, but would that really mean that it's fast? Of course not. If you want to see whether your dog is truly fast or not you would have it compete against any dog that comes along, not just other portly dogs.

Mayor Stephen Goldsmith illustrates this point well in *The Twenty-First Century City*.

Goldsmith explains how in 1991, the City of Indianapolis and its "*award-winning*" wastewater treatment system were faced with the prospect of having to spend a small fortune on "*much-needed*" improvements to the part of the system that collected and transported sewage.

The local Chamber of Commerce had identified "*more than $144 million worth of much-needed*" improvements. The city had not raised sewage rates in eight years, and Council expected they would have to raise them by 37% to pay for the upgrades and keep the system going.

Despite the fact the city's sewage system had won "*numerous*" awards, Goldsmith noted his administration considered "*the rank of 'best in class' to be somewhat meaningless, because comparisons could be drawn only with other government-run facilities.*"

His administration, just as they did with other services, decided to see if partnering with a business to help run the sewage system could reduce costs for taxpayers.

Ernst and Young were hired to do an assessment of the existing city-run wastewater system. Goldsmith noted that they, along with another firm, "*concluded that the facilities were run effectively and efficiently and noted the many awards the plants had received.*" The respected accounting firm suggested that contracting out the management of the system could only reduce costs by a mere 5%.

Despite the small benefit projected by contracting out the service, the city still decided to invite bids from businesses to test the market. The results were a delightful surprise. Note what Goldsmith said about the bid that city staff submitted in an attempt to keep their jobs and continue managing the system:

> "*Astonishingly, the proposal entered by our own in-house team – which only weeks before insisted that $30 million a year was the absolute minimum amount required to run the plant – reduced that price by 10% when subjected to competition.*"[4]

While city workers put in a good bid, the city chose a private company that provided "*$65 million in savings,*" reduced the workforce by more than 100 positions, reduced the number of effluent violations by more than 50% and allowed the city to "*avoid the proposed sewer user rate increase.*"

In other words, even though the city had an "*award-winning*" sewage system, local taxpayers received a much better service at a lower cost by partnering with a private business; a win-win for taxpayers' wallets and the environment.

Goldsmith put it best by noting:

"Privatizing operations of two exceedingly well-run facilities – and improving environmental quality and saving millions in the process – says something important about government benchmarks: If you want to find out how well government is providing a given service, do not compare yourself only to other government providers, but to the entire market – public and private, domestic and international. Especially where government is concerned, 'best in class' and 'best in the world' are two quite different concepts, and there is no reason public officials and citizens should settle for the former when the latter is readily available."[5]

Duplication of Administration

Another major problem with government is the amount of sheer duplication.

Think about how taxpayers fund municipal governments and they in turn fund province-wide municipal organizations. Then of course there is the national body, the Federation of Canadian Municipalities. On top of that there are sometimes regional municipal bodies to boot ... and provincial governments often have departments or divisions known as "Municipal Affairs" as well. Why on earth does there need to be so much duplication just to fill a pothole on your street?

The same duplication happens with education. Taxpayers fund schools, school boards, provincial school board associations, departments of education in each province and a national school boards organization.

Aboriginal organizations also fall into the same duplication trap. Each aboriginal reserve has a local administration. There are also regional aboriginal organizations, province-wide aboriginal organizations, the national Assembly of First Nations and the Department of Aboriginal Affairs and Northern Development. In addition, every provincial government seems to have mini-bureaucracies set up to interact with, and sometimes provide funding to, aboriginal reserves. Plus there are tribal councils that some reserves and governments fund.

One could go on and on with these duplication examples in government. In each case there are funds meant for a certain service – whether it be fixing roads, teaching students or for fixing homes on a reserve – that are eaten up by layer upon layer of administration. Talk to each government body and they'll tell you for hours why it's important for them to exist, push papers around and arrange meetings between other bureaucrats. But no matter how you cut it, it's not cost-effective.

Speaking of dollars getting eaten up by admin costs, how many times do you see politicians from all three levels of government in the news together wearing hard hats and turning soil for some kind of construction project announcement?

I would argue "too often."

The projects they're announcing are not necessarily a waste of money. But why are multiple levels of government needed to fund such activities?

I could understand if a couple of neighboring municipalities teamed up to fund a shared wastewater treatment plant or to share the cost of a regional community hall. That would be a good example of cooperation between government bodies that are responsible for delivering the same service.

But far too often you'll often see municipal, provincial and federal politicians smiling together and announcing projects like new bridges, a convention centre expansion or maybe a community club expansion. What's the point of having three levels of government if they each fund the same projects? Just think of the army of bureaucrats and tremendous overlap that is involved in each announcement.

Imagine you're on the board of a local community club and you want to expand.

Your board would likely have to file different funding requests with each level of government and the application process and rules may not be the same. On top of that, politicians will sometimes tell you things like *"don't just apply to this provincial program, try applying to this other provincial program as well."*

Once applications for funding are filed, each level of government then has to pay for its own army of bureaucrats to review the applications, assess the project and haggle back and forth for months with other levels of government and the applicants. At some point the politicians weigh in on the projects and give their two cents too.

Press conferences are eventually planned to announce the funding. This requires communications staff from each level of government to discuss and plan the event, while political staff from each politician's office chime in with their two cents.

Throw in the fact that most government projects lead to multiple press conferences (e.g. an initial announcement, a sod-turning ceremony to show construction has started and a ribbon-cutting ceremony when it's complete) and the entire process involves an immense amount of tax dollars burned up due to duplication, hot air and ego polishing. Think of the simplicity and cost savings if each level of government simply focused on its own responsibilities.

While we're on the topic of duplication, consider how there's often a lack of co-operation where it probably makes the most sense.

In each province in Canada you'll find a provincial curriculum division. Each year bureaucrats in that division spend millions of dollars as they tinker away at curriculum documents that are used in public schools.

The curriculum crew in B.C. will work away on material for B.C. students while next door in Alberta bureaucrats are busy doing basically the same thing. You'll find similar duplication across the country.

But are students in Victoria, B.C. really *that* different from the kids growing up in High River, Alberta?

Couldn't the two provinces get together and launch a joint organization to create the documents periodically, cutting costs dramatically at the same time? Of course they could. Right now there's no incentive to do so. No doubt the bureaucrats haven't proposed such an idea as it would mean job losses and threaten their empires. If a politician or outsider proposed the idea, the bureaucracies would have all the reasons in the world as to why it couldn't happen.

But the truth is, we could probably have a national curriculum body to serve the entire nation. It could focus on the basics – reading, writing, arithmetic, science, gym, music, etc. – and leave a bit of flexibility if there were a strong desire by one province to tinker a bit. Think of how this streamlining could save the taxpayer a fortune.

Another great example in the education sector involves school libraries. Often you'll see libraries in public schools that are located not far from public libraries operated by city governments. This means two buildings to maintain, two sets of books to keep on hand, two sets of staff, two electricity bills, etc. It's just not efficient.

Meanwhile, Vancouver's Britannia Library has been serving both the general public and elementary school students for decades. The savings racked up over the years must be immense.

These last two issues are exactly the type of inefficient spending governments should be eyeing in order to free up dollars to address our infrastructure deficit, pay for health care as our nation ages and other needs.

Zombie Spending

A big problem in government is the practice of decision makers looking at how much a division received in funding the previous year and then just rubber-stamping the same amount for the forthcoming year; plus a bit more for inflation or some other calculation.

This approach ignores several important considerations:

- The program may be ineffective so the government has just thrown good money after bad.
- A private business could potentially provide the same output (or better) for a lower cost.
- The program might be really effective and could make use of more money than, say, another program or division that is far less effective.

The rubber-stamping model is also usually devoid of data such as how much it costs to perform certain functions. For example, ask enough municipal public works directors in Canada how much it costs them to fill the average pothole in their community and you'll probably find several that still have no clue how much it costs.

Many are still focused on receiving the same funding as the previous year, not about whether they're competitive with their operations or not.

Ideally, they should be able to calculate that it costs, say, $50 to fill the average pothole. If a city had, 10,000 potholes to fix that year, it should then be able to compare the cost of having city workers do the task versus what a private business would charge for the same amount of work.

Breaking out expenses and allocating the charges to different functions is known as "activity based costing." It's one of the first steps governments should take to be able to identify areas that are ripe for reform. Once a government knows the actual cost of each activity it provides – filling a pothole, mending a broken arm in a hospital, cutting the grass in a park, etc. – then it can compare its costs with what a business would charge. As we saw in Indianapolis, this approach can encourage existing employees to reduce their cost structure as well.

Alternatively, if a government decides it needs to provide more of a service, it might keep part of the work in-house while hiring a business to carry the additional load. The Saskatchewan government started doing this with knee replacements and CT scans in 2010. They concluded it was cheaper to hire a private health firm to provide the extra procedures to patients rather than hiring more public sector employees and keeping all the work in-house.

Cost Overruns

Sadly, it has become an expectation in Canada: cost overruns with big government projects.

We've all seen it before: politicians and bureaucrats smiling and patting themselves on the back at a press conference announcing a project, only to appear before media with solemn expressions on their faces months later.

"We ran into unforeseen problems."

"There were lots of windy days that prevented our cranes from operating."

"A pack of wild dogs tormented workers on the site and stole their hammers."

The last example may be fictional (I think) but the reality is taxpayers have heard all kinds of excuses over the years as to why massive government projects have come in way over budget and behind schedule.

Whether it's Olympic Stadium in Montreal (affectionately known as "the Big Owe"), the Skydome in Toronto, Vancouver's Convention Centre, B.C.'s epic "Fast Ferry" boondoggle or smaller fiascos, governments have a terrible track record when it comes to bringing capital projects in on time and on budget.

Unfortunately, shoulder-shrugging seems to be the way governments deal with the problem. Politicians and bureaucrats often just seem to shrug their shoulders, endure a day or two of bad media, and then carry on with the "let's try harder" mantra. Again, it's not their own money that they're spending, it's just a big pot of tax dollars.

The federal government's new Canadian Museum for Human Rights is a good example of this problem. The new 160,000-square-foot museum is, according to its website:

"...a centre of learning where Canadians and people from around the world can engage in discussion and commit to taking action against hate and oppression."

It's certainly a noble initiative, but let's talk money.

When federal bureaucrats addressed the Senate of Canada on March 3, 2008, to seek approval for setting up the new museum, Lyn Sherwood, a senior official with the Department of Canadian Heritage, told the Senate the project would cost $265 million.[6] She indicated $105 million was to come from private donations, so the cost to taxpayers was to be $160 million, $100 million of which would come from the federal government alone.

Having seen the cost overrun movie before, Liberal Senator James Cowan from Nova Scotia decided to grill her a bit:

> **Senator Cowan:** *This is not one of those projects where the federal government is left to pick up anything over and above the $165 million that is contributed by other parties, is it?*

> **Ms. Sherwood:** *The total budget is $265 million. You are putting your finger on a very real risk in the current environment, which is the impact of inflation on construction budgets. That has been factored into planning and is one of the reasons for the urgency of this bill because at the moment the purchasing power of that $265 million is being eroded at the rate of between $800,000 and $1.5 million per month.*

Senator Cowan also asked about the possibility of a contingency in the event that things don't turn out as planned. Ms. Sherwood replied that the project included a *"generous contingency provision designed to stay within the budget."*

Later on during the exchange she noted it comprised *"15%"* of the cost. Ms. Sherwood was more than clear: staff had done their homework and the cost was $265 million. What could go wrong?

The Senate approved the department's request and a sod-turning ceremony was held in December of 2008. Approximately five months later, in May 2009, the government announced a hiccup. The cost for the museum had increased to $310 million, $45 million higher than Ms. Sherwood's estimate.

Clearly, her math was off a bit.

When I met with staff in 2009, after the first round of cost overruns was announced, I asked if anyone had been laid off or if there were any penalties or pay cuts for coming in way over budget. Staff shrugged their shoulders and shook their heads; no one was aware of any repercussions.

In my role with the Canadian Taxpayers Federation, I wrote to the federal government minister responsible for the project, then-heritage minister James Moore, in August 2009. I inquired as to what he had done about the cost overruns. I asked if anyone been held accountable. Was anyone let go? Any pay cuts?

Moore responded to my letter by skirting the issue, claiming all Parliament had done after the 2008 meeting at which Sherwood spoke was establish the museum as a federal museum. He claimed the newly appointed board of trustees' first task was to figure out the true cost.

In other words, when seeking approval to create the new museum, a bureaucrat told the Senate the cost was a firm $265 million. Yet, Moore claimed the government had no idea what the cost actually was. Oddly enough, the government waited five months after the ceremonial sod turning had taken place to announce the new "true" cost of the museum: $310 million. But that figure didn't last long.

A second round of cost overruns was announced in late 2011, bringing the total to over $351 million.[7]

While governments often don't discuss HR matters in public, it is on the public record that Sherwood appeared before the Senate of Canada on another matter over a year later, so it appears her job was safe.

The situation makes one wonder what *would* have to happen before heads would roll.

Cash Grabs

In 2007, two city bureaucrats in Winnipeg pitched me on one of the most bizarre policy ideas I had ever heard.

The pair claimed there had been a decrease in the number of banks around town due to the increase in the number of bank machines in the city. As a result, they suggested that the city had lost all kinds of property tax revenue due to the technology change.

To address this "problem," they proposed a new tax on bank machines. If you owned a small convenience store with a bank machine inside for your customers to use, the bureaucrats wanted you to pay a new ATM tax to the government.

The idea would be similar to putting a tax on your cable bills because many video stores have gone out of business since consumers started watching movies online. The ATM tax idea was equally ludicrous.

I can still remember being baffled by the bureaucrats' logic when they presented this "revenue idea."

I told them governments shouldn't simply go around and find something to tax for no reason. Taxes should be charged to cover the cost of a service provided. A bank machine in a store doesn't require extra government services so the owner shouldn't have to pay more. Further, I noted the storeowner would already be paying property taxes to cover the cost of city services provided to their store.

I don't think I convinced them their idea was bizarre, but the anecdote sheds a light on how liberally some inside the world of government think about wielding their taxing powers. Sadly, many have used that power in unfriendly ways towards taxpayers over the years.

In an ideal world, each tax or fee would be connected to merely covering the cost of a service that the government provides.

For example, the registration fee a government charges to register a home with a government property registry would ideally be charged to cover the cost of maintaining the registry. If the cost to maintain your name and data in their system worked out to $200, then the government shouldn't charge you $1,000 and spend the extra money on unrelated expenses like trips for politicians, nurses' salaries or tea and sugar in the staff room of a division of bureaucrats.

But that's what happens in government. Many government taxes and fees have no connection between the revenue raised and how the money is spent.

Take gas taxes as an example.

Since 1998, the Canadian Taxpayers Federation has criticized the federal government for collecting billions at the pumps in fuel taxes and putting so few of those dollars back into road construction and repair.

In 1998, the CTF estimated the federal government only spent about 2% of the billions in federal fuel tax revenue it collected on road construction and repair. In 2010, at the height of the stimulus era, and after years of holding annual events to draw attention to the problem, the CTF calculated the government dedicated more than 100% of the fuel tax funds it collected back into roads.[8] Disappointingly, since then, the CTF estimates the percentage has once again dropped off.

Why has it dropped? Why weren't the funds dedicated to road repair in the first place? Because there are no regulations in place to ensure governments simply don't go out and tax things for the sake of taxing them.

Given the federal government already applies the GST to gasoline, why should it also tax fuel with extra per-litre taxes? After all, the federal government doesn't have to maintain roads and highways like municipalities and provincial governments do.

Proponents of the gas tax argue that gas is taxed extra so that the funds can be put towards road repair. The gas tax serves as a user fee for drivers. Yet if the money isn't being fully transferred to municipalities and the provincial government for road repair then clearly the tax is a cash grab.

Certainly this problem happens at the provincial and municipal levels too. All three levels of government could do with an improvement when it comes to the "charge only enough to pay for the service" principle.

Politicians are often reluctant to address cases where funds collected for specific purposes are higher than the cost of providing the service, as many governments are dealing with enormous, unsustainable bureaucracies that need to be fed. All these cash grabs from other areas simply help feed the beast. Addressing an "inside baseball" problem that few people know about is a low priority for politicians.

Revenue Stifling

There are many different ways governments could be rolling in extra revenues right now that don't involve simply raising taxes. Those extra dollars could then be used to address some of the major problems I've mentioned in this book.

Bureaucracies just don't have the incentive to go after those extra dollars. This 2011 headline from the *Winnipeg Free Press* illustrates the problem:

"City Plans to Sell West St. Paul Riverfront Lot: 44-Acre Plot Bought in 1971, Never Used."[9]

The city bought some riverfront land four decades ago just outside the city limits. The original idea was to turn the area into recreation land, but the plan never materialized. Instead, the land sat unused for 40 years. It seems the city decided to hold onto the land and sit on it in an attempt to prevent "urban sprawl." Meanwhile, development occurred all around the parcel instead.

The problem, of course, is that by not using the land, the city's cash sat tied up in a property instead of being used to pay for infrastructure or some other necessary city service.

As this was going on, another major piece of city property was underused (in a different part of the city). A large parcel of land inside the city was being used as a snow dump despite land development exploding around it. Again, the city was slow to sell this valuable land as well.

Why do these situations happen? Because governments simply don't act like businesses or individuals when it comes to managing assets. A city can let a piece of land sit idle for decades and not have to worry because it doesn't pay property taxes. No one ever asks about the return on investment for such land or foregone property tax revenue either. In most cases, there's no visible cost to government on the books for letting land sit idle.

Investigate your own municipality's land holdings, your provincial government's land reserve or the federal government's land stock and you'll probably find more examples of land that could be sold off and developed.

Revenue stifling also comes from unreasonable regulatory environments. In plain English, when governments make it hard for businesses to operate, their costs go up, profits go down and so do income taxes. Alternatively, some businesses may choose to not locate in the jurisdiction in the first place, or perhaps they may move away.

Note that until recently it was actually illegal for people in Western Canada to buy wine in one province and transport it to another.

In Alberta, there has been much talk about the long process involved with building pipelines and the ability of activists to hijack and delay regulatory hearings by signing up everyone and their dog to speak.

Talk to business groups across the country and you'll find other tales of bureaucratic barriers that prevent reasonable commerce from happening in a timely manner.

I'm not suggesting all regulations should be eliminated, but there is plenty of room to reduce the barriers that unnecessarily slow economic growth in the country.

Another classic example of revenue stifling involves something called equalization payments.

Each year the federal government collects billions from wealthy provinces (often referred to as "have" provinces) and gives the funds to provinces it considers to be poor (known as "have not" provinces) in the form of "equalization payments." The idea behind the interprovincial financial aid program is to try to share the wealth between provinces so that there's a relatively "equal" level of services across the country when it comes to health care, education and other essential services. Again, that's the argument put forward by proponents.

For 2014-15, the equalization program will shuffle $16.7 billion from provinces deemed to be wealthy – British Columbia, Alberta, Saskatchewan and Newfoundland and Labrador – to provinces that aren't considered wealthy – Manitoba, Ontario, Quebec, New Brunswick, Nova Scotia and Prince Edward Island. Quebec is the biggest beneficiary of the program; it is expected to rake in $9.3 billion in 2014-15.[10][11]

I realize equalization payments are an extremely political topic, and not necessarily the fault of bureaucrats, but I chose to discuss the problem in this section as it's perhaps the biggest example of "revenue stifling" in the nation.

Ultimately, Canada's equalization program allows six "have not" provinces to rest on their laurels, avoid making tough financial decisions and avoid maximizing their own revenues through other legitimate means. After all, they have all kinds of cash coming in courtesy of the "have provinces."

The situation is a bit like giving a weekly allowance to a teen sleeping on your couch all summer. Give him or her a big enough cheque and you probably won't see them get off the couch and work as much as everyone else.

I'm not saying people living in "have-not" provinces don't work; I'm saying equalization dollars allow their governments to not be as cost-effective as they could. Consider a couple of ways that provinces receiving equalization payments are impacted.

First, note that the calculation behind equalization payments doesn't take natural resources into consideration when determining a province's "wealth." As a result, Quebec and Manitoba have been able to develop large volumes of hydroelectricity, sell the power at dirt-cheap rates to people in their provinces, export power to other jurisdictions to make millions, and yet still claim to be poor provinces.

According to Manitoba Hydro, as of May 1, 2013, people in Winnipeg and Quebec City paid just 8.128 and 7.036 cents per kilowatt hour respectively. Meanwhile people in Edmonton and Regina (in provinces deemed wealthy under the equalization formula) paid 12.839 and 13.827 cents per kilowatt hour respectively.[12] As you can tell, cheap hydro electricity isn't nearly as plentiful in Alberta and Saskatchewan.

Charging such low rates for power in Manitoba and Quebec would be like the Alberta government deciding to take some of the province's oil, process it and sell it at gas stations to Albertans for 50 cents per litre instead of the market rate of $1.00 per litre (or whatever the current price is in Alberta).

Yet in Manitoba and Quebec, the governments can sell dirt cheap electricity to their citizens and still count on equalization handouts from other "rich" provinces.

Table 13: Residential Electricity Rate Comparison (as of May 1, 2013)
750 kWh per month

City	750 kWh	¢/kWh
Halifax, NS	$118.55	15.807
Regina, SK	$103.70	13.827
Saskatoon, SK	$103.67	13.823
Toronto, ON	$102.52	13.669
St. John's, NL	$97.97	13.063
Edmonton, AB	$96.29	12.839
Calgary, AB	$96.06	12.808
Saint John, NB	$83.03	11.071
Vancouver, BC	$61.92	8.256
Winnipeg, MB	$60.96	8.128
Montreal, QC	$52.77	7.036

Source: Manitoba Hydro

Under a more equitable model, the federal government could expect Manitoba and Quebec to charge market rates for electricity, rates more comparable to what the rest of Canadians are facing. This would not only lead to consumers in those provinces curbing their demand as more natural prices set in, it would allow governments to increase profits by exporting the extra, surplus power. Higher profits could then be transferred to the respective provincial government to help pay for social programs.

Another way the equalization handouts stifle revenues in recipient provinces comes from the fact the handouts reduce the incentive to innovate or develop resources. Case in point, the vast amounts of natural gas deposits Quebec is sitting on – literally.

If you visit the federal government's Department of Natural Resources Canada's web site you'll find some startling numbers about natural gas resources in the province of Quebec.[13] In a section that discusses the economic impact of shale gas development in Quebec, the site notes:

"Quebec spends approximately $2 billion per year importing natural gas to meet 11% of its energy demand. At current consumption rates, and given estimates of shale gas resources, Quebec could have sufficient natural gas for decades."

Incredible. But it gets better.

"With an estimated recoverable resource between 18 and 40 trillion cubic feet if fully developed, Quebec's shale gas deposits would have a market value between $70 billion and $140 billion at current natural gas prices."

So why doesn't Quebec develop its natural resources more? Perhaps Pauline Marois, the province's former premier, explained the situation best in a video posted on her separatist party's web site: *"If one day, we produce oil and gas in Quebec, why would we let half of this wealth go down the road to Ottawa?"* *(translated)*[14]

In other words, she had no interest in developing the resource because she would have to share some of the revenues with the federal government or other provinces. She was however, happy to sit back and let her province rake in money from Alberta, Saskatchewan and other provinces that *had* decided to develop their natural resources.

In an interview with Canadian Geographic, Michael Binnion, Questerre Energy Corporation CEO and President of the Quebec Oil and Gas Association, explains just how dysfunctional natural resource development is in the French province:

"It is 100% a political battle. In 2010, when the Quebec government held the first independent environmental assessments on shale gas development, the oil and gas industry brought in experts from all over North America to explain all the things we would do in Quebec to develop the industry. But we could just as easily have been saying, 'look how safely we produce cocaine.' We thought the focus of the panel was to explain a

proposed project in Quebec that we wanted approved. But the real focus was a national debate on hydrocarbons: do we want them or don't we?

"Quebec imports 100% of its hydrocarbons from places such as Algeria, Venezuela and Norway. From an environmental point of view, it is irresponsible for Quebec to get oil and gas from overseas when it can be locally sourced. We know how the oil and gas will be produced, we can control it and we can save all of the environmental costs of transportation."[15]

Marois could easily have helped address those environmental concerns by supporting greater development of her province's natural gas deports, but again, why bother? Doing such would require sharing new revenues with the rest of Canada. Instead, she let Alberta take the environmental heat instead.

Clearly, while "poorer" provinces should be leading the way in terms of resource development, and finding ways to deliver government programs more cost-effectively, the federal government's equalization formula perverts the situation. It actually stifles revenue maximization by allowing "have not" provincial governments to act like couch-surfing teens.

The Flawed Relationship

There's a segment of Canadian society that doesn't expect much from the government. They just want a local library, a local school and hospital.

Oh, and they like the idea of a new stadium, a new arena, expanding the art gallery, putting up a new museum, building a new addition on to the convention centre, and a dog park on every fourth block. Plus, they expect their snow to be cleared every day in the winter, subways and transit all across the city, low tuition rates and "free" health care whenever they want it. But that's it.

I'm exaggerating, but you can probably see my point. People pay income taxes, property taxes, sales taxes and various other payments to the government and those dollars end up going into a big black hole. Because the funds aren't tied to any particular service, some people expect the government to pay for various luxuries they desire: *"fund the project with money from the black hole."*

In my opinion, this disconnect between what the public pays for and the services they receive from the government is a major problem that needs to be addressed.

If you think about it, few businesses operate this way. Walk into a burger restaurant, pay three dollars for a burger and that's what you're given. There's no free milkshake if you ask nicely or a side of fries if you protest. No, you pay for the burger and that's what you receive.

In government, there's often no outline of what services you'll receive for forking over half your income in taxes. Everything is up in the air, so the system is ripe for abuse.

In Canada, you could literally visit a doctor every week for the common cold and other less serious matters without a financial penalty. Heck, you can even let your body go down the tubes by eating greasy burgers every day for lunch and a tub of ice cream for dinner. Not to worry, the health care system is "free" and can perform a triple bypass if needed. Your doctor will handle everything, so no need for personal responsibility or paying attention to what's going on.

You could also let your kid watch cartoons at night instead of studying … after all, little Sarah can always take grade five over again, right? Again, no skin off your back.

You've probably also seen countless examples of groups of people "successfully" rallying to "save schools," prevent the closure of a public library or keep some kind of other government service running. Sure, the school is a quarter full, library visits may have dropped off substantially and that other service just can't be justified on a cost basis, but hey, the proponents "paid their share of taxes."

The disconnect between services demanded by citizens, and the revenues needed to pay for such services, is a significant problem that should be addressed by governments.

Solutions

Bureaucratic inefficiency in Canada is a sizable problem, but it also represents a significant opportunity for substantial savings. More than anything, I think changes need to be made to reduce duplication, inject competitive forces wherever possible, give bureaucrats the incentive to look out for the taxpayer and control spending in the first place.

Here are a few ideas that tackle the aforementioned objectives:

1) Division of Responsibilities: Governments need to stop mowing each other's lawns.

It's time for municipalities to focus on their traditional responsibilities, things like policing, roads and zoning. They should cease involvement in activities like subsidized housing, training programs and other activities that are traditionally the responsibility of other levels of government. Provincial and federal governments should do the same.

Provincial governments should stick to health care, education and social assistance to name a few responsibilities. The federal government should focus on core services such as running the military, border control, federal courts, etc.

Plain and simple, governments shouldn't overlap each other and they should each be responsible for raising the money they spend on the services they provide.

This would require some significant rejigging of revenues. For example, if the federal government stopped funding provincial health care, education and other services it would have a windfall of tens of billions of extra dollars in revenues. At the same time, provincial governments would face a financial shortfall of an equal amount. To remedy the situation, the federal government should reduce taxes by an amount equal to its current contributions while provincial governments raise taxes by the same amount. This would place full responsibility for health care, education and social services with provincial governments. There would be no more blaming Ottawa for funding shortfalls and a significant amount of bureaucracy could be eliminated at the same time.

The same process should happen with federal gas taxes. Federal gas taxes should be eliminated while provincial governments raise their gas taxes by an equal or lesser amount and then use 100% of the funds for roads.

All three levels of government should, wherever possible, connect revenue streams (e.g. gas taxes) with related services (e.g. fixing roads). A good model for this type of reform comes from Manitoba and Saskatchewan where gas tax accountability acts exist. Each province is currently required by law to spend all the money it collects in fuel taxes on road construction and repair.

The federal government should also look at significant reform to the equalization program because the status quo doesn't make sense. Provinces such as Quebec shouldn't be allowed to simply sit on their resources while collecting cash from other provinces that *have* developed their resources.

A province in Atlantic Canada, Quebec or Manitoba – all perpetual handout recipients – should be leading the nation with reform to improve the cost-effectiveness of government service delivery (like the type of reform we saw in Indianapolis nearly two decades ago). But that's simply not happening.

As long as equalization payments remain in place and act as a crutch that props up inefficient governments, leading edge reform is unlikely to happen in have-not provinces. Reforming the equalization program should place self-sufficiency as a long-term goal.

2) Managed Competition/Contracting Out: In chapter four we explored how governments can often find significant savings by hiring private companies to provide services such as road repair, snow removal and garbage pickup.

I put forward the idea of "managed competition" and contracting out as ways to reduce costs and even improve results. Governments should explore such partnerships with private businesses wherever possible. Doing so can reduce costs (and often times improve services) and ensure that everyone has a fair chance to bid on government services.

While many governments across Canada have already hired businesses to perform one service or another, one city in the U.S. has really kicked that concept into high gear.

In 2005, after decades of pushing for independence, Sandy Springs, GA finally broke free to become an independent separate city. (Search for "*The City that Outsourced Everything*" on YouTube to watch a great clip by the Reason Foundation.)[16]

The city was essentially starting with a clean slate, so instead of hiring an army of city workers, the new Sandy Springs city council decided to essentially outsource everything.

What the city did was hire a single company, CH2M, to handle the administration of almost all city services: road repair, park maintenance, zoning, building code enforcement, etc. The only services the city didn't outsource to CH2M were emergency services such as policing and firefighting; those continued to be handled by the government.

But even CH2M didn't provide all the services itself; what it did was manage a series of subcontracts.

The setup was kind of like buying a new house. You sit down with a builder, tell them what you want and they obtain estimates from various subcontractors – foundation companies, drywall companies, roofing companies, etc. – to prepare a total cost figure for the project. If you agree to the proposal, the builder hires several subcontractors to build your new home based on the agreed specs.

The Sandy Springs City Council told CH2M what they wanted in terms of services and service levels (e.g. garbage pickup to every home once a week, cut the grass in parks once every week and a half, etc.) and CH2M did the same as the builder: secure quotes from all the subcontractors and then submit a final bid.

How did it turn out? Well, in an interview with *CNBC*, the Mayor of Sandy Springs suggested they are saving around 10% by partnering with CH2M to essentially run their city.[17] 10% may not sound like much, but for a government like Sandy Springs 10% on a budget in the millions is a small fortune!

The Reason Foundation's video notes that by hiring a managing partner to run the city, Sandy Springs was able to reduce management costs alone from $50 million under a traditional government model to $25 million by partnering with CH2M.

As of 2011, the city hadn't raised taxes and was able to improve services to citizens by improving roads and fixing up old parks. Incredibly, the residents liked the improved services and the job council was doing so much that no councillor received less than 84% of the vote during the election following the partnership with CH2M.

The Sandy Springs example shows just how much could be left up to the private sector and what the possibilities could be.

3) Gainsharing: This is a great tool used by many businesses and some government bodies. Under a gainsharing model, frontline employees are financially rewarded for coming up with ideas to reduce costs.

In an August 2012 article, *Governing.com* highlighted a good example of how this can play out well in government. It described how the Montgomery County Transportation Department in Maryland tried gainsharing with their "sign and signal shop," the men and women who managed highway signs and traffic lights.

Once the employees had the incentive to think of ways to reduce costs, they proposed selling scrap signage to a recycling outfit instead of paying a trash hauler $430 per month to take away the material. *Governing.com* noted:

> *"By separating metals with resale potential from those that had no value, the sign and signal shop was able to generate $1,819 from the salvager the first time it tried out the system. Once the program went into effect, documented savings were $15,000, with $7,500 to be divided among 65 employees."[18]*

Under gainsharing models, some employers split savings 50/50 with employees while other organizations use different formulas. Regardless of how governments fine-tune the rewards program, the key to gainsharing is to give employees the incentive to come forward with ideas to save money, while requiring the same level of output or better.

Just think how this model could play out in the broader public sector. Picture a paper-pushing division in government with 10 employees and an annual budget of $1 million.

Under a gainsharing model, the employees might determine they really only need seven full-time employees instead of ten. There might not be much savings in year one as some employees are bought out, but the benefit would be significant by year two. The group of seven employees might also determine they only need five laptops and three cell phones instead of equipping everyone with such devices (a common practice in government).

The smaller, leaner unit might also start looking for a smaller office area. Who knows, they may even decide that they don't need any office space at all. Perhaps the type of paperwork they do could be done in a "work from home" setting, renting a hotel board room twice a month for meetings.

Again, a condition for any of these innovative ideas is that the staff must still produce the same level of output or better. If they can find ways to meet the same output, but at a lower cost, a sizable cheque awaits them while the government (taxpayers) also benefits.

4) Privatization: In some cases it makes sense for the government to ask if they even need to be involved in commercial activities.

In this day and age, should the Alberta government really own and run a bank? Should the government of Saskatchewan really own and subsidize a bus company? Should taxpayers really have to buy their alcohol from the government? Should the federal government still own Via Rail, a passenger train company? Should taxpayers have to subsidize money-losing golf courses operated by municipalities?

Couldn't the government sell some of those ventures off? Of course they could.

In chapter one, I began by noting the lunacy of governments running Tim Hortons cafeterias that lost millions of dollars. Here's a solution.

In 2013, the Canadian Taxpayers Federation blew the whistle on losses at Victoria Hospital's government-run cafeteria in Winnipeg. In 2011-12 the hospital lost an astounding $186,851. Like we saw with the Tim Hortons example, government employees were paid a fortune to make sandwiches, well above what private sector counterparts were making.

Yet in 2012-13, everything changed. The government stopped running the cafeteria and instead allowed a business to come in and set up shop. Instead of losing $186,851, the hospital actually made $25,591 from the new deal (presumably by charging rent to the private company).[19] In total, the hospital saw a $212,442 turnaround, money that could now go towards hiring a couple of nurses or a surgeon.

All kinds of other opportunities exist like this across the country. Governments should pursue them.

5) Public-Private Partnerships (P3s): As discussed, governments have a terrible track record when it comes to managing complex capital projects such as stadiums, museums and other projects.

"Public-private partnerships," also known as "P3s," are an option that governments across the world have used to help bring projects in on time and on budget.

This process involves governments partnering with a private sector partner to manage the project and take on some of the risk. P3s come in all shapes and sizes, but one common element is a responsibility for the private partner to cover cost overruns (or a portion of).

P3s are often successful because they take advantage of private sector know-how when it comes to managing complex projects and the profit incentive for the private sector partner to carefully manage costs.

The Confederation Bridge (the structure that connects New Brunswick and Prince Edward Island) is an example of a successful P3. The Library of Parliament praised it for coming in *"on time and on budget."*[20]

Another good example is the Anthony Henday Drive; a ring road project in Edmonton. According to the government of Alberta, the innovative partnership will lead to the motorway being completed three years ahead of schedule and $370 million less than what it would cost if the government had managed the project.[21]

There are all kinds of other examples of P3s in Canada, from fire halls and arenas to hospitals and office towers.

To be sure, P3s are not the panacea that some claim. Governments can still negotiate a bad deal with a business just as they can negotiate a bad deal with their unions. In that respect, P3s are a bit like shopping around: you can get a great deal or lose your shirt. However, especially for larger scale projects, P3s should be an option that policy makers consider.

6) Open Tendering: Some governments actually stipulate that only unionized companies are allowed to bid on their projects.

Such stipulations certainly aren't fair to those who work for or own non-union companies. At the same time, the barrier also impacts taxpayers negatively through higher costs.

Requiring businesses to be unionized workplaces means there are fewer bidders on projects as non-union companies are shut out, reducing competition. According to Merit Canada, a national organization that pushes for open bidding, approximately 70% of Canadians working in construction are non-union.[22] Clearly we're not talking about a small group of people who are being discriminated against.

Appearing before a parliamentary committee studying tendering procedures, the president of Merit Canada, Terrance Oakey, had this to say in 2013:

> "...the federal government recently contributed $28 million in stimulus funding to a project in the city of Hamilton. Of the approximately 260 qualified contractors, only 17 had workers registered with the union that the city rules require. The other 243 contractors, or 94% of the available workforce – some of your constituents – were not even allowed to bid or work on this project."[23]

The whole situation is kind of like when you sell your house. When you put your home on the market, you'd rather have 10 people bidding on it than five; more people bidding means there's a greater chance you'll be offered more than your asking price. It's a similar situation with government tenders – except instead of lots of bidders resulting in high bids, lots of bidders means more competition and lower bids tend to come forward, saving taxpayers money.

Oakey described to the committee how restricting bids results in higher costs:

> "In construction, most reputable studies that have been done on the issue show a premium of between 12% and 18%. That's overall. When you

*look at specific regions where there's further shrinkage of competition, it
can be as high as 30% to 40%.* "[24]

While some may think that non-unionized companies simply pay their
employees less and that's how they can afford to put in lower-priced bids,
Oakey corrected such claims by noting:

*"A lot of our members pay well above the union rate. A lot of the cost
associated with closed shops actually has nothing to do with wage rates.
It's increased cost that had to do with paying into an endowment fund, a
sports and entertainment fund, a hunting fund, a social justice fund, a
political action fund – none of which goes to the worker. It's simply a tax
on the employer and the project that gets funded through the local union.*

*"If our members paid less, or if our members treated their workers poorly,
there's an alternative. They would likely go and work in a union shop. But
they choose not to. In the industry, 70% of the workers, despite all legal
opportunities available to them, choose to be union-free. The numbers
speak for themselves."*

The solution to this problem is simple: governments should not require
any businesses bidding on projects to be unionized. Both unionized and non-
unionized businesses should have the right to bid on government tenders. It
just makes sense.

7) Ability to Pay: Statistics Canada regularly publishes data that shows
changes to the average person's income in different parts of the country.

At the very least, governments should be forced to consider such data
as they work on their budgets each year. This is especially necessary at the
municipal level, where property tax increases are an annual practice.

Beyond simply considering changes to taxpayers' incomes, an alternative
approach would be to actually cap any tax increases to no higher than the
community's increase in average weekly earnings.

So if the average weekly earnings in Ontario only went up by, say, 2% the previous year, then municipalities in Ontario would not be allowed to increase taxes any higher than 2%. The model might require some tweaking, but on the whole, governments should be forced to take into account what the average taxpayer can actually afford and make tough spending decisions.

8) Economic Performance Bonuses – A lot of businesses have bonuses for employees if the company exceeds forecasts in a given year. Such measures are put in place to ensure everyone works hard to row in the same direction, so to speak.

As we've already discussed, governments rarely have such incentives in place.

There is nothing to encourage the bureaucrat at the city arena to maximize ad revenues by providing great customer service. There was also nothing incenting City of Winnipeg bureaucrats to sell valuable real estate that was being used as a snow dump half the year. Again, once developed, the land could have provided the city with additional property tax revenue on an ongoing basis.

But not only do you often find such lax attitudes among bureaucrats, sometimes government unions even work to oppose growth. CTF B.C. Director Jordan Bateman wrote about this problem:

> *"It's an all-too-regular occurrence in this province. Government employees, whipped up by their union leaders, marching against whatever economic development opportunity is being proposed.*
>
> *"Pipelines to the coast? Opposed. Gas exploration? Opposed. Companies creating investment revenue for pensions? Opposed. New mine? Opposed. Coal exports? Opposed."*[25]

Bateman went on to describe an interesting initiative by B.C.'s government to encourage everyone to row in the same direction.

What the government did was set up a system whereby employee unions receive higher pay if the economy does better than expected. So if the government forecast the economy to grow by 1.5%, but it actually grew by 2.5%, the unions would get half of the difference: a 2% wage increase.

As Bateman notes in his column, the model isn't perfect. Instead of granting permanent pay increases, the incentive should be treated as a bonus that needs to be earned each year.

Further, the B.C. model doesn't include disincentives if targets aren't met.

But the overall concept has merit. Governments could even tweak it to suit different goals. For example, staff at a city-run arena could be incentivized with a bonus based on revenues. If they provide a friendly atmosphere that encourages people to come back and rent out more ice time and buy more advertising, perhaps staff could receive a share of additional revenues.

City bureaucrats managing zoning, permits and other barriers to business expansions could potentially receive bonuses if the number of commercial properties coming online exceeds targets. Wouldn't that speed up the lethargic permit process!

9) A Ray of Sunshine Wipes Out Grime: Greater transparency in government could actually help keep a lid on spending.

To see what I mean, note that governments often have massive electronic accounting systems behind the scenes. When an expense occurs, someone has to log it in the system and it is filed under a division's budget.

For example, when a provincial bureaucrat in the department of highways' southern regional office approves the purchase of a new computer it gets logged into the system under their division's budget. So do things like travel costs for conferences.

Now think back to the bureaucrat I mentioned in chapter four who sent me an anonymous note describing how colleagues went on inappropriate trips.

Instead of sending me (as an employee of a taxpayers' watchdog organization) an anonymous note to encourage an investigation of the expense, imagine if the giant bureaucratic expense system was available for the public to see. The bureaucrat could find the link online to the expense in question and then send it anonymously to politicians, the media and others. Such a model would make it 10 times easier for bureaucrats, and even the public, to expose wasteful spending; leading to more prevention.

Another initiative that should happen is on the pay and benefits side. Many governments have what are known as "sunshine lists," reports that disclose how much government employees are making. For example, in Manitoba and Saskatchewan, you can go online (in most cases) and find the salaries of provincial employees who make more than $50,000 per year. (Note: Crown corporations are not usually as keen to disclose the information online.) In Ontario, the earnings threshold is $100,000.

Unfortunately, some governments haven't enacted such transparency – including the federal government. Further, disclosure lists could be improved by including the cost of employee benefits and pension contributions made by the government (taxpayers) for each employee. Politicians and bureaucrats know that as disclosure lists are made public each year, throwing money around needlessly can hurt the government's image.

10) Medical Savings Accounts: There is no government service in Canada that uses up more tax dollars than health care. Open up your provincial government's budget and you'll find health spending alone typically gobbles up more than 40% of total expenditures. On top of that, municipalities spend millions, if not billions, on ambulance costs annually.

From 911 calls to nursing home expenses, the system is quite costly for governments to maintain.

Of course, many people don't think of it that way, as they aren't provided with a bill for visiting an emergency room or popping by a walk-in clinic. Many think of, and often refer to our system as being "free," as if some Texas oil tycoon had kindly covered the tab for us.

Obviously that's just not the case. Our "free" system is one of the main reasons why our taxes are so high. But our "free" system is in jeopardy over the long haul.

As I noted in chapter one, the Canadian Institute of Actuaries estimated in 2013 that health costs could represent as much as 103% of total provincial expenditures by 2037 unless there are significant changes. The Fraser Institute offered similar, dire concerns.

Substantial reform is needed to ensure the health care system is there for us when we need it most.

While health care reform is a complex topic, too big to tackle in this book, it's also too big to ignore, especially as I identified rising health care costs as one of the four main financial storm clouds facing our country. I also described earlier in this chapter how patients don't have to worry about how often they use the health care system or what type of shape they keep their bodies in. Our system is almost completely devoid of personal responsibility. At the same time, the system lacks competitive forces to keep costs down.

One way that we can revamp the system is to move to a model proposed by Dr. David Gratzer in his bestselling 1999 book *Code Blue: Reviving Canada's Health Care System*.

Gratzer recognized both the failure of governments to contain costs as well as the unlimited demands on our "free" system. He also acknowledged the strong desire among Canadians for universality, the notion that even the poorest should receive basic, necessary health services.

Gratzer put forward "medical savings accounts" (MSAs) as a possible solution.

In short, an MSA model has two parts.

The first part would see each Canadian given a health care account by the government. Each year the government would deposit money into the account – say, $2,000. People would then use those funds to pay for routine health services; things like visiting a family doctor or having your knee X-rayed after a fall while playing soccer.

If you only used $1,500 on such routine services, the remaining $500 would be rolled over into your account for next year. Alternatively, some MSA models allow people to withdraw and spend funds they don't use. Perhaps a Canadian model might allow people to do the same, or to take out a percentage of your savings and use it for eyewear, hearing aids and other medical devices. Obviously this detail would have to be ironed out by policy makers.

Conversely, if you used *more* than $2,000 worth of health care services before the year was done, you would start paying out of pocket for routine procedures. If you happened to use the health care system willy-nilly, you would be held accountable for your actions.

The second part of the model deals with catastrophic events such as being hit by a bus or being diagnosed with cancer. For catastrophic events you would be covered by government insurance through a high deductible; perhaps $1,000. This deductible could be covered by any surplus you had built up in your medical savings account.

An MSA approach would help curb demand. Those who abuse the system would face a cap on the amount of "free" health care they received each year. People would think twice about visiting the doctor after coming down with the sniffles. At the same time, if a doctor tried to needlessly prescribe a costly procedure, more patients would no longer just go along with it. Many would ask questions and possibly seek a second opinion.

Patients would also take more interest in their health. After all, everyone in Canada would know that if they ate properly, exercised and lived a healthy life, then there would be a greater chance they could avoid using the health care system and save up more money in their medical savings account for when they truly needed it. Again, if the government allowed you to withdraw a portion of unused funds in your medical savings account, that would also serve as an incentive to live a healthier lifestyle.

If you don't believe incentives would have much of an impact, consider a 2009 article on health reform that appeared in the *Wall Street Journal* by Steven Burd, CEO of Safeway Inc. and founder of the Coalition to Advance Healthcare Reform.[26]

Burd noted: "*70% of all health care costs are the direct result of behavior*" and "*74% of all costs are confined to four chronic conditions; cardiovascular disease, cancer, diabetes and obesity.*" The article goes on to say that between 60-90% of the aforementioned chronic conditions are preventable.

Burd's piece tells how the grocery chain Safeway (in the U.S.) modified its health insurance system to incentivize good behavior. The firm reduced family health insurance premiums by up to $1,560 if employees didn't smoke, had healthy weights, and maintained good blood pressure and cholesterol levels. The firm's CEO believes these incentives are directly correlated to the company's employees having smoking and obesity rates that are only 70% of the national average.

Further, the company was able to keep per capita health insurance costs constant over a four-year period while *"most American companies' costs ... increased 38% over the same four years."*

I'm not aware of a single provincial department of health in Canada restraining per capita health expenses like this.

Back to the MSA model. Not only would it encourage people to take better care of their health, it would also encourage patients to shop around between providers, injecting more competition into the mix. Doctors who overbilled or ordered unnecessary follow-up visits would have a harder time doing so under an MSA model. Word would spread quickly among patients as to who to avoid. Patients would be in the driver's seat once again.

There is obviously more to the MSA model than I've described here, but I hope it gives you food for thought about a system that could work in Canada. After all, it has had success among various private insurers in the United States, Singapore and even in communist China.

If you're thinking such a proposal would never fly here, that no politician would ever agree to such a systemic change, the quote on the back cover of Gratzer's book is worth noting:

"Gratzer proposes a workable solution for the biggest public policy problem of the coming generation — our government-controlled health care monopoly. Our health care system isn't just sick; it's killing people. Canada needs Gratzer's new prescription."

That endorsement came from none other than Stephen Harper ... prior to becoming prime minister.

11) User Fees: Another great takeaway from Gratzer's book *Code Blue*, is an anecdote that he calls the *"supervalue phenomenon."*

Gratzer describes one manner in which the former western grocery chain "SuperValu" differed from Safeway, its main competitor in the 1990s. SuperValu required customers to bag their own groceries at the checkout, keeping labour costs down and prices low.

However, as the shopping bags were free, customers would often abuse the privilege, taking far more than they truly needed to bag their groceries. Gratzer described how in some cases *"yellow bags became packed with other yellow bags."* In other words, in a "free" system, demand for bags was off the charts.

This eventually led the store to introduce a small user fee for the bags, just four cents per bag. Gratzer notes:

> *"Even though the fee was small, the result was startling. People began to bring their old bags back. Others opted to use canvas bags. And most paused a moment to consider how many bags they really needed at the checkout. In short, even very modest user fees provide an incentive to economize."*

If a mere four cent charge could have an impact on the services people demand, imagine how small user fees could curb public demands for new government services. User fees may not make sense for every government service, but there are plenty of cases where such a tool could help.

CHAPTER 8

The Politicians

Politicians are the fourth 'force' that leads to wasteful and inefficient government spending. You might think this topic is a bit like shooting fish in a barrel – surely we can all think of examples of politicians spending our money inappropriately. However, the problems run much deeper than what we see on the surface. I believe our political system is broken and needs reform.

In this chapter I describe what I think the role of a politician should be, several problems with our democratic system and how these problems contribute to higher costs for taxpayers. Just like chapters five through seven, I'll explore some solutions worth considering.

Before we discuss why we elect politicians in the first place, recall the anecdote involving the massive auto bailout from 2009. GM and Chrysler asked for and received a whopping $13 billion in taxpayer-funded loans and assistance from the government of Ontario and the federal government.[1]

I've already demonstrated why corporate welfare isn't effective. What I want to draw your attention to is public support for the bailout decision – or rather, the lack of it.

After the first part of the auto bailout was announced – an initial loan of "just" $4 billion – pollster Angus Reid asked Canadians what they thought about the government's decision. Their national poll found a majority of Canadians – 51% – opposed the deal while only 43% were in favour and 6% were unsure.[2]

Even in Ontario, home of the auto sector, more people opposed the bailout than supported it. A surprising 48% were opposed while only 46% supported the handouts.

On the other hand, perhaps the Ontario polling numbers shouldn't be surprising. Ontarians more than anyone had seen the *"give us money or we'll close up shop"* movie before. Perhaps they opposed the bailouts because they knew the firms required significant restructuring rather than another dump truck full of cash, courtesy of taxpayers.

Either way, the bigger question is: if a majority of Canadians opposed the bailout deal, how did both governments still approve the measure?

How is it that 51% of Canadians opposed the auto bailout, yet of our country's 310 Members of Parliament no one was vehemently opposed in public?

Given a majority of Canadians opposed the deal, we should have seen a majority of our nation's 310 MPs speaking out publicly in opposition to the bailout. At the very least, there should have been a large group of MPs opposing the deal and speaking out publicly. Much smaller stories – such as the $16 glass of orange juice famously expensed by former MP Bev Oda – got a bigger rise out of our parliamentarians. Why didn't the majority of Canadians have a stronger voice in Ottawa on the $13-billion auto bailout issue? Surely parliament could have mobilized some kind of a ruckus?

The reason we didn't see a ruckus is because our political system is broken; and not just in Ottawa, there are problems at the municipal and provincial levels too. In order to fix the situation, let's first look at some of the good apples and bad apples that we've elected.

The Highs and Lows of Our Elected Class

Politicians are often rated as one of the least trustworthy occupations in the eyes of the public so it would be easy to launch into a tirade of criticisms. The job has earned our mistrust as politicians across the political spectrum have burned taxpayers many times in the past.

However, it wouldn't be fair to simply paint everyone with the same brush as many good politicians enter politics for the right reasons.

In fact, I would bet most people who run for office do so with a sincere hope of improving their community. Sure, some candidates break the public's trust along the way, but I think most people enter public life with the right intentions.

With that said, let's highlight a few examples of current and former politicians who have pursued some positive, under-reported activities. Again, I don't want this book to sound *all* doom and gloom!

Consider Shelly Glover, a Winnipeg MP. During my time with the Canadian Taxpayers Federation I didn't have much involvement with federal issues; the CTF's Ottawa office handles most of those matters.

However, I've met with Glover a few times on different matters and we inevitably ended up talking about other activities she has been working on in Ottawa. She'd tell me of some example of wasteful spending she observed in Ottawa and then explain how she worked to put a stop to it.

She has also proudly told me how she regularly flies economy class rather than billing costly first class tickets. While MPs' expenses are hidden from the public, ask someone who regularly flies to Ottawa and they'll tell you they've seen MPs sitting right up at the front of the plane in the prime seats.

While I encouraged Shelly Glover to share those stories with her constituents, she doesn't seem like the type of person to seek such public praise. Glover seems to figure looking out for the taxpayer is just part of her job – so I decided to give her kudos in this book. However, that's not the only reason why I think she's sincerely concerned for the little guy.

Here's what she said to the House Standing Committee on Finance in October 2011:

> *"You might be surprised to know that some of us actually do believe that we need to move towards adjustments in pensions and whatnot. And some of us actually, when we got elected, tried to waive the federal pension but we're not allowed to because of prior decisions by previous governments. So be careful about painting us all with the same brush because some of us have some pretty innovative ideas and I would hope you put some faith in us as we move forward."[3]*

Glover's claim about being unable to turn down her MP pension is true. Note what *Sun News* indicated in January 2012: *"In 2000, former prime minister Jean Chretien ushered in modest pension reform, which included making it mandatory for MPs to collect their federal entitlements."[4]*

Glover's efforts to reject the golden pensions available to MPs are reminiscent of Preston Manning, Lee Morrison and Werner Schmidt. The three gents are former Reform Party MPs who turned down the golden pensions before they became "mandatory." Yes, even after many of their colleagues refused the plans – only to opt back into the plans later on – Schmidt, Manning and Morrison stuck to their guns.

It takes a lot of principle to turn down literally hundreds of thousands of dollars from the government! Glover's attempt to do the same is worth praise as well.

Another great example comes from the Standing Buffalo First Nation in Saskatchewan.

Shortly after winning a by-election in 2012, Councillor Stella Isnana was presented with all kinds of outrageous perks and benefits for serving on her band's council. The situation was obscene. Her reserve had less than 500 people, but annual spending on council pay and expenses was close to $1 million. Incredibly, her Chief's pay ($174,862 tax-free) rivaled that of Stephen Harper's and other council members made more than Saskatchewan's premier, Brad Wall (once calculations were made to take into account the tax-free nature of aboriginal politicians' pay).[5]

Isnana felt such extravagance was inappropriate, especially as social programs were being cut on the reserve. Tragically, people were told there was no money available to address the community's youth suicide problem or to help young people with training programs.

Isnana blew the whistle in 2013 and the news eventually led to a power struggle within the band. Chief Redman was eventually re-elected, but Isnana's efforts helped shine a big spotlight on the problem, eventually forcing the band's council to cut total spending on council pay and expenses in half.

But it's not just pay that often becomes an area of abuse for politicians; those in power often abuse their expense accounts as well. From a politician in Nova Scotia expensing an Xbox video game to Alison Redford expensing a $45,000 trip to attend Nelson Mandela's funeral in South Africa, taxpayers have been burned time and time again by those in public office.[6][7]

For leadership in this area, note the actions of Michelle Simpson, Liberal MP for Scarborough Southwest from 2008 to 2011.

When Simpson was elected, most governments in Canada required disclosure of their elected officials' expenses. However, the expenses of politicians in Ottawa were still under lock and key (and are still confidential as of publishing this book).

Disclosure was only done in the form of annual totals for each MP by category, say, "$90,234 –Travel." This format obviously doesn't tell you important details such as where the trips occurred, for what purpose, what class the person flew, that sort of thing.

Simpson felt the secrecy was inappropriate and began disclosing her expenses online in July 2009.

In the Summer 2011 edition of *The Taxpayer*, official magazine of the Canadian Taxpayers Federation, she wrote a column describing how taxpayers loved her leadership in this area. She described receiving hundreds of emails and letters from across the country after posting her expense details online. Simpson noted:

> *"The commonality in the messages was astounding ... not one commented on how I spent the money, just the fact they were delighted I shared the detail of expenditures at all."*

While the public loved what she did, several MPs were none too pleased. They chided her disclosure efforts, some claiming the public *"wouldn't understand and couldn't put MP spending in proper context."* Others accused her of *"opening a can of worms."*

Odd comments indeed, especially when one considers a politician's expenses are one of the easiest things about government to understand.

While the aforementioned politicians represent examples of elected officials trying to do the right thing, there are many cases of Canadian politicians misleading the public or taking advantage of the taxpayer. Someone could write an entire book on that subject alone.

Sadly, we're all too familiar with such stories, but for good measure, here are a few tidbits to get your blood boiling.

Consider Len Goucher, the Nova Scotia MLA who expensed the afore-mentioned Xbox video game.[8] He was also caught expensing 11 computers, 12 printers, five digital cameras and four video cameras over a three-year period. Goucher was actually the "star" of a massive expense scandal involving several MLAs in 2010. Some of his colleagues were even caught expensing generators for their homes.

Taxpayers only found out about the scandal after the province's auditor investigated. Oddly enough, people were told there were no problems with the system before the auditor came in to have a look. Right.

In Alberta, a 2012 scandal provoked similar anger from taxpayers.

The situation exploded after the Canadian Taxpayers Federation gave a committee of Alberta MLAs one of its annual government waste awards. What did the MLAs do to deserve the award? Nothing. Literally. Then CTF Alberta director Scott Hennig discovered how 21 MLAs were being paid $1,000 per month to be part of a committee that hadn't met in 39 months.

The "no-meet committee" scandal went gangbusters. Unfortunately for the governing Progressive Conservative Party, the story hit the news just before the provincial election. Leading up to the vote, the *Edmonton Sun* said the issue *"could be the hinge the April 23 provincial election hangs on."*[9]

At the federal level, scandals and shenanigans have also left the public shaking their heads in disgust.

Recall the Senate expense scandal. For years, taxpayers were told that although federal MPs and senators' expenses were under lock and key, the public need not worry: strict rules prevented any kind of abuse of the system.

In a 2010 *Globe and Mail* story, columnist John Ibbitson described the situation:

> *"In the past, defenders of these secret practices have said that strict internal controls prevent any abuse by MPs and senators of their office budget."*[10]

Fast forward a couple of years and too many stories put lie to such a claim. Conservative Senator Mike Duffy was caught expensing ineligible expenditures and ended up paying back a whopping $90,000.[11] Tiny mistake right?

Liberal Senator Mac Harb was charged with fraud and breach of trust and Senators Patrick Brazeau and Pamela Wallin were suspended. Former Liberal MP Joe Fontana was convicted in 2014 for expensing a bill for his son's wedding.[12] As the *London Free Press* noted:

"Fontana was convicted of breach of trust by a public official, fraud and uttering forged documents after the Mounties probed the longtime former MP's expense claim."[13]

These examples may strike a nerve, but the cost of politicians' compensation, their trips and other direct expenses are actually a drop in the bucket of the government's overall budget.

However, it's important to pay attention to how politicians use their expense accounts for the simple reason that if they grossly abuse their own pay and benefits, they're probably not people we want to control the rest of the public purse. Just think of the damage their carefree, "money is no object" attitude could do to the federal government's $250-billion-plus budget, a provincial budget in the billions or even a municipality's budget.

So how do we elect more "good" politicians and fewer of the "not-so-good" variety? Let's look at the system that elects our politicians in the first place.

The Candidates

When people put their names forward for election, they're applying to be on the board of directors of a multi-million- or multi-billion-dollar organization in the case of big cities, provincial governments or the federal government.

Once elected, their role, at least in theory, is even more powerful if they're selected to be part of a provincial or federal government's cabinet.

Yet, many who are elected, and even many of those who are chosen for cabinet, simply don't have experience running anything of significance prior to entering public office. They're suddenly elevated to a position with significant power and responsibility, and tasked with making significant decisions without a lot of experience to draw on.

This problem is especially true of NDP candidates as they often come from the union movement (many from the public sector) and tend to have less business or managerial experience.

That's not to say that having been a CEO or senior executive is a prerequisite to being a good politician. Some very good politicians have emerged from fairly modest prior positions.

However, it would help if our governments were comprised of more people who had achieved leadership roles prior to entering public life. I think we need more people who can critique proposals while drawing from similar decision-making experiences prior to being elected.

To be clear, politicians should come from a mix of different backgrounds: CEOs, small business owners, teachers, branch managers of a store or bank, police sergeants, etc. After all, governments make decisions not only on fiscal issues, but also social issues such as guidelines for sentencing criminals, rules around adoption, prostitution laws and the legalization of marijuana, to name a few. But the biggest part of government is management.

How well does our health care system treat patients? How do Canadian students fare compared with students in other countries? Should a city expand its subway system or go with light rail transit? Are road construction crews operating efficiently? Is the chief administrative officer doing a good job? How does he or she compare with peers? Those are the types of questions politicians need to ask of civil servants, and more importantly, be able to evaluate the responses they hear.

If a party's caucus is full of people with no experience running anything of significance, it's going to be a lot harder to achieve results than a team that has a fair number of elected officials with experience running a human resources department, working on an organization's budget, leading a sizable project, etc. A team composed of rookies would probably make more mistakes than a team with a healthy mix of experience. Needless to say, more mistakes lead to higher bills for taxpayers.

And to be clear, inexperience running large organizations is not unique to the NDP. All parties have faced the challenge of attracting candidates with great experience.

One stumbling block that seems to prevent good, qualified people from running for office is the fact that it often requires successful people to take a large pay cut.

Sure, some highly successful people from business, government and the non-profit sector run for office because they either love politics or want to play a role in shaping their community for the better. I'm not saying it doesn't happen. Former prime minister Paul Martin is a great example of someone who took a sizable pay cut after entering politics.

But many talented people don't run for office because they don't want to take a sizable pay cut and suffer all the drama that comes with public life: living in fishbowl, having to adhere to political correctness, kissing babies and so on.

I've talked to many talented people over the years about the possibility of running for office. Time and time again I've heard people dismiss the idea, citing the loss of income as a big reason.

Another major challenge for outsiders is the power of incumbency. Plain and simple, incumbents can be extremely difficult to knock off. After all, they not only have four years to campaign while being paid, they typically enjoy greater access to media publicity than an unknown challenger. Throw in access to public funds for sending out flyers to voters and the deck is stacked in their favour.

For some politicians, getting elected is likely the best job they'll ever have. Thus, they keep running again and again; not because they have a strong commitment to public service. They keep running because they know they'll never find another job as good as the one they've got.

Think of a teacher's assistant or a clerk at a local business who makes $45,000 per year before entering politics. Once elected, they're suddenly making anywhere from $80,000 to $160,000 annually. Not only that, they have a couple of assistants who are at their beck and call all day long, they're invited to all kinds of special functions, people wine and dine them and they contribute to some pretty senior government decisions.

Who wouldn't enjoy such a boost in status, pay and benefits? It's easy to see why they keep running again and again.

Shifting Convictions

Once elected, many politicians compromise their convictions while some outright morph into Play-Doh-like creatures. The latter become so soft that they can literally be moulded into standing for, and doing, almost anything if they think they can get a few votes; politicians who cross the floor and join another party would be a good example.

Granted, politics requires a degree of compromise. For example, if every elected official waited for a budget they thought was perfect it would simply never happen; no one would ever agree 100% on something as complex as a budget.

Unfortunately, I think we see too much compromising of principles.

Prime Minister Stephen Harper deserves credit for keeping major election promises; such as reducing the GST, introducing income splitting, following through with tough on crime legislation and scrapping the wasteful long-gun registry to name a few. However, one area where I wish he had stuck to his guns concerns government-run regional economic development bodies.

Prior to becoming prime minister in 2006, Prime Minister Harper supported dismantling such bodies; he wanted to eliminate the regional development agency in Atlantic Canada (ACOA) and others like it in other parts of the country.[14] Yet after being elected prime minister, he not only kept all of those slush fund agencies, he created two new regional development agencies; one in Ontario and one in Northern Canada!

Make no mistake, Prime Minister Harper is not alone in making an about-turn on an issue once elected. Politicians across the spectrum often make such "transitions."

Many elected officials seem to know which difficult decisions are required, but worry that reform could be hard to communicate and could potentially cost them votes. This is especially true about cutting spending. Someone is benefitting from such spending and will no doubt cry out publicly against the politician cutting their funding.

Politicians who don't view the job as a career probably aren't as worried about such a backlash. But others who hope to stick around for the long haul are more likely to avoid making such tough decisions.

Further, I believe difficult decisions are avoided because politicians often seem to lack effective communications strategies. They may have a solid rationale to cut wasteful spending, but often don't seem to know how to properly defend such a difficult decision publicly. As a result, they worry about losing votes and simply move along to the next issue.

This generates too many shortsighted politicians focused on the next election and not so much on long-term matters such as the big-picture issues I've raised in this book.

Beyond funding projects and programs that may not make sense, some politicians will do virtually anything in the name of self-preservation. Think about one of the granddaddies of such costly decisions: former Ontario premier Dalton McGuinty's gas plant saga from 2011.

In short, the McGuinty government announced deals to move forward with two gas-fired electricity plants in 2009; one in Mississauga and one in Oakville.

After environmentalists organized, they put enough pressure on the malleable McGuinty government to cancel the Oakville plant in 2010. Not long after, during the middle of the 2011 election, the McGuinty team announced it would also cancel the Mississauga plant as the Liberals realized not doing so could cost them a seat or two. The only problem was construction had already started, so the cancellation costs would be anything but cheap.

When all was said and done, Ontario's provincial auditor estimated the gas plant boondoggle could cost the government as much as $1.1 billion.[15] Again, the entire move was done not in the name of the public good, but to help the Liberal Party keep a couple of seats.

Beyond outright schemes like this, politicians also dream up expensive programs to win votes more broadly.

Throne speeches and budget speeches often include new programs and tax credits concocted to help political parties appeal superficially to targeted demographics. Need more votes from seniors? Create a tax credit for seniors. Need more votes from soccer moms? Create a program to target that demographic. Yes, politics is that calculating. Good public policy decisions often take a backseat to political needs.

The Chretien government's decision to create a national gun registry is a great example. No doubt it helped the Liberals win a few votes among those thinking with their hearts and less with their heads. How could anyone believe a hardened criminal would pop by a government office to register his or her guns? They're criminals; breaking the law is what they do.

A 2009 *CBC* story notes the gun registry was originally predicted to cost taxpayers $2 million (most of the cost was to be covered by registration fees).[16] In fact, the project ended up costing taxpayers more than a billion dollars and was ultimately scrapped by the Harper government due to its ineffectiveness.

Need Outside the Box Thinking

Instead of dreaming up ways to spend more money, politicians need to spend more time focusing on dreaming up ways to reduce costs. Politicians could connect with voters by showing they understand their challenges and are working hard to keep the tax burden down.

The story of Suvir Murchandani, a 14-year old boy from the Pittsburgh area, is a great example of the type of thing politicians should be spending more time doing.

According to a 2014 *CNN* story, Suvir was interested in applying his computer science knowledge to promoting environmental sustainability for a science fair project.[17] He decided to investigate ways his school could reduce paper and ink costs.

Suvir examined the standard fonts used by his school and compared the amount of ink they used with the amount of ink used in alternative fonts. A simple enough exercise, but the results were surprising. Suvir concluded his school division could choose a slightly less ink-dependent font and reduce ink consumption by 24%, saving the division approximately $21,000 annually.

Encouraged by an academic journal to think even bigger, Suvir researched and concluded that a combined $370 million in ink costs could be saved by the U.S. federal and state governments if they merely switched fonts.

If you find yourself smiling at the simple, yet cost-effective analysis by 14-year-old Suvir, imagine your local politician announcing similar analysis of an issue and acting on the idea to save taxpayers money.

A lot of people would love seeing such outside the box thinking. What senior or soccer mom wouldn't have liked such an idea? The point is, a politician showing he or she is committed to finding savings (rather than announcing lofty spending plans) will also score points with the electorate.

Strict Party Discipline

There is simply not enough independence for our local provincial and federal politicians. The men and women we elect at the local level often go off to Ottawa or provincial capitals and become enmeshed in strict, partisan caucuses. While party caucus discussions are fairly confidential, the exterior results are disappointing.

It is quite rare to see a politician with a governing party vote against one of his or her party's bills. Similarly, it's rare for a politician with an opposition party to break rank and vote with a government bill. If you think about it, it just doesn't make sense.

Could politicians in opposition really believe the governing party's legislation is really "*that bad*" all the time? Could politicians in the governing party really believe their own legislation is "*that good*" all the time? The answer in both cases is "no."

Even private member's bills – legislation tabled by individual politicians rather than a governing party – are often voted on along party lines rather than the old tradition of letting politicians vote on such matters as they see fit.

Unfortunately, politicians seem to spend more time trying to find something wrong with their opponents' ideas rather than evaluating what's right. At the same time, if their own party makes a mistake ... well, they keep quiet.

So what causes such strict party discipline in the first place?

Each party has a "whip" who regularly meets with his or her colleagues to make sure they fall in line during party votes. From the outside, that's sometimes seen as a symbol of party discipline.

However, more than anything, what seems to keeps politicians in line is the power and pay top up that comes with a cabinet post, and the need to retain their party's nomination for the next election.

Overall, many politicians in partisan environments feel marginalized. They complain about being treated as drones that simply show up and vote as they're told, kiss babies at public events and help secure the seat at election time. Many politicians complain about not having a meaningful role in the drafting of legislation that's put forward.

In partisan environments, governments often seem to be run by a few key people: the premier or prime minister, a couple of trusted advisors and a few key cabinet ministers. Beyond that, there seems to be a lot less power exercised by our local provincial and federal politicians than what many think.

Consider a snippet from a June 6, 2013, *Globe and Mail* story on Brent Rathgeber, an MP who quit the federal Conservative Party caucus:

> *"The Alberta MP said he ultimately grew tired of the [prime minister's office's] authority, and of bowing to 'masters half my age' who give back-bench MPs instructions about how to vote, treating them like 'trained seals'."*[18]

Rathgeber isn't alone when it comes to believing politicians are often treated like "trained seals." In fact, it's not just a concern with the Parliament of Canada or even one particular party.

If you visit the Cable Public Affairs Channel's website (CPAC.ca) and watch *Whipped: The Secret World of Party Discipline* you'll hear the "trained seals" term used several times in the documentary about B.C. politics.[19]

Former journalist Sean Holman put the documentary together and it describes, as its name suggests, the high degree of party discipline in B.C.

politics. However, Holman probably could have put together the same video in any province in Canada; the system seems to be broken across the country.

The documentary starts off with a stunning fact: a government bill in British Columbia hasn't been defeated since March of 1953.

Could all the pieces of legislation that have come before the B.C. legislature over the last 60 years really be that well crafted? Or could it be that the province suffers from a democratic deficit? Holman leads viewers to conclude the latter and I would agree. In fact, I would think most people would come to that conclusion after watching his work.

But not only are government bills never defeated, politicians rarely break rank with their parties. Holman's documentary notes that from June 2001 to April 2012, of 32,328 votes cast by politicians in the B.C. legislature, just 80 were cast by MLAs voting against their own party – about 0.25% of the time.

One interesting segment features an interview with Dennis Mackay, a former Liberal MLA. During the discussion, Mackay describes how he had announced he would be voting against his government's proposed land claim with the Tsawwassen First Nation. He received plenty of media attention, once news broke that he would not support the bill.

Mackay notes how prior to the vote, one colleague told him: *"I support you and I would like to vote with you, but I can't."* Frustrated by what he heard, Mackay pressed his colleague, asking why he wouldn't vote against the bill. According to Mackay he was told: *"I'm looking for a cabinet post and I don't want to be seen as a maverick."*

Another interesting anecdote from *Whipped* was a look at Bob Simpson, a former NDP MLA who sat as an independent during his final few years in office. Holman crunched the numbers and found that while Simpson sat as an NDP MLA, he voted with the party 100% of the time. However, after leaving the party and sitting as an independent, he voted with the opposition Liberals 22% of the time.

So why does all this matter in a chapter about how politicians contribute to higher costs than necessary for taxpayers?

Well, think back to the auto bailout. Canadians opposed the bailout, but there was no movement among MPs to try to stop the multi-billion-dollar handout. Ideally, MPs should have tried to amend the budget bill that year or introduce their own legislation to stop the move, but that simply didn't occur.

It's not clear how each caucus decided to support the auto bailout, but once the party's position was established, the MPs all fell in line like … trained seals.

Question Period

Watch question period at the federal or provincial level and it should be clear it's a fairly useless exercise. For those who enjoy watching politicians yelling back and forth, and political drama, it's pretty entertaining. But if you like accountability you'll be disappointed.

No longer do we have gentlemen (and ladies) engaged in civil debates; question period has turned into a chance for the opposition to ask barbed questions and the government to respond with rhetoric. Seldom do opposition parties obtain any kind of useful answers to help them do their jobs.

It's not uncommon to see exchanges like the following:

Opposition politician: "Mr. Speaker, when did the minister find out about the expense scandal at the Oak Hills Hospital and what action did she take?"

Cabinet Minister: "Mr. Speaker, this government believes in building new health care infrastructure. That's why we're building a new state of the art hospital in…"

Such nonsensical exchanges defy the whole concept of a daily question period while legislatures (and parliament) are in session. The idea was to give opposition parties a chance to ask the government about various matters, hear meaningful answers and hold them accountable. It's supposed to be a check and balance within our system. But it's broken.

Many observers regard it as theatre more than anything. But does it really make sense to take dozens of highly-paid people and put them in a room where they waste an hour of time each day? Of course not.

But not only is it a waste of money, clips on TV of the raucous environment also likely lead many good people to say "no thanks" when asked to consider running for politics.

In an ideal world, the opposition should be able to obtain details on just about anything the government is working on, learn about mistakes, help identify weaknesses and hopefully prevent a few boondoggles. But when information simply doesn't flow as freely as it should, it's a lot harder for opposition parties to do their jobs and save the taxpayer a few bucks.

Advertising

Governments waste a lot of money on advertising. Why? Because politicians know they can inject rhetoric subtly into government ads and use those large ad budgets to get their message out.

For example, in 2008 the Workers Compensation Board (WCB) in Manitoba had an actor in one of its ads describe the province as having a "booming" economy while discussing workplace injuries.

At the time, the province's economy was growing by about 3% annually; a good clip, but it certainly wasn't "booming." Economists tend to reserve that term for economies like China and others that see growth in the 6% range or higher.

Political apparatchiks often inject themselves into administrative matters, so one can imagine how that rosy language made it into the WCB ads. The government could subtly suggest that the economy was doing quite well. And if people think the economy is doing well, it reinforces in the minds of some voters that there's no need to change governments.

From a politician's perspective, if they can run ads talking about a positive new program, why not? The taxpayer pays the bill for the ads and it helps the party in power connect with voters in a positive light.

Other governments in Canada have pulled similar stunts with ad buys. The federal government has been relentless over the years with advertising its "Economic Action Plan" and other programs. Here are some ad spending numbers from the feds:

Table 14: Federal Ad Spending

Year	Amount
2002-03	$110.0 million
2003-04	$69.8 million
2004-05	$49.5 million
2005-06	$41.3 million
2006-07	$86.9 million
2007-08	$84.1 million
2008-09	$79.5 million
2009-10	$136.3 million
2010-11	$83.3 million
2011-12	$78.5 million
2012-13	$69.0 million

Source: *2008-09 and 2012-13 Annual Report on Government of Canada Advertising Activities.*
Note: *2003-04 spending restricted due to auditor's review, 2004-05, 2005-06 and 2008-09 spending restricted due to elections*

Beyond the appropriateness of the messages in some ads, many question the role advertising can have with media influence. In short, if a government spends a ton of money on advertising, will ad-supported news media treat it a little bit better than a party that talks about cutting such spending? The situation reminds one of the saying, *"don't bite the hand that feeds you."*

How would you react if you were a news manager and knew that 10% of your revenues were from a certain government? Would you want to rock that boat?

I'm not saying that governments shouldn't spend money on advertising. I'm also not saying all media outlets are easily swayed by government ad spending. I'm just flagging these common concerns and identifying them as possible unfair advantages to governing parties (not to mention the cost).

Four-Year Blank Cheque

Imagine you've just heard back from a company you interviewed with and they want you to come in and negotiate the terms of your contract.

You sit down with your future boss and slide a piece of paper across the table with a few demands.

First, you want a four-year contract regardless of how poorly you perform. Second, you want to be able to miss a lot of work annually. Third, you want a company credit card for personal expenses and you don't want to be challenged on what you purchase. Finally, you want to be able to lie to your boss if you feel the need to do so.

No employer would ever agree to such absurd demands, would they? Well, actually *we* do as taxpayers.

When we elect politicians in Canada we're hiring them to do a job. Yet, the relationship affords them a blank cheque of sorts for four years. Sadly, there's not a lot we can do as taxpayers if they turn sour once elected.

While politicians may not abuse their power as much as they technically could, there is still a lot of abuse that occurs. Such taxpayer-unfriendly actions often happen early in a politician's four-year term; in fact, it's a well-known strategy in politics to make difficult decisions during the first or second year of your term.

Why? Because if you're going to ruffle anyone's feathers, the hope is that if you do it early in your mandate, by year four – the next election – many people will have forgotten about your unfavourable decisions (or perhaps will have forgiven you).

Regardless, it doesn't make much sense for taxpayers to be powerless against such occurrences until the next election. Here are a few examples of broken promises or questionable decisions right after politicians were elected:

Table 15: Post-Election Broken Promises

Politician	During the Election
Premier Gordon Campbell (BC)	Promised no harmonized sales tax during May 2009 election, brought in a harmonized sales tax two months later
Premier Dalton McGuinty (ON)	Promised in 2003 election to not raise taxes or create new ones without voter approval, brought in a new health tax less than a year later
Premier Alison Redford (AB)	Promised to balance the budget by 2012-13, ran multiple deficits
Premier Greg Selinger (MB)	Said the suggestion he would raise the sales tax was "ridiculous" in the October 2011 election, raised sales tax in 2013 budget

To be clear, broken promises and questionable decisions right after an election aren't just limited to provincial premiers. Plenty of councillors, mayors, ministers and prime ministers have done the same over the years.

Unfortunately, whether it's tax changes or questionable decisions after a politician is elected, taxpayers are the ones who end up with the short end of the stick.

Solutions

I've discussed several ways politicians lead to inefficient and wasteful spending, and unaccountable activities. From a system that attracts too many unqualified candidates in the first place, to party discipline and politicians having four-year blank cheques, there are plenty of things that should change.

I'll discuss some solutions to these problems a bit more in chapter nine, but in the meantime, here are a few thoughts on how we can improve on the status quo:

1) **T4 Pay Model:** Some politicians keep running again and again because they're unlikely to find a better job, not because their heart is actually in the

work. At the same time, there are plenty of really good people who choose not to run because they would have to take a significant pay cut if they won.

Simply raising the pay level for everyone may help recruit *some* better candidates, but it would also encourage stale politicians to linger on in the job even more.

Some will say that there's a better approach: pay politicians based on results. I couldn't agree more.

If a politician were part of a team that delivered a balanced budget, lowered health care wait times, improved road conditions, contributed to better student test results and lowered taxes, I would support paying them a big bonus. I think a lot of people would.

However, it's highly unlikely that our elected officials would ever agree on such a performance matrix. Politicians who want higher taxes would balk at having their pay tied to reducing taxes. Politicians who don't care about balancing the budget each year would also balk at such measures deciding their pay.

So why not try a totally different approach? Why not use a model that is based on what a politician makes before he or she is elected. So if you were a successful person making $250,000 per year, you wouldn't have to take an $85,000 pay cut to be an MP ($163,700 as of 2014).[20] At the same time, if you were making $70,000 per year before entering politics, then that's what you would earn once elected. You wouldn't suddenly "win the lottery" by seeing your pay jump by over $160,000.

This approach would obviously need some tweaking and safeguards, but you can see where I'm going with it.

For example, if NHL star Sidney Crosby ran for office and won, the public probably wouldn't stand for paying him $10 million per year (or whatever he currently makes) to be a politician. Therefore, governments would probably be wise to put a cap on the system. At the federal level, where MPs currently make $165,000 per year or so, a cap of, say, $330,000 might be appropriate (double the current pay).

The government would need a way of determining someone's pay prior to being elected to public office. For this, I would suggest looking at the person's income from their annual income tax statements. To ensure someone couldn't somehow spike their pay just before being elected, perhaps the government could take the most recent three-year average from their T4 slips. Alternatively, an arbitrator could even be used to help determine a fair amount.

Further, in the case of someone who took time off for maternity or paternity leave, there would probably need to be a provision to address that type of circumstance. The same would be true for students coming out of school. If a university student were somehow elected to Parliament, it wouldn't be reasonable to pay them $9,000 per year or whatever they earned while working part-time as a student. It would probably make sense to establish some kind of pay floor. Perhaps what the average Canadian earns each year.

One tweak to this approach might be to keep the status quo, but allow elected officials to apply for a top-up if they can demonstrate they were earning more before being elected.

Either way, once a pay amount is determined for each elected official, it should be adjusted each year to increase with Statistics Canada's average weekly earnings index. That way someone's pay wouldn't become stale once elected, it would rise as the paycheque of the average citizen rises.

The goal of this approach is to reduce the deterrents that keep the best and brightest from running for office while reducing the incentive for burned-out politicians to keep running again and again. Again, this idea would require further analysis to work out some of the kinks but I think it has merit.

2) Citizen Initiative Legislation: Earlier I described several examples of provincial premiers breaking their promises shortly after being elected.

One of them didn't get away with it.

In the May 2009 B.C. election, Gordon Campbell's Liberal Party promised it wouldn't bring in a harmonized sales tax (HST). Yet, just a couple of months after re-election, he dropped a bombshell on taxpayers. He announced in July 2009 that his government would be bringing in an HST the following year.[21]

Thankfully, voters didn't have to sit back and accept the broken promise. You see, B.C. is unique in that voters have two tools available for holding politicians accountable.

The first tool is known as "initiative" and it allows citizens to force a province-wide referendum on an issue if they collect enough petition signatures. This measure was created after 83% of voters approved of the idea in a province-wide referendum in 1991.[22]

So, if a political party broke a major promise, taxpayers could try to force a referendum to reverse it. And that's exactly what happened after Campbell brought in an HST.

Former B.C. premier Bill Vander Zalm led a charge to collect petition signatures across the province. Under Elections B.C. rules (the body that regulates elections and initiative), Vander Zalm and company were required to collect the signatures of 10% of registered voters in each riding.[23] That worked out to 299,611 signatures.[24]

However, given the deep-rooted anger towards the HST, Vander Zalm and his team were able to collect more than double the threshold, 713,883 signatures. A referendum was later held and voters shot down the HST. This resulted in the legislature tabling and passing a bill to eliminate the HST – the people won!

B.C.'s initiative process isn't perfect. Many feel the 10% threshold is way too high and note that only one effort to achieve a province-wide vote has been triggered since 1995.

By contrast, in California, citizens have the same initiative tool, but they only need to collect 5% of the number of voters who actually voted.

Notice the distinction.

While B.C.'s threshold of 10% is based on the number of people on the voting list, California's is based on a smaller number – the number of people who actually voted.[25] And again, California only requires 5% to sign a petition versus B.C.'s threshold of 10%.

I'm not holding California up as an ideal model. Their low threshold allows for too many referendums. But somewhere in between B.C.'s high threshold and California's low one is probably a threshold that is "just right." A level needs to be determined that makes the tool more accessible to hold politicians accountable, but not to the point that it's a nuisance.

One other shortcoming with B.C.'s system is that the results are not binding. There is still the chance voters could go to the all the trouble of collecting enough signatures across the province to force a referendum, win that vote, then see the legislature shoot down a subsequent piece of legislation.[26]

While the referendum may not be a binding vote, it certainly would be extremely difficult for any party to ignore the results and get away with it.

Despite the shortcomings of B.C.'s initiative system, it's a tool that other provinces, municipalities and the federal government should look at implementing nation-wide (with improvements). As we saw in B.C., it helped keep politicians in check.

3) Recall: The other tool that British Columbia voters approved in that 1991 referendum is "recall." It too passed by a large margin of voters, 81%.

Recall allows voters to collect enough signatures in a particular constituency to remove a politician from office, forcing a by-election. So if a politician breaks a promise or performs poorly, recall provides voters with a tool to do something about the politician's defiance. The tool brings an end to the "four-year blank cheque" approach.

Some people might think such a tool would be abused, but the numbers suggest otherwise.

According to Elections B.C., since 1995, there have been 24 registered attempts to try to collect enough signatures to force a member of B.C.'s legislative assembly to step down. Of those 24 attempts, not one provincial politician has been successfully recalled.[27] However, the province's elections body notes on its site that one MLA did resign after petition signatures had been handed in and were being verified. In other words, the politician likely saw the writing on the wall and decided to leave office before being forced out by voters in a by-election.

Others speculated that if Gordon Campbell had not stepped down after his HST boondoggle, he too would have been recalled. Thus, only two politicians potentially could have been recalled since 1995 – that's hardly a tool that has been abused!

In terms of the signature threshold to remove a politician from office, proponents need to collect signatures from 40% of registered voters. Again, this threshold might also be a bit too high, but the tool is still worth replicating nation-wide.

4) Referendums: Our electoral system is largely still based on a society from more than 100 years ago.

Back in 1900, it made more sense for communities to vote for politicians and send them off to provincial capitals or Ottawa to take care of the day-to-day affairs of government. News travelled slowly and it could take people hours to get to the nearest town. Citizen involvement in the daily activities of government would have been much more difficult as most people (especially in rural parts of the country) didn't have hours to spend travelling to and from polling stations each month.

However, everything has changed since that period. The Internet allows people across the country to get access to immense piles of information on public policy issues with the click of a mouse. Similarly, there have been significant advances in transportation. Cars and buses are extremely common and thousands of kilometres of paved roads and highways help most people in rural parts of the country get to a voting station with ease.

Technology has made it possible for someone in Thunder Bay, Ontario, to stay on top of what's happening at the provincial capital in Toronto just as easily as someone in Mississauga can. Someone living two hours by horse and buggy from an Estevan, Saskatchewan, community hall can now likely arrive there in a few minutes by car if there were a need to vote on something.

Despite these significant changes in technology and transportation that make it possible for more people to be involved in government decisions, politicians have been reluctant to embrace more citizen involvement through tools such as referendums.

Not only should the public be included in making more decisions – especially decisions such as spending $200 million on a non-essential project like a stadium or arena – more inclusion could actually help politicians.

A story from the *USA Today* in 2010 (when the U.S. was still in a recession) illustrates the tendency of voters to be fiscally responsible:

> *"Three times since 2002, voters in affluent Marblehead, Mass., have approved building new schools or renovating old ones. Not this year. Voters said 'no' last week to a plan to build an elementary school that would replace a 1916 building that has all its bathrooms in the basement. In a sign of the times, Marblehead voters rejected not just the new school but all 10 projects on the ballot – from environmental cleanup of the dump to artificial turf at the local football field. Voter reluctance to approve new projects during hard times has played a big role in a drop in spending on schools, roads, sewers and other infrastructure."*

> *"'If it had been an emergency, people might have dug deep. But artificial turf? In these times?' says Jack Buba, an opponent of the Marblehead projects."*[28]

According to *The Bond Buyer*, a daily publication that follows municipal finance, voters approved 66.8% of public votes for various spending initiatives at the municipal and state level in the U.S. in 2010.[29] That approval number was a significant drop from 2006 and 2008, when voters approved over 80% of projects put to a vote.

In other words, voters were more likely to recognize that during tough times, the government should postpone spending money on such luxuries as artificial turf. Yet, in Canada, many politicians (at all three levels) saw the slowdown as a chance to spend a boatload of "stimulus" money on all kinds of luxury projects.

Simply put, the government should leave more decisions up to voters and we'd probably see more responsible spending decisions being made. As a side bonus, we would probably see more people get engaged in politics and consider running as well.

5) Taxpayer Protection Acts: This safeguard makes it harder for governments to simply raise taxes. Taxpayer Protection Acts (TPAs) come in all shapes and sizes, but a common feature of the measure is to require governments to hold a referendum before raising or creating major taxes.

For example, Alberta's TPA prevents the introduction of a provincial sales tax without first holding a referendum. In Manitoba, legislation calls for holding a referendum prior to an increase of a sales tax, personal income taxes or the province's payroll tax.

While TPAs aren't bulletproof – governments can simply pass legislation to remove the acts or to get around referendum requirements – the acts do carry a lot of weight in the court of public opinion. In other words, politicians pay the price if they fool around with these measures.

In 2013, Manitoba's NDP government raised the province's sales tax and effectively bypassed the taxpayer protection law by tabling legislation to exempt their tax increase from triggering a referendum.

While the NDP may have thought the move would be fairly easy, they faced a tremendous public backlash. The premier's approval rating tanked and so did support for his party. The public turned on the government and many expect a loss for the NDP in the upcoming election.

In my role with the CTF, I received several calls and emails from people who identified themselves as NDP supporters, but they too were fed up. They felt the government removed their right to vote on the matter and they were furious.

Time will tell if Manitobans forgive the government by the time the next election rolls around, but what is clear is the NDP, and all parties for that matter, have realized if you meddle with this measure, you'll feel the wrath of the public. It definitely makes it harder for governments to simply raise taxes.

6) Balanced Budget Legislation: This legislation is fairly simple: governments can't spend more on operations than they take in through revenues each year. If they do, then there is usually a penalty that kicks in.

In the case of Manitoba's legislation, cabinet ministers have to take a 20% pay cut the first time they run a deficit. The second time they do so, and until the budget is balanced, the penalty increases to 40%.

Like taxpayer protection acts, this measure isn't bulletproof either. Governments can simply water down the legislation. However, each time they do they'll pay a price in the court of public opinion.

As long as the legislation is adhered to, it helps force governments to control spending and make tough decisions. (Note: such legislation does allow for exceptions in times of war or natural disasters.)

7) Full Disclosure of Expenses: Politicians are at the top of the food chain in any government. So who holds the politicians accountable for their expenses? Is it reasonable to ask a lowly bureaucrat to have to stand up to a politician and tell him or her that one of their expenses is out of order and won't be reimbursed? No.

All politicians should have to disclose their expenses to the public. Incredibly, federal politicians, and some provincial politicians, still refuse such disclosure.

The best models in the country for politicians' disclosure are found at City Hall in Toronto and with the Alberta government. Both governments actually take each receipt that is expensed by a politician, scan it and post it on the Internet.

It may sound like a bit much, but simply noting *"Meeting at George's Steakhouse; $125.46"* or *"Accommodations for municipal conference; $199.35"* doesn't really tell you much. Was the meeting at the steakhouse all alcohol? Did the hotel bill include a bunch of movie rentals and expensive room service?

Some argue this level of disclosure and worrying about such trivial expenses is a waste of time. However, I disagree.

If a politician is going to try to expense something really inappropriate, he or she probably isn't the type of person taxpayers want deciding a government's overall budget.

8) Truth in Politics Act: Andrew Coyne put forward a great idea in a 2011 column in *Maclean's*: *"Time for a Truth in Politics Act."*

Coyne noted how Elections Canada surveys had found mistrust in politicians to be the root cause of low voter turnout in the country. After documenting countless examples of politicians lying and breaking their promises, he floated an interesting solution commonly found in business: allow politicians to "*opt in to legal liability if the claims they are making prove false.*"

In other words, let them put their money where their mouth is. Coyne notes:

> "*Again, there are examples of this in private life: from bonded couriers to sworn affidavits, people have found ways to show they are trustworthy, by willingly assuming certain penalties if they are not. Suppose, then, there were a provision of the Elections Act, which a candidate could invoke at his discretion to cover particular statements or documents – such as a platform – with provisions for fines or other sanctions if they are found to be materially false. No gotchas over some stray comment on the campaign trail, but when they really needed to be believed they'd have some means of persuading people.*"[30]

The process could work much in the same way a performance bond works with private contractors. In business, when you hire someone for a major project (e.g. to build a 10,000-square-foot building with certain specifications) you make sure the builder is bonded first. If they don't meet the agreed upon specifications for the building, you can cash in the bond they put up in the beginning.

A party leader could do the same. They could make a promise like the following:

> "*If elected to government our party will not raise the sales tax or personal income taxes during our next term.*"

The leader's party could put up a bond of $200,000 or whatever amount they determine would be sufficient to convince voters they're serious. If the party breaks its promise, then the party has to cough up the money.

Alternatively, politicians themselves could be allowed to put up some of their own personal collateral.

Coyne notes politicians' promises covered under such a model:

"…would no doubt be drafted with caution, as they are in private life, with conditions attached to cover different eventualities: 'we will balance the budget, provided the economy grows by more than 2% annually.' Fine. Voters could decide how much weight to attach to them accordingly – as they could any declarations issued without such backing."

9) Advertising Reform: In 2004 the Ontario government passed a positive piece of legislation called the *Government Advertising Act*.[31] The legislation attempts to mitigate the advantage governing parties have with controlling massive government ad budgets and the act requires major ads to be first be approved by the provincial auditor.

This approach helps prevent taxpayers from having to fund partisan messaging in government ads. The process has been efficient for government bodies wishing to get information out in a timely manner. According to a 2012 Ontario auditor's report, of the 565 ads that were brought to its attention in 2011/12, all 565 received a decision within seven business days.[32]

Two improvements to the rules would be to have them apply to ads appearing outside Canada (a lot of Canadians watch TV feeds from U.S. cities) and to have ads vetted by opposition parties, who are more attuned to partisan nuances than the auditor.

10) Report Cards: One way to address the incumbent advantage would be regulate the taxpayer-funded flyers that politicians send out. I'm referring to the flyers politicians send out with all kinds of pictures of them in the community.

Winnipeg activist Todd Dube once suggested a good way those documents could be reformed: require the flyers to include report card-like information. For example, politicians could be required to disclose their attendance in the legislature, how they voted on important matters and other information such as how much they've spent on meals and trips.

Provincial politicians' flyers could also be required to disclose the government's total debt, how income taxes compare with other provinces, how the test scores of students compare with kids in other provinces, wait times for health care and other benchmarks.

At the municipal level, the reports could disclose data on things like road conditions, property tax comparisons, and the percentage of homicide cases solved by local police to name a few examples.

As long as politicians are given taxpayer dollars to send out brochures, it makes sense to at least require some neutral information in such documents. It would be another tool to help hold politicians accountable and keep them focused on results.

11) Answer Period: Question period needs a complete makeover. For starters, that daily activity should be called "answer period" and the speaker should be given the power to compel the premier (or prime minister) and cabinet ministers to actually answer questions.

That would put an end to opposition parties asking straightforward questions and hearing responses that completely skirt the issue.

To ensure politicians actually have to answer questions, the speaker should be awarded powers similar to a judge in a court trial.

If a speaker felt a politician wasn't answering a basic question, perhaps the speaker could compel him or her to sit in the legislature until they provided an adequate response. Or perhaps the speaker could financially penalize a politician who refuses to answer a basic question. Either way, there needs to be more teeth in the system so that opposition parties can do their jobs more effectively.

Of course, reform can't stop there.

The speaker of each legislature and parliament is almost always a member of the governing party. Thus, they won't want to crack down on their colleagues; doing so could hurt the party's brand and the speaker's own chances of getting re-elected under the party banner.

To ensure the speaker would hold the government accountable, I recommend moving to a system whereby the public votes for a speaker during an election.

Under such a model, the public would likely seek out a non-partisan candidate, someone who they thought would do a good job of serving as a judge no matter what party was elected.

How will this save taxpayers money? If opposition parties had a greater ability to get information and answers from governing parties, boondoggles could potentially be avoided. Some financial problems could be stopped before they spiraled out of control and governments could no longer refuse to release unflattering information until after they're re-elected.

Just as governments that require politicians to disclose their expenses don't seem to have as many problems as jurisdictions that allow hidden expenses (e.g. the Senate), greater accountability for day-to-day government activities would be a good thing.

12) More Disclosure, More Accountability: When journalists, taxpayer watchdog organizations and think tanks want information from the government we often have to sit down, fill out a "freedom of information" request form, and carefully articulate what information we are seeking.

In many cases the systems work. This process is how journalists in Alberta obtained documents that detailed the penthouse suite being designed on the top floor of a government building for former Premier Alison Redford. At the federal level, this process allowed the *Canadian Press* to expose former federal minister Bev Oda's famous $16 glass of orange juice and her swanky hotel bills.[33]

Numerous stories come to light each year because of the FOI process. It's a valuable tool, but it could be a lot better.

Countless research efforts over the years have hit informational brick walls, as if the Great Wall of China suddenly went up in front of your eyes. Governments put up these walls by using excuse clauses in FOI legislation to refuse public access to sensitive information. Bureaucrats and politicians know that challenging refusals to release information (through an Ombudsman's office or in court) can take time and is often fruitless; ultimately embarrassing information is kept behind closed doors. (Unless you want to spend thousands of dollars going to court to try to pry the info loose, a route that, for obvious reasons, isn't used too often.)

However, some government bodies in Canada run the risk of having information pried out of their hands. According to a 2008 report by the Canadian Association of Journalists, five out of 10 provinces have information commissioners armed with "order-making power."[34]

This power allows independent information commissioners to force government bodies to release information if the commissioner believes the excuse to withhold the records is unsubstantiated.

However, five provinces, as well as the federal government, don't have information commissioners with order-making power.

By now you can probably tell where I'm going with this – the federal government, and the five provinces without "order making power" should enact it. Improving the ability of opposition parties, journalists, taxpayer groups and others to watchdog governments could help prevent boondoggles and stop other financial problems in their tracks.

13) Break the Law? No Pension: On the heels of an expense scandal involving politicians in Nova Scotia, its NDP government passed a law in 2013 that would strip any politician of their golden government pension if they were convicted of committing a serious crime while in office.

MP John Williamson, a former federal director of the Canadian Taxpayers Federation, tabled a similar bill in Ottawa. He indicated one of his inspirations for the bill was former Senator Raymond Lavigne.[35] As noted earlier, Lavigne was convicted and jailed in 2011 for expense account fraud and for using his government staff to cut down trees on his cottage property during the workday.

To be sure, under both bills, politicians wouldn't lose their pensions for things like littering or other less serious offences. Their pensions would only be stripped if they were caught for serious crimes such as fraud and breach of trust.

The penalty sends a strong message to legislators that serious crimes come with serious penalties for politicians. It would also help weed out some of the people we wouldn't want running for office in the first place.

CHAPTER 9

The Public

Margaret Thatcher once said:

Marxists get up early to further their cause. We must get up even earlier to defend our freedom.

I love that quote because it's true. Every day there are thousands of people across Canada who wake up early and work hard to find ways to get their hands on the money you give to the government.

They may not all be Marxists per se, but you can see the point: their success in obtaining your tax dollars from the government ends up hurting your financial freedom. Higher taxes are the result.

As I've demonstrated over the last few chapters, special interest groups and government employee union bosses are great at getting their paws on your earnings. Not only do politicians often cave in to their demands, the elected class are also guilty of wasting funds by dreaming up new ways to spend money, often in the cause of self-preservation.

And then there are bureaucracies ... what else needs to be said about bureaucratic inefficiencies and empire building? Not much. Although I am reminded of the famous Oscar Wilde quote, *"the bureaucracy is expanding to meet the needs of the expanding bureaucracy."* In other words, it's a beast that will always, always, always be hungry for more money.

The four aforementioned groups lead to a bloated tax bill for taxpayers. Recall what I noted in chapter three: the Fraser Institute calculated the typical Canadian household gave "just" 33.5% of their income to the government in 1961, but now pays approximately 42.7% as of 2013.

So what have Canadians done about the situation? We've largely rolled over and taken the financial abuse. The public are the fifth force behind wasteful and inefficient government spending.

Note that nearly four in 10 Canadians didn't even vote in the 2011 federal election; turnout was just 61.1%.[1] In Ontario, election turnout has been even worse; a record low of just 48.2% in 2011 and 52.1% in 2014.[2][3] Things weren't much better in the last elections held in B.C. and Alberta – just 55.3% (2013) and 54.4% (2012) respectively.[4][5] Turnout is down across the country.

But it never used to be this bad.

According to Elections Canada data, an average of 75.2% of eligible voters came out to the polls in federal elections between 1954-1984.[6] Over the past 30 years (1984-2014) that figure shrunk to only 66.6%. If we drill down even further and just focus on the last five general elections, that number shrinks even more – an average turnout of just 61.3%.

To be clear, I don't think voting is a magic solution. I can see why people don't vote; the public has been burned many times in the past by politicians of all stripes. It's easy to become jaded towards the system. Not to mention, our voting system is structured so that many people know their vote really doesn't count; if, say, you happen to live in a constituency where the party you support doesn't stand a chance of winning the local seat.

However, I do think the drop in voter turnout is indicative of the public becoming less engaged in politics and government decisions.

In this chapter I'll discuss why a less engaged public is troublesome for taxpayers and why we need to treat our politicians like our employees. Finally, I'll also discuss what we can do as citizens to start impacting government decisions for the better and how we can move some of the recommendations I've outlined in this book from ideas on paper into reality.

Why Ignorance and Apathy Are Bad for Taxpayers

"What's the difference between ignorance and apathy? I don't know and I don't care." While the popular joke makes for a good chuckle, ignorance about, and apathy towards, politics and government activities actually hurts your

pocketbook. The system is impacted by ignorance and apathy in three main ways:

First, fewer people paying attention means the pool of potential candidates dwindles. If someone has decided to not follow politics and government decisions, they're probably not going to run for office either. And fewer people interested in running for office means less competition.

Just like in business, less competition is not a good thing for consumers – in this case, voters.

To be clear, I'm not saying there are no good candidates that run for public office; I'm just inferring that, overall, we're probably not seeing as good a crop as we could be seeing.

The second reason why apathy is a major concern is that if the public isn't paying attention, then they have no idea what governments can and can't afford. Such ignorance lets politicians get away with claims like *"we had no choice but to raise taxes,"* rather than making difficult decisions to address inefficient spending. This ignorance also allows unions and special interest groups to fear-monger with claims like *"there will be cuts to health care if taxes don't go up."*

When the public doesn't pay attention to a government's financial picture, then some will demand more in services than the government's budget can afford. Recall, the fortune the masses pay in taxes each year often just goes into a black hole. Many people feel this entitles them to demand the government spend money on things the individual personally wants, whether it's a new stadium, an expansion to the local art gallery or keeping an underused library or school open.

If people have no idea the government is running a massive deficit, then why not demand funds for their pet cause?

The third reason why apathy is a major problem is that it means fewer people are going to write, call or email their politicians or engage in other ways to hold them accountable in between elections.

Some people think their civic duty is to vote once every four years for each level of government and that's it.

But that's not enough.

Think about how vocal unions, special interest groups and others can be at urging politicians to do what they want. Turn on the nightly news and you'll see unions and special interest groups routinely holding rallies, strikes or some kind of other demonstration. Such groups are known to fire out emails to all their members and supporters to encourage them to call politicians and put pressure on them for one reason or another.

They're effective at giving politicians the feeling that *"everyone"* is upset about the issue the special interest groups are pushing.

Unions also have huge war chests full of money for advertisements to put the heat on politicians. Behind the scenes, lobbyists also regularly woo politicians with steak dinners, tickets to sporting events and all kinds of other perks.

Remember, the livelihood of the aforementioned groups at the government trough depends on convincing the politicians to keep the money flowing. As a result, they're more than persistent and motivated.

That's why the public needs to become just as vocal and engaged with what's happening or things will never change. Politics and governance is about a lot more than just voting once every four years.

Monitor Your Employee

Your local politician is your employee. Along with your neighbours and the people in your community, you hire a local politician to work for you over a four-year period. That person is paid with your tax dollars and is expected to work to represent the views of the community.

Yet so many people treat the relationship quite differently, akin to hiring someone to cut their grass for the summer and then ignoring the person's performance. Meanwhile, the lawn-cutting boy becomes sloppy as time marches on. He stops trimming around the birdbath and cutting the small patch of grass behind the garage.

But then, just before summer is over, he pulls up his socks to wow you with his services. He wants you to hire him for next summer too!

In real life, if your lawn boy missed a spot repeatedly or did a shabby job, you would probably speak up and correct the problem. After all, you've just paid him $20 or so to cut your grass.

Why someone would give nearly half their income to the government and then not speak up when a mistake occurs is beyond me.

It boggles my mind how people will take ten minutes to quibble with a store clerk if their receipt is off by $5 or $10, but they won't take five minutes to call their politician about a $50-million or $100-million government boondoggle in the news.

Public apathy towards politics, especially between elections, is probably the number one reason why things continue the way they are in Canada.

Consider that we're the last developed, reputable, respectable country in the world that still allows one individual to appoint an entire class of politicians: Canada's Senate. Sure, it's great if you're a friend of the prime minister, but come on! It's farcical that we let a politician appoint his or her friends to positions for life with great pay and little in the way of responsibilities.

It's even worse when unelected senators start meddling with legislation drafted by people who were elected – our local MPs in the House of Commons.

When the Supreme Court of Canada came down with its decision on Senate reform in April 2014, Saskatchewan Premier Brad Wall had a good tweet:

> *"The following have unelected upper houses: Thailand, Antigua, Burkina Faso, Jordan, St. Lucia, Trin&Tob, Belize, Fiji, Grenada, Canada."*

Premier Wall's tweet reminds me of the phrase *"one of these things is not like the other."*

So how did Canada end up in such odd company? How are we in the 21st century and yet Canadians still allow the prime minister to appoint friends to the Senate? How were MPs able to ratchet up their own pensions to such golden levels? How did Prime Minister Chretien get away with not eliminating the GST like he promised? How did Dalton McGuinty get away with raising taxes despite signing a pledge that he wouldn't? How did Bob Rae become an MP after he helped bring Ontario to its knees when he was the province's NDP premier in the early 1990s?

Why do we allow governments to continue to operate like Prada-wearing, high-end car-driving, latte-sipping, money-burning organizations?

We could continue with all kinds of questions about how politicians and governments get away with abusing the public's trust, but in each case the answer is the same: because we let them.

As a society we've turned a blind eye to too many problems for too long. It's time for action.

What You Can Do

In the introduction to this book I told you about the Wilsons, a couple from Winnipeg. Katie and Mitch Wilson don't live in Winnipeg's core, but they don't live in a ritzy suburb either. They have three kids, a mortgage and a car loan. Mitch is an electrician and Katie watches the kids and teaches music to local kids in their converted garage.

In many respects, they're like the average Canadian household. Katie and Mitch try to pay attention to the news, but like 99.9% of Canadians, they're not the type to sit down on a Friday night and read through a dry government report about demographic changes. Nor do they graze through government budget documents in their spare time. They're normal people.

Like many Canadians, the Wilsons are fed up with unaccountable politicians who keep raising taxes instead of making tough spending decisions. Like many Canadians, they don't know what they can do about the situation.

That's why I wrote this book.

I started off by telling you about some of the big-picture problems in this country: an aging demographic, rising health care costs, the nation's infrastructure deficit and government employee pension problems. I described how governments have known about these problems for years but haven't bothered to save up or plan for them.

As a result, these financial challenges have our nation on course for higher taxes and poorer services.

I then presented the good news; governments, on the whole, are pretty inefficient with the money we provide them right now. If we can force our governments to improve their operations we can mitigate some of the pressure to raise taxes. I've described at length why governments are inefficient with the money we give them, but I've also put forward all kinds of policy changes that could address inefficiencies and reduce costs. Such changes would free up funds to counter the big picture problems headed our way instead of just raising taxes.

Well, now it's time to talk about how we get from A to B.

It's time to explore how we can take the policy ideas I described in this book and turn them into reality. It's time to talk about five things that you, your friends and loved ones, the Wilsons and the general public can do.

1) Stay Informed

The first step towards change is for more people to be informed about what's happening. Fortunately, you don't have to spend your weekends and spare time plodding through government reports to unearth some of the details I've talked about in this book.

It's great if you want to conduct such research, but why not take advantage of work that is already being done by others? I'm talking about the media, taxpayer watchdog groups, bloggers and other organizations who regularly pore through government studies and data and then report on the main points in short columns, blog entries, YouTube clips and other means.

Figure out which journalists you feel do a good job of reporting on government and then pay attention to what they write, watch them on TV or tune them in on the radio. Find journalists, news outlets and opinion leaders who believe in reasonable tax rates and responsible government spending rather than those who blindly accept politicians' claims that tax increases are "needed."

Clicking on stories written by like-minded journalists will not only help you stay informed, you'll help those journalists and media outlets as well. Remember, the more you and your friends click on their stories, the more ad revenues the news outlet receives.

At the same time, I would urge you to click responsibly. If you feel a journalist is too biased in favour of raising taxes or too friendly to government employee unions and special interest groups, then don't click on their stories. If enough people stop clicking on that journalist's work then his or her managers will likely notice the low website traffic, lower revenues and they'll have no choice but to address the problem.

Tools like Twitter and Facebook can also help you to stay informed. For example, you can "follow" and "like" journalists and media outlets and see their opinions when they post content online.

Further, you can follow the work of the Canadian Taxpayers Federation, Fraser Institute, Manning Centre, Frontier Centre for Public Policy, CFIB and other groups I've mentioned in this book – we're all on Twitter, Facebook, YouTube and other social media sites. Give us a "like" or "follow" and it will be easy to see our reports and news as soon we put out information.

2) Speak Out

I've worked for several politicians in the past, from being an assistant in their local offices to advising them on policy matters. In fact, I still regularly converse with politicians on various issues.

Regardless of party affiliation, they all seem to have one common habit: when a controversial matter pops up, they ask their assistants, "*how many calls are we receiving on this issue?*"

The fact of the matter is very few people actually contact their politicians throughout the year – or even throughout a term in office. As a result, it doesn't take many calls on an issue to attract a politician's attention. Anecdotally, I can tell you that city councillors in Winnipeg have told me it takes just five or 10 calls or emails to get their attention. Obviously it would take more calls to force a federal politician to take note (they represent much larger areas and more people) but you see the point.

Given the low threshold to get a politician's attention, it's not hard to imagine the reaction when union bosses or special interest groups mobilize their members and start lobbying a politician in droves.

Well, it's time for the general public to become just as active at contacting their politicians with phone calls, letters, emails, tweets, popping by their office, approaching them at public functions, etc. That's probably the one thing I can't stress enough in this book. The squeaky wheel really does get the grease and taxpayers need to be a lot more squeaky … er, vocal.

If a politician raises taxes, tell him or her your story. Explain how it will hurt your household budget.

Ask why they didn't pursue some of the solutions I've talked about in this book instead of raising taxes.

But don't stop with the politicians; you can pressure bureaucrats as well. Email or call civil servants working on different issues and let them know what you think. They're human; if they receive a lot of calls, they too will feel the pressure and it will be communicated to higher-ups.

It's also important for you to write letters to the editor of your local paper, post comments online, call in to radio talk shows and send feedback to local TV news stations. I've been bumped from radio interviews after stations' switchboards lit up with calls over a hot topic scheduled before my segment. As a result, the previous segment was extended because the host could tell it was a hit with the audience. Again, if the public speaks out, people are more likely to listen and take note.

Finally, I would stress that it's important to not just criticize: positive reinforcement can do wonders. When a politician does something good, give them a call and say "great work." When a journalist writes a really good column or story, send them an email and tell them you loved it.

If you don't think speaking out makes a difference, here are a few cases where the public speaking out helped changed politicians minds.

In 2000, the federal government mused publicly about bailing out NHL teams with millions of dollars in public funds. Many people reacted furiously to the idea of giving tax dollars to professional hockey teams which paid their players millions of dollars to chase a puck around on the ice.

Radio talk shows lit up with calls and newspapers had a field day. Even many die-hard hockey fans thought the idea was irresponsible. The Canadian

Taxpayers Federation responded to the government's idea by starting a "puck off" campaign that urged the public to send their MPs a hockey puck in protest of the subsidy idea.[7]

To the Chretien government's credit, it heard the public's anger loud and clear and backed away from the idea. Victory: vocal taxpayers.

More recently, in December 2008, opposition parties attempted to take over Parliament.

Just a couple of months prior, Canadians elected a Conservative government, the third minority government in a row, falling on the heels of Paul Martin's in 2004 and Stephen Harper's in 2006.

The election results didn't sit well with the NDP, Liberals and Bloc Quebecois so they announced an agreement to form a coalition government and seize the reins of power from the Conservatives.[8]

There was nothing illegal about what the parties did, but the move didn't sit well with the public. Many Canadians objected to the idea of a coalition government propped up by a separatist party. Others saw the whole move as a desperate attempt to grab power.

Ultimately, the polls showed the public didn't like what the opposition parties were trying to do. Talk radio shows lit up with calls, newspapers ran reams of letters to the editor and rallies took place in different parts of the country against the coalition. In no time at all, the opposition politicians listened and backed down.

I highlight this anecdote not because of the partisan dynamic, but because it represents another good example – on a national level – when the public spoke out and the politicians listened. Victory: vocal taxpayers.

A final anecdote I'll share occurred at the municipal level in Winnipeg. In late 2013, Winnipeg's city council voted 9-7 in opposition to auditing the new police headquarters project. The decision shocked many as the project was $75 million over budget and council had just received a damning audit related to the construction of four new firehalls ($3 million over budget).

I knew a couple of councillors planned to push for a second vote on the matter, so I contacted labour groups to see if they would like to put aside our differences and work together in support of an audit (some of their members were facing layoffs so they were eager to hold the mayor accountable).

Of the nine councillors who voted against an audit the first time, I worked with the Winnipeg Labour Council to target two in particular. Labour focused on the labour-friendly candidate and I focused on the one who was more taxpayer-friendly.

Both our organizations sent out emails to our supporter lists urging them to speak out. We also spoke with contacts who knew the two targeted councillors personally and asked them to contact the councilmen. After the joint press conference, I actually went out door-knocking with a couple of volunteers in the ward of one councillor, urging his constituents to call him.

The very next day, the two targeted councillors announced they would now support an audit. Within days, most other councillors had flipped as well; like dominos they fell, one by one. An audit motion passed later that month 14-1. It was another classic case of the public speaking out and the politicians listening. Victory: vocal taxpayers.

3) Educate and Mobilize Your Friends, Family, Contacts, Etc.

It's not enough to just pay attention to what's going on and call your elected officials. We have to wake up Canada's sleepy electorate and get them tuned in to what's happening and mobilize them to speak out too.

Thankfully, it's easier than you think.

In the anecdote on the police headquarters audit, I described how I worked with labour groups to put pressure on nine councillors who opposed an audit the first time.

Through Facebook and Twitter, I circulated the names and phone numbers of all nine councillors and I had an email sent to everyone in Winnipeg who had signed up for email updates from the CTF. The email included the councillors' names and phone numbers to make it easy to take action: no digging in phone books for the numbers or having to Google the info.

Technology allowed me to reach thousands of people without leaving my desk.

Most people reading this book probably have access to email, Facebook, Twitter and other Internet tools. When you read a good article about some of the issues I've discussed, post it on Facebook and Twitter and email a link to your friends. At the same time, share your local politician's contact info to make it easy for your friends to take action.

There are also plenty of things you can do that don't involve the Internet. Clip an article in the paper that you feel is important and show it to friends and family. Alternatively, you could photocopy the article along with your local politician's number and then deliver it to people on your street. Or perhaps you could hand it out to your friends when you gather for cards or coffee.

Regardless, each of us needs to work hard to spread the word on important issues and encourage others to take action.

4) Get Involved

You're not alone. There are plenty of other people in Canada who are just as frustrated by the issues I've talked about in this book.

No doubt you have a neighbour or colleague or acquaintance who is also ready to take action. Or perhaps you have a relative who likes to chat about these issues when you gather at family functions.

People should band together with like-minded individuals or join existing groups to work toward change. Government employee unions are good at mobilizing their members to speak out. Well, taxpayers who want reasonable tax rates and responsible government also need to band together and become more vocal.

I encourage you to join the Canadian Taxpayers Federation and get involved as a taxpayer. If you're a business owner and belong to an industry association, ask what they're doing about the big picture issues I've mentioned in this book. If the answer is "nothing," then perhaps you should think about sending your donation or dues somewhere else.

Think tanks such as the Fraser Institute, Frontier Centre for Public Policy, Manning centre, C.D. Howe Institute, Atlantic Institute for Market Studies and Macdonald-Laurier Institute produce good research each year and also need your support. I would encourage you to visit their websites and see what events they have coming up and learn about other ways that you can help out.

Of course all of the advocacy groups and think tanks I've just mentioned need donations to survive. Big government employee unions have millions at their disposal as funds are automatically deducted off the paycheques of millions of government employees every week. Their side never has to worry about finding funds to pay staff or run a big ad campaign.

Well, our side doesn't have such an automatic cash flow; we face an uphill battle when it comes to collecting voluntary donations. Every dollar helps.

Another way you can take action is to start your own organization. This is especially valuable at the municipal level, where larger organizations simply don't have the resources to carefully examine what's going on. After all, there are literally thousands of municipalities across Canada.

If you do decide to fight a local issue, there are all kinds of free tools on the Internet that can help you take action. For example, you can set up petitions and blogs online for free. YouTube is great for posting videos and Facebook groups can really help too. The bottom line is advances in technology are making it much, much easier for taxpayers to connect with each other, mobilize the public and speak out.

Finally, you can have an impact on government policies by becoming involved with a political party or local municipal politician's campaign. After all, they're the ones who ultimately vote on government decisions.

While political parties can seem intimidating from the outside, the truth is they're heavily dependent on volunteers and are usually easy to join. Apathy being at an all-time high means it's usually not too hard to rise to a position within a political party that allows you to have a voice as a delegate at a convention and on a local politician's constituency association board of directors.

In chapter eight I described how our political system is broken and how partisan politicians often vote in blocs or take direction from party leaders rather than listen to their local constituents. Partisan politicians often get away with doing whatever their leaders want because their local party associations often just go with the flow.

If you do decide to get involved in a local party's association, bring a few friends along and stir things up.

Find a party or candidate about whom you're passionate and help them succeed. You can sell memberships to help the candidate earn the party's nomination, put up lawn signs for them, deliver brochures or help in some other way.

If they're successful and are elected to public office, don't take your foot off the gas pedal. Organize a small group of like-minded individuals and make sure the politician stays on the right track. Encourage them and regularly monitor their activities. When a government waste story pops up, grill your representative to find out what he or she is going to do about it. When they tell you about something great they've done, share the news on Facebook to support them.

Alternatively, you could even organize something within a party like a coalition of "taxpayers for responsible spending." So if you're, say, a member of the B.C. Liberal Party, you could band together with others who share similar views and create a voting bloc that supports fiscally responsible candidates. Such a bloc could become so powerful at volunteering, donating and helping out that the party's elite simply couldn't ignore it.

The other avenue for party influence comes during their regular policy review processes. Such processes often include conventions where delegates vote on party policy. Why not work with others to try to push some of the ideas in this book? Someone has to do it.

5) Vote

Our personal and financial freedoms can quickly erode if we're not mindful of those we elect.

Years ago, the Canadian government arrested Saskatchewan farmers for – wait for it – selling wheat across the border in the U.S. instead of to the government's mandatory wheat marketing board.[9] In Toronto, a storeowner and two relatives were charged after they caught a thief who stole from their store.[10] One would think police would have thanked the trio for capturing a crook, but instead they took exception to the trio locking the thief in a delivery van until the boys in blue could arrive.

Across Canada, "human rights" commissions have been handing out bizarre punishments as well. From forcing people to apologize for things they clearly aren't apologetic about to cracking down on those who say or do things that might "offend" someone, these commissions are all for freedom of speech as long as they agree with your point of view.

Financially, our freedoms have eroded as well. The government used to focus on the basics. Now, in many cases, it has become all things to all people. Needless to say, the "sky is the limit" approach to government has come with a huge cost; that is, ever-higher taxes.

Personally, I think it's important to vote and support parties that advocate fiscal responsibility, personal responsibility, freedom of the individual and other important values.

However, that doesn't mean you have to like the choices on the ballot. Even if you spoil your ballot, in your own small way you can still have your voice heard.

I think it's important to not just vote, but to vet party platforms and local candidates. Try to nail them down on specifics. Heck, you can even ask them to put their promises in writing. If a candidate tells you something verbally that isn't in his or her platform, write it up and ask the candidate to sign his or her name beside it. Alternatively, you can whip out your phone and ask if they'll let you take a short video clip with them committing to the position in question.

If politicians give you vague answers on something, probe them for details. Remember, it's a job interview. Candidates shouldn't be able to just show up on your door and take off within a minute; ask how they would respond to different scenarios.

Tell them that if you agree with their plans, you'll phone your friends and spread the word to help get the candidate elected. Again, positive reinforcement helps more than a curt response.

CHAPTER 10

Conclusion

In late December 2009, I was working at my desk when the mailman brought in a brown envelope from a whistleblower.

A lady named Phyllis Sutherland from the Peguis First Nation in Manitoba sent the Canadian Taxpayers Federation, all three national parties in Ottawa and the auditor general the pay information for her chief and council. The numbers were off the charts.

Her chief and council were serving a community of just a few thousand people, yet they were all making more than the prime minister of Canada ($310,800 in 2008-09) by the time you took into account the fact chief and council pay is income tax-free. One of the band councillors made the equivalent of a whopping $439,745 for someone living off reserve and paying income taxes.

Sadly, like most reserves, Peguis had its share of social problems at the time; addiction, mouldy homes, unemployment, etc.

When we discussed the issue internally, I suggested calling for change instead of just releasing the data to the media and criticizing the reserve's politicians. Phyllis was able to obtain her community's pay information (although she thought the figures were low-balled), but I had heard numerous stories from people living on other reserves who couldn't obtain the pay data for their communities. Many told me about being bullied and physically assaulted for speaking out and asking questions about how public funds were spent on their reserve.

I suggested we call on the federal government to post online the salary details for every chief and councillor in the country as well as each band's annual financial statements. The move would bring aboriginal politicians in line with municipal, provincial and federal politicians who had done the same for years.

As Ottawa already received each band's pay and financial information annually, all it had to do was pass a law so that it had the legal right to post the information online. Most importantly, by putting the financial information online, band members could access it anonymously and not have to worry about retribution. We ended up deciding to call for such a change.

When we released the Peguis pay information to the media, the story went wild.[1] I found myself doing news interviews with radio stations and newspapers across the country as well as *CBC*'s *The National* and *Global News*' national broadcast. One of my former colleagues discussed the problem on *CTV*'s *Power Play*. The nation was aghast at the obscene salaries.

In each interview I kept repeating the message: "*the public needs to speak out. Tell your Member of Parliament you want chief and council pay data posted online each year, just like it is for federal, provincial and most municipal politicians.*"

We knew that disclosure of band financial material wasn't a magic solution to solve all the problems on reserves. However, it was a step in the right direction that almost everyone would agree with in the short term: where was the money going?

From the time I drafted the news release that called on the federal government to start posting the info online to the time Parliament actually voted on the legislation, many cynics said to me along the way: "*I love the idea, but it'll never happen*" or "*the feds won't touch this with a 10-foot pole.*" The skeptics suggested the issue we raised was simply too racially charged for Ottawa to do anything. For far too long politicians had been reluctant to do anything meaningful to address problems on reserves, as many chiefs would often throw temper tantrums and play the "race card" to quell discussions about policies they didn't like.

Well, this time it was different.

In no time at all, we started to receive more and more brown envelopes from other communities with outrageous pay data. A whistleblower from the Enoch Cree Nation in Alberta smuggled out his or her community's pay info (the chief and many councillors earned more than Alberta's premier) and sent it to us with a letter that read:

> *"I am writing this letter out of pure frustration. I live on the Enoch Cree Nation and we should have no problem providing for our people. The problem is the greed of our leadership and the lack of motivation. They know that there is nothing we can do to change the policies. We are under a different system than the real world … I have requested copies of the budgets for several years from both [the Department of Indian and Northern Affairs] and Chief and Council and have never received anything."*[2]

We released the Enoch pay info to the media and that story also attracted plenty of media attention and even more brown envelopes. We released those too and kept repeating our message in the media that the public needed to speak out.

In late September 2010, Kelly Block, an MP from Saskatchewan, tabled a private member's bill to improve disclosure on reserves. The bill had a number of shortcomings, but as I noted to a former colleague, it would establish a beachhead for *"furthering debate on the problem."* I immediately started conversations with Block's office and the Minister of Aboriginal and Northern Affairs' office about the legislation and explained what I thought were shortcomings in the bill.

While Block's bill passed second reading with the support of the Conservative Party and 15 Liberal MPs, it died when an election was triggered in 2011. Fortunately, the government tabled Bill C-27, *The First Nations Financial Transparency Act* later that year, legislation that was very similar to Block's bill but incorporated the changes we recommended.

After organizing meetings with politicians and grassroots aboriginal people who wanted the bill passed, countless efforts to keep the story in the news (writing newspaper columns, holding press conferences, releasing data, etc.), sending emails to CTF supporters urging them to speak out, and providing testimony before Senate and House of Commons committees, *The First Nations Financial Transparency Act* passed in early 2013.

Soon after, Phyllis Sutherland and I were invited to the prime minister's office to receive signed copies of the new bill. Salary details for aboriginal reserve politicians began being posted on the federal government's website in the summer of 2014 and I'm proud to report there are already stories of how the new law has changed things for the better.

I bring up the story of *The First Nations Financial Transparency Act* because it shows how we accomplished "the impossible."

We took on one of the most politically sensitive issues in Canada, mobilized the masses to speak out and eventually put enough pressure on politicians to address the problem. Grizzled pundits, media veterans and other "experts" told me it would "*never happen.*" But we did it.

The *First Nations Financial Transparency Act* story is similar to the "impossible" challenges outlined in this book. Instead of simply raising taxes to meet our country's future challenges, we need politicians to start making some very tough decisions.

Just like we did with the *First Nations Financial Transparency Act*, we need to make the politicians realize the status quo is not an option. They need to know that taxpayers simply will not stand by and accept large tax hikes while so much wasteful and inefficient spending persists in government.

Many special interest groups will be aghast at my suggestion that governments cut off their funding. They'll be furious at the thought of having to roll up their sleeves and ask *you* for a voluntary donation to their project, to invest in their company or buy their product. It's just so much easier for them to walk into a government office, present a few spurious numbers describing "economic benefits" that will come from funding their proposal and then walk out with a cheque.

If politicians *do* decide to start cutting back on special interest group funding, don't be surprised to see the latter speak out through the media. You will need to do your part to help educate your friends, family and others that it's the right decision; the public is more than capable of deciding for themselves which projects to support financially. Plain and simple, governments need to stop funding special interest groups.

Government employee union bosses will also howl at many of the changes I've suggested. In fact, they will be the most difficult opponents we face when it comes to our war on higher taxes. Scaling back the powers provided to government employee unions, and scaling back their unsustainable benefits, will be similar to one of those epic battles from the Lord of the Rings movies.

The only way we will win is if taxpayers work even harder than the unions.

Government employee union bosses will use their huge financial war chests to run million-dollar ad campaigns against any politician or political party that dares to try to scale back unsustainable compensation levels. Like generals overseeing a war, the union bosses will also deploy loyal foot soldiers (government employees who are benefitting from the status quo) to campaign door-to-door against politicians who refuse to bow down to union boss demands.

The unions will fear monger and use phoney claims to defend their immense power and overly generous contracts.

You will need to fight back with the truth. The public needs to understand that what's going on with government employee compensation isn't fair for taxpayers and it isn't sustainable. Things *need* to change.

You can help by writing letters to the editor of your local paper, calling into talk shows and leaving comments on news sites online. Praise journalists who talk about the same problems I've described and call your local politician to pressure them for change. And perhaps most importantly, help politicians who aren't afraid of taking on big government employee unions. Volunteer on their campaigns or provide them with a financial donation. They're going to need all the help they can get.

Bureaucracies across the nation will also be a formidable force – they have so much inertia behind them! Too many politicians will continue to hear budgetary "needs" from senior civil servants each year and then simply raise taxes to pay for it.

You will need to play an important role in tackling this problem by educating politicians and the public about alternatives to tax increases. Reforming the way governments operate can save money and even improve results at the same time.

Call your local politician and tell them about the positive reforms from Indianapolis, Sandy Springs and other examples I've highlighted. Speak out publicly as well. Don't let lethargic notions of "necessary tax hikes" go unchallenged in the media.

Finally, the relationship between taxpayers and politicians needs a fundamental rethink. Canada has seen some great politicians over the years, but as a whole, taxpayers have been let down. Politicians have piled up mountains of government debt while failing to prepare our nation for the four major financial problems I've described in this book.

Systemic changes need to occur so that better candidates decide to seek public office in the first place. Change needs to be implemented to improve accountability and transparency in government decisions and to rebuild trust with the public. Balanced budget acts need to be passed (and enforced) across the country and taxpayer input should be sought more frequently through well-planned referendums. Politicians who fail to perform should be subject to recall in between elections.

While I've put forward several ideas as to how governments can cut wasteful spending instead of simply raising your taxes, there are certainly other good ideas that I didn't cover. My goal with this book was not to touch on every possible solution. What I hoped to do was establish a beachhead in the minds of readers as to the major challenges facing our nation, as well as ways governments can reduce costs or spend our tax dollars more effectively.

Earlier, I wrote about Thomas Malthus, the British economist who in 1798 famously predicted that food shortages and misery would occur in the not too distant future as people were reproducing faster than food production was rising.

More than 200 years later that prediction hasn't come true, because Malthus didn't take into account improvements in technology and a drop in the birth rate.

Similarly, it's hard to know what unforeseen changes may occur between now and the next decade, never mind the next couple of hundred years.

Could there be an enormous oil or gold discovery in your province that could drive up government revenues and save you from significant tax increases? Maybe. Could there be a giant leap forward in technology, leading to machines running nursing homes and providing other government services at a fraction of the cost? Seems a bit far-fetched, but sure, let's go with it as a possibility.

However, I certainly wouldn't bet on those dreams. Most respectable experts on this matter aren't expecting such miracles either.

We also have to remember that unforeseeable changes can work both ways. The public could elect politicians who pursue even wilder spending decisions and make things much worse. Similarly, another serious recession could come along and so could a natural disaster. Both could further decimate public treasuries.

While I'm convinced we're headed for higher taxes unless we make serious changes, there is a bright side to starting to cut the fat now. If governments start to pursue some of the ideas I've suggested in this book, and if the cost pressures I describe somehow don't materialize, we'll all save money and have a stronger democracy as a result. A win-win prospect for taxpayers, no matter how you cut it.

I wrote this book as a call to action. I don't want to just make you aware of the problems facing our country; I want you to help address the problems. If you don't feel like you can have an impact, let me leave you with a great quote from the late anthropologist Margaret Mead:

"Never doubt that a small group of thoughtful, concerned citizens can change the world. Indeed it is the only thing that ever has."

ACKNOWLEDGEMENTS

Throughout *The Government Wears Prada*, I have referenced numerous studies, reports and articles. I want to thank the authors of those sources; especially those working for like-minded think tanks, advocacy organizations such as the Canadian Taxpayers Federation and others who are fighting the good fight. A big "thank you" to my editor Bruce Annan for his patience and careful review of my first book and Mark Milke for taking the time to go through my first draft and provide constructive criticism and advice. I also want to thank my friends and family who helped in various capacities along the way; including those who helped shape my beliefs about government and the need for fiscal responsibility. Finally, I want to thank my wife for supporting me during this process in so many different ways.

ENDNOTES

Chapter 1: The Age of Denial

1   "Nero Biography." Biography.com article, accessed December 1, 2014. http://www.biography.com/people/nero-9421713#awesm=~oDS48NyXT8cZkx

2   "Tim Hortons at St. John's hospital awash in red ink." CBC News, May 29, 2012. Accessed December 1, 2014. http://www.cbc.ca/news/canada/newfoundland-labrador/tim-hortons-at-st-john-s-hospital-awash-in-red-ink-1.1136260

3   IBID

4   Pearson, Craig. "Tim Hortons with $26/hour servers putting Windsor hospital $265k in the hole." National Post, May 31, 2012. Accessed December 1, 2014. http://news.nationalpost.com   /2012/05/31/taxpayers-picking-up-the-tab-as-windsor-tim-hortons-drains-hospital-of-265k-a-year/

5   Grant, Rick. "Taxpayers top up money-losing Tim Hortons at Halifax hospital." CTV News, January 11, 2013. Accessed December 1, 2013 http://atlantic.ctvnews.ca/taxpayers-top-up-money-losing-tim-hortons-at-halifax-hospital-1.1109211

6   Lu, Vanessa. "Shade audit finds risky spots for kids." Toronto Star, August 26, 2010. Accessed December 1, 2014. http://www.thestar.com/life/health_wellness/2010/08/26/shade_audit_finds_risky_spots_for_kids.html

7   Yuen, Jenny. "Wanted: Fake homeless." Toronto Sun, March 23, 2009. Accessed December. http://www.torontosun.com/news/torontoandgta/2009/03/23/8848476-sun.html

8   Donovan, Kevin. "TDSB's $143 school pencil sharpener just the beginning." Toronto Star, December 6, 2012. Accessed December 1, 2014. http://www.thestar.com/news/canada/2012/12/06/tdsbs_143_school_pencil_sharpener_just_the_beginning.html

9   Walsh, Moira and Kevin Donovan. "Toronto schools pay high prices for small jobs." Toronto Star, June 21, 2012. Accessed December 1, 2014. http://www.thestar.com/news/gta/2012/06/21/toronto_schools_pay_high_prices_for_small_jobs.html

10 "City launches slippery sidewalk bulletin." Winnipeg Sun, February 16, 2012. Accessed December 1, 2014. http://www.winnipegsun.com/2012/02/16/smith-set-to-launch-safe-walking-index-surefoot

11 Gaudet, Kevin. "13th Annual 'Teddy' Government Waste Awards Winners." Canadian Taxpayers Federation News Release, February 8, 2011. Accessed December 1, 2014. http://www.taxpayer.com/news-releases/13th-annual–teddy–government-waste-awards-winners

12 Staples, David. "Haiku boosts transit / City contest raises ire / Critics in a flap." Edmonton Journal, February 9, 2011. Accessed December 1, 2014. http://www.canada.com/story_print.html?id=225aaf56-2ca8-4f35-9885-b89b951a8d43&sponsor=

13 Martel, Laurent and France-Pascale Ménard. "The Canadian Population in 2011: Age and Sex." Statistics Canada 2011 Analytical product. Accessed December 1, 2014. http://www12.statcan.ca/census-recensement/2011/as-sa/98-311-x/98-311-x2011001-eng.cfm

14 "Total fertility rate in Canada, 1926 to 2005." Statistics Canada, 2007. Accessed December 1, 2014. http://www.statcan.gc.ca/pub/91-003-x/2007001/figures/4129893-eng.htm

15 Denton, Frank T. and Byron G. Spencer. "Demographic Developments in Canada." Berlin-Institut Report, December, 2010. Accessed December 1, 2014. http://www.berlin-institut.org/online-handbookdemography/canada.html

16 "Total fertility rate (number of children per woman), Canada, provinces and territories, 1981 to 2011." Statistics Canada, Table 2, Survey 3231.

17 Martel, Laurent and France-Pascale Ménard. "Generations in Canada." Statistics Canada Census in brief report. Accessed December 1, 2014. http://www12.statcan.gc.ca/census-recensement/2011/as-sa/98-311-x/98-311-x2011003_2-eng.cfm

18 Askari, Mostafa and Russell Barnett, Jeff Danforth, Chris Matier and Stephen Tapp. "Fiscal Sustainability Report 2011," September 29, 2011. Office of the Parliamentary Budget Officer. http://www.parl.gc.ca/pbo-dpb/documents/FSR_2011.pdf

19 "Income of individuals, by sex, age group and income source, 2011 constant dollars." Statistics Canada, CANSIM table 202-0407.

20 Friesen, Joe. Budgets, boomers and ticking time bombs." The Globe and Mail, February 25, 2010. Accessed December 1, 2014.http://www.theglobeandmail.com/news/politics/budget/budgets-boomers-and-ticking-time-bombs/article4311854/

21 "National Health Expenditure Trends, 1975 to 2011." Canadian Institute for Health Information report, Table E.1.1, P. 159.

22 IBID P. 41

23 "Health Care in Canada, 2011: A Focus on Seniors and Aging." Canadian Institute of Health Information, 2011, Page 37.

24 "National Health Expenditure Trends, 1975 to 2011." Canadian Institute of Health Information, 2011. Page 10.

25 Palacios, Milagros and Nadeem Esmail. "The Unfunded Liability of Canada's Health Care System." Fraser Institute, December, 2012, Page 2.

26 Esmail, Nadeem. "Aging population and changing demographics mean Canada's health care system facing a funding gap of more than $537 billion." Fraser Institute news release, December 10, 2012. Accessed December 1, 2014. http://www.fraserinstitute.org/research-news/news/news-releases/Aging-population-and-changing-demographics-mean-Canada-s-health-care-system-facing-a-funding-gap-of-more-than-$537-billion/

27 "Sustainability of the Canadian Health Care System and Impact of the 2014 Revision to the Canada Health Transfer." Canadian Institute of Actuaries, September 2013 report, Page 1. Accessed December 1, 2014. http://www.soa.org/Canadian-Health-Care-Sustainability/ (page?)

28 Mirza, Saeed. "Danger Ahead: The Coming Collapse of Canada's Municipal Infrastructure." Federation of Canadian Municipalities, November 7, Page 2.

29 Powers, Lucas. "Urban flooding likely to worsen, say experts." CBC News, July 11, 2013. Accessed December 1, 2014. http://www.cbc.ca/news/canada/story/2013/07/10/f-floods-rain-engineering.html

30 Statistics Canada Cansim Table 280-0026

31 Mallett, Ted. "Public Sector Pensions: A Runaway Train." Canadian Federation of Independent Business report, 2012, Page 3.

32 Laurin, Alexandre and William Robson. "Ottawa's Pension Gap: The Growing and Under-reported Cost of Federal Employee Pensions." C.D. Howe Institute, December 13, 2011. Accessed December 1, 2014. http://www.cdhowe.org/pdf/ebrief_127.pdf

33. OMERS 2012 Annual Report. http://www.omers.com/pdf/OMERS_AR_2012_-_ENG_Highlights.pdf

34. "Regina Civic Employees' Superannuation & Benefit Plan: December 31, 2012." Regina Civic Employees' Superannuation and Benefit Plan. Accessed December 1, 2014. http://www.reginapensions.ca/uploads/2012_Civic_Annual_Report.pdf

35. Saskatchewan Teachers' Superannuation Commission website. Accessed December 1, 2014. http://www.stsc.gov.sk.ca

36. Local Authorities Pension Plan, 2012 Annual Report, Page 2

37. Teachers' Pension Plan, website. Accessed December 1, 2014. http://www.pensionsbc.ca/portal/page/portal/annual_reports/teachers_annual_reports/tpp_2012_ar/2011_actuarial_valuation/

38. Government of Manitoba 2014 Budget, Page 20.

39. "After months of protest, parliamentary hearings on pension reform begin." CTV News, August 20, 2014. Accessed December 1, 2014. http://montreal.ctvnews.ca/after-months-of-protest-parliamentary-hearings-on-pension-reform-begin-1.1967834

40 "Saint John fire union slams planned cuts." CBC News, January 20, 2012. Accessed December 1, 2014. http://www.cbc.ca/news/canada/new-brunswick/saint-john-fire-union-slams-planned-cuts-1.1165863

41 "The Gazette's View: Time to take action on municipal pensions." Montreal Gazette, December 29, 2011. Accessed December 1, 2014. http://www2.canada.com/business/time+action+municipal+pensions/5924379/story.html?id=5924379

42 Fair Pensions for All website. Audio recording. Accessed December 1, 2014. http://fairpensionsforall.net/wp-content/uploads/2011/11/robbreakenridgepodcastoct28-3.mp3

43 "Table 15: Gross and net debt." Government of Canada: Fiscal Reference Tables (2012) Accessed December 1, 2014. http://www.fin.gc.ca/frt-trf/2012/frt-trf-1203-eng.asp#tbl15

44 Government of Canada, Budget 2014, Chapter 4.2: Fiscal Outlook. Accessed December 1, 2014. http://www.budget.gc.ca/2014/docs/plan/ch4-2-eng.html

45 "Borrowing and Debt History." Government of Ontario, Ontario Financing Authority. Net Debt and Interest on Debt. Accessed December 1, 2013. http://www.ofina.on.ca/borrowing_debt/borrowhistory.htm

46 Government of Manitoba 2001 Public Accounts, Page 61

47 Government of Manitoba 2014 Budget, Page 20

48 "Heritage Fund – Frequently Asked Questions." Government of Alberta, Treasury and Finance. Accessed December 1, 2014. http://www.finance.alberta.ca/business/ahstf/faqs.html

49 Mertz, Emily. "Alberta government unveils balanced 2014 budget." Global News, March 6, 2014. Accessed December 1, 2014. http://globalnews.ca/news/1192585/alberta-government-unveils-balanced-2014-budget/

50 Canadian Federation of Independent Debt Clock, Accessed February 22, 2015 http://www.cfib-fcei.ca/english/article/6066-debt-clock.html

51 Lammam, Charles and Milagros Palacios. "Your share of Canadian government debt: more than $34,000." Fraser Institute, December 14, 2012. Accessed December 1, 2014. http://www.fraserinstitute.org/publicationdisplay.aspx?id=19098&terms=immigration

Chapter 2: Storm Clouds Raining on Your Wallet

1 "Catalogue 91-520-X" Statistics Canada Tables 10 and 12: Population by age group and sex, low-growth and high-growth forecasts.

2 "Federal Support to Provinces and Territories." Department of Finance, Canada. Accessed October 1, 2014. http://www.fin.gc.ca/fedprov/mtp-eng.asp

3 Rosenberg, Matt. "Thomas Malthus on Population." About.com. Accessed December 1, 2014. http://geography.about.com/od/populationgeography/a/malthus.htm

4 Paul Vieri. "Canada's demographic time bomb." Financial Post, April 2, 2011. Accessed October 1, 2014. http://www.financialpost.com/news/Canada+demographic+time+bomb/4544389/story.html

5 "Canada's crumbling municipal infrastructure." Toronto Star Opinion Editorial, December 16, 2014. Accessed October 1, 2014. http://www.thestar.com/opinion/editorialopinion/2012/11/23/canadas_crumbling_municipal_infrastructure.html

6 Niels Veldhuis and Milagros Palacios. "Unfunded liabilities dwarf public debt and are growing." Opinion editorial published in the Calgary Herald, May 22, 2008. http://www.canada.com/story_print.html?id=d254af34-6191-4989-8d36-54a3b23be2ce

7 Scott Cameron, Helen Lao and Trevor Shaw. "2014 Fiscal Sustainability Report." Office of the Parliamentary Budget Officer, Fall, 2014, Page 4.

8 IBID. Page 2.

9   "Chapter 4.2: Fiscal Outlook." Government of Canada budget, Table 4.2.5. Accessed October 1, 2014. http://www.budget.gc.ca/2014/docs/plan/ch4-2-eng.html

10   "MLI Paper: Canada's Looming Fiscal Squeeze." Macdonald-Laurier News Release, November 3, 2011. Accessed October 1, 2014. http://www.macdonaldlaurier.ca/mli-paper-released-today-canadas-looming-fiscal-squeeze/

11   IBID

12   Christopher Ragan. "Canada's Looming Fiscal Squeeze." Macdonald-Laurier Institute Report, March, 2012, Page 3. http://www.macdonaldlaurier.ca/files/pdf/Canadas-Looming-Fiscal-Squeeze-November-2011.pdf

Chapter 3: The Government Taketh ... and Taketh ... and Taketh

1   Argitis, Theophilos and Greg Quinn. "Canadians with more debt than U.S. spark policymakers' warning." Bloomberg, December 14, 2010. Accessed December 1, 2014.   http://www.bloomberg.com/news/2010-12-14/canadians-with-more-debt-than-u-s-spark-policy-makers-warning.html

2   Bill Curry and Jeremy Thorobin. The Globe and Mail, January 17, 2011. Accessed October 1, 2014. http://www.theglobeandmail.com/news/politics/flaherty-moves-to-put-brakes-on-consumer-debt/article562315/

3   "Archived – Speech by the Honourable Jim Flaherty, Minister of Finance, at a symposium hosted by the Institute of Research on Public Policy." Government of Canada Website, Speech Delivered May 4, 2010. Accessed October 1, 2014. http://www.fin.gc.ca/n10/10-041_1-eng.asp

4   Mark Milke. Tax Me I'm Canadian! Calgary: Thomas and Black Publishers, Page 2.

5   Ontario. Employer Health Tax web page. Accessed October 1, 2014. http://www.fin.gov.on.ca/en/tax/eht/

6   Nick Bergamini. "15th Annual Gas Tax Honesty Day Report." Canadian Taxpayers Federation, May 16, 2013. Accessed October 1, 2014. http://www.taxpayer.com/media/2013-GTHD-Report-CTF.pdf

7   Milagros Palacios and Charles Lammam. "Taxes versus the Necessities of Life: The Canadian Consumer Tax Index." Fraser Institute, April 2013. Accessed October 1,

2014. http://www.fraserinstitute.org/uploadedFiles/fraser-ca/Content/research-news/research/publications/canadian-consumer-tax-index-2013.pdf

Chapter 4: What's the Role of Government?

1   Craig, Colin. "Fiacco loses bet, taxpayers pay for it." Canadian Taxpayers Federation blog post, August 21, 2012. Accessed October 1, 2014. http://www.taxpayer.com/blog/fiacco-loses-bet%2C-taxpayers-pay-for-it

2   "Hero's welcome for Alouettes." CBC News, November 30, 2009. Accessed October 1, 2014. http://www.cbc.ca/mobile/text/story_sports-football.html?/ept/html/story/2009/11/30/alouettes-back-home.html

3   Annable, Kristin. "Alberta City's $280,000 taxpayer-funded Starbucks grounds for controversy." March 8, 2012. Accessed October 1, 2014. http://news.nationalpost.com/2012/03/08/st-albert-starbucks/

4   Boswell, Randy. "Hockey jersey owner wants sweater shown across Canada." Canwest News Service, June 22, 2010. Accessed October 1, 2014. http://www2.canada.com/topics/news/national/story.html?id=3185962

5   Marchand, Francois. "Punk band draws ire of heritage minister." Vancouver Sun, May 19, 2011. Accessed December 1, 2014. http://www2.canada.com/vancouversun/news/story.html?id=406a240c-ee88-43ef-a52d-53e64514a55c

6   Redekop, Bill. "$5-million loan; plant never used." Winnipeg Free Press, December 17, 2012. Accessed December 1, 2014. http://www.winnipegfreepress.com/local/5-million-loan-plant-never-used-183746621.html

7   Goldsmith, Stephen. The Twenty-First Century City. Regnery Publishing. Page 9.

8   IBID, Page 10

9   Canadian Taxpayers Federation website; posted pdf file. Accessed March 15, 2015. http://www.taxpayer.com/media/garbageFOI.pdf

10 "Translink spends $500k on faulty TVs, says CTF." CBC News, June 5, 2012. Accessed December 1, 2014. http://www.cbc.ca/news/canada/british-columbia/translink-spends-500k-on-faulty-tvs-says-ctf-1.1210227

11 Government of Canada, Senate Debate, May 5, 2009. Accessed December 1, 2014. http://www.parl.gc.ca/Content/Sen/Chamber/402/Debates/031db_2009-05-05-e.htm

12 City of Winnipeg Economic Opportunity Commission Final Report, 2007. Page 20.

13 Mallett, Ted. CFIB report - Wage Watch: A Comparison of Public-sector and Private-sector Wages and Benefits. March 2015. Accessed March 23, 2015. http://www.cfib-fcei.ca/cfib-documents/rr3348.pdf

14 Thomas, Gregory. "Pension Gap Astounding in Canada." Canadian Taxpayers Federation news release, August 29, 2012. Accessed December 1, 2014. http://www.taxpayer.com/news-releases/pension-gap-astounding-in-canada

15 Murphy, Jessica. "Fire porn-surfing bureaucrat: Watchdog." Toronto Sun, September 9, 2011. Accessed December 1, 2014. http://www.torontosun.com/2011/09/08/fed-staffer-axed-for-porn-habit-back-on-job

16 Canadian Taxpayers Federation custom purchase of Statistics Canada data. 2013.

Chapter 5: Special Interest Groups

1 YouTube clip of John Stossel news clip, ABC. Accessed December 1, 2014. http://www.youtube.com/watch?v=UPmo2e-bAMQ

2 Maclean's Magazine, December 18, 2008. Accessed 2013. http://www2.macleans.ca/2008/12/18/auto-workers-make-a-lot-of-money%E2%80%94but-not-that-much/

3 Levs, Josh. "Big three auto CEOs flew private jets to ask for taxpayer money." CNN News, Nov. 19, 2008. Accessed Dec. 1, 2014. http://www.cnn.com/2008/US/11/19/autos.ceo.jets/

4 Walkom, Thomas. "Toyota latest winner from Canada's corporate socialism: Walkom." Toronto Star. January 23, 2013. Accessed December 1, 2014. http://www.thestar.com/news/canada/2013/01/23/toyota_latest_winner_from_canadas_corporate_socialism_walkom.html

5 Walkom, Thomas. "Kellogg subsidies another bad deal for Ontario: Walkom." Toronto Star, December 11, 2013. Accessed December 1, 2014. http://www.thestar.com/news/canada/2013/12/11/kellogg_subsidies_another_bad_deal_for_ontario_walkom.html

6   Munsey and Suppes. Ballparks.com. Accessed December 1, 2014. http://www.ball-parks.com/baseball/american/nyybpk.htm

7   Ballparks.com. Accessed December 1, 2014. http://www.ballparks.com/baseball/index.htm

8   Ballparks.com. Accessed December 1, 2014. http://football.ballparks.com/NFL/DallasCowboys/newindex.htm

9   Kives, Bartley. "Millions to aid True North." Winnipeg Free Press, March 2, 2012. Accessed December 1, 2014. http://www.winnipegfreepress.com/local/millions-to-aid-true-north-141154603.html

10 Winnipeg Sun, November 25, 2013. Accessed December 1, 2014. http://www.winnipeg-sun.com/2013/11/25/jets-value-rises-significantly-according-to-forbes-list

11 Curry, Bill. The Globe and Mail, March 6, 2012. Accessed December 1, 2014. http://www.theglobeandmail.com/news/politics/ottawa-notebook/disappointed-flaherty-scoffs-at-ontarios-nhl-ticket-subsidy-gambit/article551376/

12 Brodbeck, Tom. "$52.5 million stadium lie." Winnipeg Sun, May 10, 2010. Accessed December 1, 2014. http://www.winnipegsun.com/news/colum-nists/tom_brodbeck/2010/05/10/13901221.html

13 Coates, Dennis and Brad R. Humphreys. "Do economists reach a conclusion on subsidies for sports franchises, stadiums, and mega-events?" Econ Journal Watch, September 2008, Page 296.

14 "British Columbia Film and Television Tax Credit." Government of British Columbia Tax Bulletin, February 2011.

15 "Canadian Film or Video Production Tax Credit Program." Canada Revenue Agency, Government of Canada. Accessed December 1, 2014. http://www.cra-arc.gc.ca/tx/nnrsdnts/flm/ftc-cip/menu-eng.html

16 Bailey, Ian. "B.C. wants truce with Ontario, Quebec on film tax credits." The Globe and Mail, June 17, 2013. Accessed December 1, 2014. http://www.theglobeandmail.com/news/british-columbia/bc-wants-truce-with-ontario-quebec-on-film-tax-credits/article12626487/

17 IBID

18 Luther, William. "Movie Production Incentives: Blockbuster Support for Lackluster Policy." Tax Foundation, January 2010 Special Report. Accessed December 1, 2014. http://taxfoundation.org/sites/taxfoundation.org/files/docs/sr173.pdf

19 Tannenwald, Robert. "State Film Subsidies: Not Much Bang For Too Many Bucks." Center on Budget and Policy Priorities News Release, December 9, 2010. Accessed December 1, 2014. http://www.cbpp.org/cms/index.cfm?fa=view&id=3326

20 "Artist hopes to float giant banana over Texas." CTV News, January 10, 2007. Accessed December 1, 2014. http://www.ctvnews.ca/artist-hopes-to-float-giant-banana-over-texas-1.223313

21 "Rabbit corpses core of new art exhibit." CBC News, September 10, 1999. Accessed December 1, 2014. http://www.cbc.ca/news/canada/rabbit-corpses-core-of-new-art-exhibit-1.188421

22 Barber, Bruce, Serge Guilbaut and John O'Brian. Voices of Fire: Art, Rage, Power, and the State. University of Toronto Press Incorporated. Preface Page 8.

23 Speirs, Doug. "Banana split divides Melita." Winnipeg Free Press, April 7, 2010. Accessed December 1, 2014. http://www.winnipegfreepress.com/local/banana-split-divides-melita-90071517.html

24 "Breaking News: Crazy Horse Memorial Foundation Announces Major Gift." Crazy Horse Memorial Website. December 12, 2013. Accessed December 1, 2014. http://crazyhorsememorial.org/4750/breaking-news-crazy-horse-memorial-foundation-announces-major-gift-2/

25 Hansen, Darah. "Poodle installation delights, confuses on Main Street." Vancouver Sun, January 9, 2013. Accessed December 1, 2014. http://www.vancouversun.com/travel/Poodle+installation+delights+confuses+Main+Street/7798434/story.html

26 "HFHGV & B.C. Housing Partner on Richmond Project." Habitat for Humanity Website. Accessed December 1, 2014. http://www.habitatgv.ca/project.aspx?asset=190

27 Craig, Colin. "Friendly Reports From Funding Recipients." Canadian Taxpayers Federation Website. Accessed December 1, 2014. http://www.taxpayer.com/blog/friendly-reports-from-funding-recipients

28 Kirby, Jason, Mika Rekai, Nick Taylor-Vaisey, Rosemary Westwood, and Tamsin McMahon. Maclean's Magazine, January 7, 2013. Accessed December 1, 2014. http://www.macleans.ca/news/canada/99-stupid-things-the-government-did-with-your-money-part-i/

29 "Disclosure of Grants and Contribution Awards Over 25,000." Government of Canada Website. Accessed December 1, 2014. http://www.pch.gc.ca/eng/1360356760939/1360357040397

30 "Award Recipients." Government of Canada Website. Accessed December 1, 2014. http://www.sshrc-crsh.gc.ca/results-resultats/recipients-recipiendaires/index-eng.aspx

Chapter 6: Government Employee Unions

1 "Firefighters drop complaint about city workers who fought fire." CBC News, June 6, 2007. Accessed December 1, 2014. http://www.cbc.ca/news/canada/saskatchewan/firefighters-drop-complaint-about-city-workers-who-fought-fire-1.638800

2 YouTube clip posted. Accessed December 1, 2014. http://www.youtube.com/watch?v=-bJZKuxGMZc

3 "In Brief." St. Petersburg Times Online, March 16, 2003. Accessed December 1, 2014. http://www.sptimes.com/2003/03/16/news_pf/Worldandnation/It_s_so_cold_in_Canad.shtml

4 Macdonald, Nancy. "The $100,000 club: Who's really making big money these days." Maclean's Magazine, April 15, 2013. Accessed December 1, 2014. http://www2.macleans.ca/2013/04/15/the-new-upper-class/

5 Table 2 Union Membership, 2010." Statistics Canada, Labour Force Survey. Online Catalogue 75-001-X.

6 Manitoba Nurses Union YouTube Ad. http://www.youtube.com/watch?v=L8TTGdN_sJk

7 "Constitution of the New Democratic Party of Canada. Effective April 2013." NDP Website. Accessed December 1, 2014. http://xfer.ndp.ca/2013/constitution/2013_CONSTITUTION_E.pdf

8 Lambert, Steve. "Unions fall short on delegates for Manitoba NDP leadership: sources" Global News, February 27, 2015. Accessed March 1, 2015. http://globalnews.ca/news/1854509/unions-fall-short-on-delegates-for-manitoba-ndp-leadership-sources/

9   Elections Saskatchewan, 2011-12 official New Democratic Party return. Accessed December 1, 2014. http://www.elections.sk.ca/resources/new-democratice-party-sk-section-fiscal-period-return.pdf

10 Elections Saskatchewan, 2011-12 official Saskatchewan Party return. Accessed December 1, 2014. http://www.elections.sk.ca/resources/sask-party-fiscal-period-return.pdf

11 McElroy, Justin. "Interactive chart: Who donated to the NDP and Liberals last election?" Global News, August 20, 2013. Accessed December 1, 2014. http://globalnews.ca/news/790499/who-donated-to-the-ndp-and-liberals-last-election-find-out-with-our-interactive-charts/

12 Den Tandt, Michael. "Funding system making politics meaner and dumber as cash-starved parties beg for money." National Post, January 5, 2014. Accessed December 1, 2014. http://fullcomment.nationalpost.com/2014/01/05/michael-den-tandt-funding-system-making-politics-meaner-and-dumber-as-cash-starved-parties-beg-for-money/

13 Smith, Joanna. "NDP returned $344,468 in advertising income after Conservatives complained to Elections Canada." Toronto Star, August 26, 2012. Accessed December 1, 2014. http://www.thestar.com/news/canada/2012/08/26/ndp_returned_344468_in_advertising_income_after_conservatives_complained_to_elections_canada.html

14 Elections Ontario. "Annual Report 2011-12: Report by the Chief Electoral Officer of Ontario."

15 "Letter on the Resolution of Federation of Federal Employees Against Strikes in Federal Service." The American, Presidency Project. Accessed December 1, 2014. http://www.presidency.ucsb.edu/ws/?pid=15445

16 Labour Agreement British Columbia Public School Employers' Association, Board of School Trustees of School District No. 61 (Greater Victoria) and British Columbia Teachers' Federation (BCTF) and Greater Victoria Teachers' Association. British Columbia Public School Employers' Association Website. Accessed December 1, 2014. http://www.bcpsea.bc.ca/documents/sd-collective-agreements/61-LB-2006-2011 FINAL District Draft March 7 2011.pdf

17 "Grading the Teachers: Little Connection Between Teacher Pay and Performance." StateImpact report, July 17, 2013. Accessed December 1, 2014. http://stateimpact.npr.org/ohio/2013/06/17/grading-the-

teachers-analysis-shows-little-connection-between-pay-and-value-added-performance/

18 "Grading the Teachers: Using Value-Added Scores to Evaluate Ohio Teachers." StateImpact backgrounder. Accessed December 1, 2014. http://stateimpact.npr.org/ohio/tag/value-added/

19 Statistics Canada. 2001 Census. Catalogue no. 97F0019XCB2001003

20 Statistics Canada. National Household Survey: Data tables. Catalogue no. 99-014-X2011042.

21 Statistics Canada. Cansim table 280-0026

22 Rushowy, Kristin. "Teacher sick days rising as end of school year nears." Toronto Star, June 5, 2013. Accessed December 1, 2014. http://www.thestar.com/your-toronto/education/2013/06/05/surge_seen_in_teachers_taking_sick_days_as_end_of_school_year_nears.html

23 Statistics Canada. Custom data purchase by the Canadian Taxpayers Federation. News release, August 29, 2013. Accessed December 1, 2014. http://www.taxpayer.com/news-releases/labour-day-reality-check--a-look-at-government-employee-sick-time

24 Eisenhower, Dwight. "Farewell radio and television address to the American people, January 17th, 1961." Dwight D. Eisenhower Presidential Library, Museum and Boyhood Home (Website). Accessed December 1, 2014. http://www.eisenhower.archives.gov/all_about_ike/speeches/farewell_address.pdf

25 Bloomberg, Michael. Speech to the Economic Club of New York, December 18, 2013. Accessed December 1, 2014. http://www.econclubny.com/events/Transcript_Michael_Bloomberg_December_2013.pdf

26 O'Toole, Megan. "Municipalities rally behind bill to tax Ontario's 'broken arbitration system." National Post, September 27, 2012. Accessed December 1, 2014. http://news.nationalpost.com/2012/09/27/municipalities-rally-behind-bill-to-fix-ontarios-broken-arbitration-system/

27 State of Indiana. Accessed December 1, 2014. http://www.in.gov/legislative/bills/2011/SB/SB0001.1.html

28 "Study: Right-to-Work Laws Lead to More People, More Jobs and Higher Pay." Michigan Capital Confidential, August 28, 2013. Accessed December 1, 2014. https://www.mackinac.org/19069

Chapter 7: The Bureaucracy

1   Weston, Greg. "March madness spendfest for federal bureaucrats: Weston." Toronto Sun, March 14, 2010. Accessed December 1, 2014. http://www.torontosun.com/news/columnists/greg_weston/2010/03/14/13225201.html

2   Ibbitson, John. Ottawa gets a pre-budget warning cut the spending sprees. The Globe and Mail, February 2, 2012. Accessed December 1, 2014. http://www.theglobeandmail.com/news/politics/ottawa-gets-a-pre-budget-warning-cut-the-spending-sprees/article543275/

3   Craig, Colin. "Nothing says poverty like a spa retreat." Canadian Taxpayers Federation news release, February 14, 2012. Accessed December 1, 2014. http://www.taxpayer.com/news-releases/sk–nothing-says-poverty-like-a-spa-retreat

4   IBID, Page 205

5   IBID, Page 210

6   Senate of Canada Hansard. March 2, 2008. Accessed December 1, 2014. http://www.parl.gc.ca/Content/SEN/Committee/392/huma/03evb-e.htm?Language=E&Parl=39&Ses=2&comm_id=77

7   "Museum's bold idea worthy." Winnipeg Free Press, December 30, 2011. Accessed December 1, 2014. http://www.winnipegfreepress.com/opinion/editorials/museums-bold-idea-worthy-136420543.html?device=mobile

8   Fildebrandt, Derek. "Taxpayer Supply and Government Demand." Canadian Taxpayers Federation report, May 2010. http://www.taxpayer.com/media/GTHC_May2010.pdf

9   Kives, Bartley. "City plans to sell West St. Paul riverfront lot." Winnipeg Free Press, July 14, 2011. Accessed December 1, 2014. http://www.winnipegfreepress.com/local/city-plans-to-sell-west-st-paul-riverfront-lot-125550543.html

10   Government of Canada 2014 budget. Accessed December 1, 2014. http://www.budget.gc.ca/2014/docs/plan/ch4-2-eng.html

11   Government of Quebec 2014 budget. Accessed December 1, 2014. http://www.fin.gc.ca/fedprov/mtp-eng.asp#Quebec

12   Manitoba Hydro. Electricity bill comparison as of May 1, 2013. https://www.hydro.mb.ca/regulatory_affairs/energy_rates/electricity/utility_rate_comp.shtml

13 "Shale Gas: Key Facts." Natural Resources Canada. Accessed December 1, 2014. http://www.nrcan.gc.ca/energy/natural-gas/5687

14 Parti Quebecois Website. http://pq.org/video/la-souverainete-cest-payant/

15 Rosano, Michael. "13+ things you didn't know about energy." Canadian Geographic, June 2013. http://www.canadiangeographic.ca/magazine/jun13/energy_in_canada4.asp

16 Reason TV YouTube Channel. Accessed December 1, 2014. http://www.youtube.com/watch?v=f8qFvo2qJOU

17 CNBC News Clip posted on City of Sandy Springs YouTube channel. http://www.youtube.com/watch?v=O1-JFfp0j7M

18 Barrett, Katherine and Richard Greene. "Gainsharing Falls Victim to Tight Times." Governing, August, 2012. Accessed December 1, 2014. http://www.governing.com/columns/smart-mgmt/col-gainsharing-falls-victim-to-tight-times.html

19 Craig, Colin. "Hospital cafeterias losing millions." Canadian Taxpayers Federation news release, August 13, 2013. Accessed December 1, 2014. http://www.taxpayer.com/news-releases/mb--hospital-cafeterias-losing-millions

20 Padova, Allison. "Public-Private Partnerships: Why, Where, When and How." Government of Canada, Industry, Infrastructure and Resources Division, May 12, 2010. Accessed December 1, 2014. http://www.parl.gc.ca/Content/LOP/ResearchPublications/2010-18-e.htm#txt15

21 "Northeast Anthony Henday Drive." Government of Alberta, Ministry of Transportation. Accessed December 1, 2014. http://www.transportation.alberta.ca/3787.htm

22 Parliament of Canada, Standing Committee on Transport, Infrastructure and Communities, April 30, 2013. Online Hansard accessed on December 1, 2014. http://www.parl.gc.ca/HousePublications/Publication.aspx?DocId=6121810&Language=E&Mode=1&Parl=41&Ses=1

23 IBID

24 IBID

25 Bateman, Jordan. "Could a government worker actually grow the economy." Canadian Taxpayers Federation, November 28, 2013. Accessed December 1, 2014. http://www.taxpayer.com/commentaries/bc--could-a-government-worker-actually-grow-the-economy-

26   Burd, Steven A. "How Safeway is cutting health-care costs." Wall Street Journal, June 12, 2009. Accessed December 1, 2014. http://www.wsj.com/articles/SB124476804026308603

Chapter 8: The Politicians

1   Milke, Mark. "Canada's auto bailout: still waiting for payback." Financial Post, May 31, 2013. Accessed December 1, 2014. http://opinion.financialpost.com/2013/05/31/canadas-auto-bailout-still-waiting-for-payback/

2   Brennan, Richard J. "Most oppose taxpayer auto bailout." Toronto Star, April 9, 2009. Accessed December 1, 2014. http://www.angusreidglobal.com/polls/35733/canadians_disagree_with_help_for_auto_makers/

3   Fildebrandt, Derek. "CTF Report on MP Pensions." Canadian Taxpayers Federation report, January, 2012, Page 8. Accessed December 1, 2014. http://www.taxpayer.com/media/CTFMP-PensionReport-WEB.pdf

4   Murphy, Jessica. Parliamentary Bureau, Simcoe Reformer, January 20, 2012. Accessed December 1, 2014. http://www.simcoereformer.ca/2012/01/20/pension-double-dip-may-be-possible-for-some-mps-2

5   Craig, Colin. "Chief Redman needs to pack it in." February 11, 2013 column. Accessed March 23, 2015. http://www.taxpayer.com/commentaries/chief-redman-needs-to-pack-it-in

6   "NDP's expense challenge to Libs is small step to transparency." Canwest News editorial, August 18, 2013. http://www.canada.com/theprovince/news/story.html?id=4f65b0b2-bc47-4282-b352-c3723966c7d6

7   Gerson, Jen. "Alison Redford repays $45,000 spent to fly to South Africa but MLA quits in protest. National Post, March 12, 2014. http://news.nationalpost.com/2014/03/12/alison-redford-says-she-will-pay-back-45000-spent-to-fly-to-south-africa/

8   "Former MLA Goucher biggest spender." CBC News, February 10, 2010. Accessed December 1, 2014. http://www.cbc.ca/news/canada/nova-scotia/former-mla-goucher-biggest-spender-1.901037

9   Larson, Jackie L. "No-meet" committee pay could be vote factor." Edmonton Sun, April 15, 2012. Accessed December 1, 2014. http://www.edmontonsun.com/2012/04/15/no-meet-committee-pay-could-be-vote-factor

10   Ibbitson, John. "Silence speaks volumes in thwarted quest to audit Parliament's expenses." The Globe and Mail, April 26, 2010. Accessed December 1, 2014. http://www.theglobeandmail.com/news/politics/silence-speaks-volumes-in-thwarted-quest-to-audit-parliaments-expenses/article4316364/

11   Press, Jordan. "Senator Mike Duffy vowed to bring down high-ranking Tories if expense scandal led to charges: new book." National Post, March 2, 2014. Accessed December 1, 2014. http://news.nationalpost.com/2014/03/02/mike-duffy-vowed-to-bring-down-high-ranking-tories-if-expense-scandal-led-to-charges/

12   Payton, Laura. "Mac Harb fraud, breach of trust case put off to April 22." CBC News, March 18, 2014. Accessed December 1, 2014. http://www.cbc.ca/news/politics/mac-harb-fraud-breach-of-trust-case-put-off-to-april-22-1.2576986

13   Sims, Jane. "London Mayor Joe Fontana found guilty on all charges." London Free Press, June 13, 2014. Accessed December 1, 2014. http://www.lfpress.com/2014/06/12/judgment-day-for-joe

14   Curry, Bill. "Conservatives cut 100 jobs at Atlantic development agency." The Globe and Mail, October 19, 2011. Accessed December 1, 2014. http://www.theglobeandmail.com/news/politics/ottawa-notebook/conservatives-cut-100-jobs-at-atlantic-development-agency/article618427/

15   Canadian Press. "Auditor-General report puts total cost of Liberal gas plant cancellations as high as $1.1-billion." National Post, October 8, 2013. Accessed December 1, 2014. http://news.nationalpost.com/2013/10/08/auditor-general-report-puts-cost-of-liberal-gas-plant-cancellations-as-high-as-1-1-billion/

16   "The gun registry debate." CBC News, October 9, 2009. Accessed December 1, 2014. http://www.cbc.ca/news/canada/timeline-the-gun-registry-debate-1.786548

17   Stix, Madeleine. "Teen to government: change your typeface, save millions." CNN News, March 29, 2014. Accessed December 1, 2014. http://www.cnn.com/2014/03/27/living/student-money-saving-typeface-garamond-schools/index.html?iref=allsearch

18   Wingrove, Josh. "Harper's office treats MPs like trained seals': Ex-tory MP." The Globe and Mail, June 6, 2013. Accessed December 1, 2014. http://www.

theglobeandmail.com/news/politics/tories-have-lost-their-way-mp-writes-after-quitting-conservative-caucus/article12377182/

19 Holman, Sean. "Whipped: The Secret World of Party Discipline." Public Eye Mediaworks Production available at CPAC.ca. Accessed December 1, 2014. http://www.cpac.ca/en/digital-archives/?search=whipped

20 "Indemnities, Salaries and Allowances." Parliament of Canada website. Accessed December 1, 2014. http://www.parl.gc.ca/parlinfo/lists/Salaries.aspx?Menu=HOC-Politic&Section=03d93c58-f843-49b3-9653-84275c23f3fb

21 "B.C. moves to 12 per cent HST." CBC News, July 23, 2009. Accessed December 1, 2014. http://www.cbc.ca/news/canada/british-columbia/b-c-moves-to-12-per-cent-hst-1.850374

22 "British Columbia recall and initiative referendum, 1991." Wikipedia. Accessed December 1, 2014. http://en.wikipedia.org/wiki/British_Columbia_recall_and_initiative_referendum,_1991

23 Elections B.C. website. Accessed December 1, 2014. http://www.elections.bc.ca/index.php/referenda-recall-initiative/initiative/#F

24 Elections B.C. website. Accessed December 1, 2014. http://www.elections.bc.ca/docs/init/Summary-Initiatives-1995-2013.pdf

25 Marr, Anthony. "Making BC's Referendum Act Workable." Accessed December 1, 2014. http://bcinitiative.albernirealty.com/bc-recall-and-initiative-act

26 Elections B.C. website. Accessed December 1, 2014. http://www.elections.bc.ca/index.php/referenda-recall-initiative/initiative/

27 Elections B.C. website. Accessed December 1, 2014. http://www.elections.bc.ca/docs/rcl/Summary-of-Recall-Petitions.pdf

28 Cauchon, Dennis. "Voters just say 'no' to spending initiatives." USA Today, June 25, 2010. Accessed December 1, 2014. http://usatoday30.usatoday.com/news/nation/2010-06-24-just-say-no_N.htm

29 "The Bond Buyer's 2010 in Statistics." BondBuyer.com. Accessed December 1, 2014. http://www.bondbuyer.com/pdfs/2010yrend.pdf

30 Coyne, Andrew. "Time for a truth in politics act." Maclean's Magazine, April 7, 2011. Accessed December 1, 2014. http://www.macleans.ca/general/time-for-a-truth-in-politics-act/

31 "Government Advertising Review Guidelines." October, 2012. Office of the Auditor General of Ontario. Accessed December 1, 2014. http://www.auditor.on.ca/adreview/guidelines_oct2012.pdf

32 "Chapter 5: Review of Government Advertising." 2012 Annual Report of the Office of the Auditor General of Ontario. Page 411.

33 Ditchburn, Jennifer. "Five-star hotel not good enough, Bev Oda opts for posh hotel favoured by royalty." Canadian Press article on Toronto Star, April 23, 2010. Accessed December 1, 2014. http://www.thestar.com/news/canada/2012/04/23/fivestar_hotel_not_good_enough_bev_oda_opts_for_posh_hotel_favoured_by_royalty.html

34 Welch, Mary Agnes, John Dickins and Stanley Tromp. "Canada's access to information act fails to meet global standards, report finds." Canadian Association of Journalists news release, October 1, 2008. Accessed December 1, 2014. http://www.caj.ca/?p=1007

35 "MPs to debate pulling pensions from convicted colleagues in Commons and Senate." Canadian Press article on Victoria Times Colonist website, December 9, 2014. Accessed December 1, 2014. http://www.timescolonist.com/opinion/blogs/mps-to-debate-pulling-pensions-from-convicted-colleagues-in-commons-and-senate-1.751742

Chapter 9: The Public

1 "Voter Turnout at Federal Elections and Referendums." Elections Canada website. http://www.elections.ca/content.aspx?dir=turn&document=index&lang=e&section=ele

2 "Statistics from the records." Elections Ontario website – wemakevotingeasy.ca. http://www.wemakevotingeasy.ca/media/EO_Site/Statistics from the Record.pdf

3 "Ontario election 2014 saw the highest number of declined ballots since 1975." Canadian Press article via National Post, June 19, 2014. Accessed December 1, 2014. http://news.nationalpost.com/2014/06/19/ontario-election-2014-saw-the-highest-number-of-declined-ballots-since-1975/

4   Elections B.C. 2013 General Election Report. Accessed December 1, 2014. http://www.elections.bc.ca/docs/rpt/2013-General-Election-Report.pdf

5   "Voter turnout in recent Alberta provincial elections." Elections Alberta website. Accessed December 1, 2014. http://www.elections.ab.ca/Public Website/927.htm

6   "Voter turnout at federal elections and referendums." Elections Canada website. Accessed December 1, 2014. http://www.elections.ca/content.aspx?dir=turn&document=index&lang=e&section=ele

7   Robinson, Walter. "Are you upset mail the PM a puck." Canadian Taxpayers Federation news release, January 19, 2000. Accessed December 1, 2014. https://www.taxpayer.com/news-releases/are-you-upset--mail-the-pm-a-hockey-puck

8   "Liberals, NDP, Bloc sign deal on proposed coalition." CBC News, December 1, 2008. Accessed December 1, 2014. http://www.cbc.ca/news/canada/liberals-ndp-bloc-sign-deal-on-proposed-coalition-1.700119

9   "Harper pardons farmers arrested under old wheat board law." CBC News, August 1, 2012. Accessed December 1, 2014. http://www.cbc.ca/news/politics/harper-pardons-farmers-arrested-under-old-wheat-board-law-1.1146436

10   "Toronto Chinatown grocer found not guilty." CBC News, October 29, 2010. Accessed December 1, 2014. http://www.cbc.ca/news/canada/toronto/toronto-chinatown-grocer-found-not-guilty-1.931466

Chapter 10: Conclusion

1   Craig, Colin. "Band chief and council pay higher than prime minister." Canadian Taxpayers Federation news release, December 21, 2009. Accessed December 1, 2014. https://www.taxpayer.com/news-releases/mb--band-chief-and-council-pay-higher-than-prime-minister

2   "Alberta reserve chief makes more than Stelmach." Canadian Taxpayers Federation news release, April 20, 2010. Accessed December 1, 2014. https://www.taxpayer.com/news-releases/fed--alberta-reserve-chief-makes-more-than-stelmach

ABOUT THE AUTHOR

Colin Craig served as a taxpayers' watchdog for the Canadian Taxpayers Federation from 2008 to 2015. While working for the CTF, his advocacy efforts led to public policy reform at the municipal, provincial and federal levels, including the federal government's *First Nations Financial Transparency Act*.

Colin's work has been published in newspapers across Canada, most notably by the National Post, Sun newspapers nation-wide, the Calgary Herald, Winnipeg Free Press, Regina Leader Post and Saskatoon Star Phoenix.

Colin has a degree in economics and an MBA from the University of Manitoba. He has policy experience from inside government, having previously served as a policy advisor to a former Ontario minister of finance, a research assistant in the Manitoba government and as a project director for a commission focused on finding efficiencies at the City of Winnipeg. Colin currently works for the Manning Centre in Calgary.

In his spare time he enjoys running, playing baseball, travelling with his wife and two dogs, and cheering for the Los Angeles Dodgers (this could be their year).

Colin can be contacted through his website (www.ColinCraig.net) and on Twitter (@colincraig1).

Note: If you would like to help a young Canadian receive a copy of this book, the author is working with various youth organizations and donors to provide copies at cost. Please contact Colin through his website for details.

Index:

Ability to Pay Act, 125-126

Ackerman, Gary, 79

Anthony Henday Drive, 160

Art subsidies, 89-94

Atlantic Canada Opportunities Agency, 77-78, 179

Auto bailout, 78-80, 170-171, 184-185

Balanced budget legislation, 196-197

Basic personal amount, 37-38

Bateman, Jordan, 57, 163-164

Binnion, Michael, 152-153

Bloomberg, Michael, 124-125

Brazeau, Patrick, 176

Breakenridge, Rob, 20

Brodbeck, Tom, 85-86

Broken Window Fallacy, 72-73

C.D. Howe Institute, 18, 216

Campbell, Gordon, 189, 191-192, 193

Canada Council for the Arts, 90

Canada Post, 134-135

Canadian Centre for Policy Alternatives, 94

Canadian Federation of Independent Business, 18, 22, 63, 211

Canadian Football League, 85-86

Canadian Institute for Health Information, 11-14

Canadian Museum for Human Rights, 106, 143

Canadian Taxpayers Federation
- First Nations Financial Transparency Act, 219-222
- Corporate welfare, 75-78
- Email updates, 214, 221
- Formation, 40-41
- No meet committee, 175
- Pension research, 64
- Road repair research 146-147
- Skytrain, 57
- Teddy Awards, 55-56, 90
- Whistleblowers, 60-61
Canadian Union of Public Employees, 99-100
Cato Institute, 81-82
Centre on Budget and Policy Priorities, 89
Chrysler, 78-79, 170
Churchill Northern Studies Centre, 57-58
City of Detroit, 104-105
City of Edmonton, 6, 160
City of Winnipeg, 5, 53, 59, 62, 134, 145-146, 148, 163, 213-214
- public private partnership 160
Clement, Tony, 132
Coates, Dennis, 86
Confederation Bridge, 160
Conservative Party of Canada, 109, 183, 213, 221
Contracting out, 99, 137, 156-157
Core government, 44-49, 155
Corporate Welfare, 73-89, 97
Cost Overruns, 106, 142-145, 160
Coyne, Andrew, 197-199
Crazy Horse, 93
de Jong, Mike, 88
Debt (Government), 13, 21-22, 24-25
Dependency Ratio, 9, 24-25

Dube, Todd, 199-200
Duffy, Mike, 176
Equalization 26, 149-153, 156
Esmail, Nadeem, 14
Expense disclosure, 174, 197
Federation of Canadian Municipalities, 16-17
Fiacco, Pat, 42-43
Film subsidies, 87-89
Flaherty, Jim, 35, 39
Floating banana, 90
Fontana, Joe, 176
Forrest, Alex, 104
Fraser Institute, 13-14, 22, 39, 166, 204, 211, 216
Gainsharing, 158-159
General Motors, 78-79, 102
Glover, Shelly, 172-173
Goldsmith, Stephen, 49-54, 136-138
Goucher, Len, 175
Government of Alberta, 21, 22, 38, 159, 160, 175, 196, 201
Government of Manitoba, 19, 21, 22, 26, 36, 149, 156, 165, 196
Government of Ontario, 21, 22, 26, 36, 38, 78, 80-81, 83, 88, 149, 165, 170, 180, 199
Government of Saskatchewan, 22, 25, 127, 133-134, 142, 149, 156, 165
Government employee pay, 60-63, 118-119, 163-164
Gratzer, David, 166-168, 169
Harb, Mac, 176
Harper, Stephen, 21, 37, 168, 173, 179
Harris, Mike, 97
Hazel, Jimmy, 5, 100
Hennig, Scott, 175
Holle, Peter, 48
Holman, Sean, 183-184
Holtmann, Felix, 90-91

Hudak, Tim, 110, 129
Humphreys, Brad, 86
Infrastructure deficit, 15-17, 24, 28, 141
Initiative, 191-193
Isnana, Stella, 173
Kaminski, Vickie, 3-4
Keating, Raymond, 81-82
Kellogg, 80-81
Lavigne, Raymond, 202
Liberal Party of Canada, 109, 181, 213, 221
MacDonald-Laurier Institute, 30-31, 216
Mackay, Dennis, 184
Mackinac Centre for Public Policy, 128
Malthus, Thomas, 26-27, 224
Managed Competition, 54, 156
Manitoba Hydro, 59, 150-151
Manning Centre, 211
Manning Foundation, 216
Manning, Preston, 173
March madness, 130-133
McGuinty, Dalton, 21, 180, 189
Medical Savings Accounts, 165-167
Melita Banana, 92-93
Merit Canada, 161-162
Milke, Mark, 36, 81-83, 96
Monstrance, 90
Montreal Alouettes, 42-43
Moore, James, 145
Morrison, Lee, 173
Morrison, Shannon, 40-41
Mosaic Stadium, 86
Murchandani, Suvir, 181-182
National Gallery of Canada, 91

National Hockey League, 82-85, 212

Natural gas (Quebec), 151-153

New Democratic Party, 21, 108-111, 127, 177-178, 184, 196, 202, 209, 213

Oakey, Terrance, 161-162

Oldridge, Cliff, 73-76

Ontario English Catholic Teachers Association, 100, 110

Parliamentary Budget Officer, 9, 28-29

Peel District School Board, 121

Peguis First Nation, 219-220

Pensions

- Canada Pension Plan, viii, 9

- Canadian Museum for Human Rights, 106

- Government employee Plans, 17-20, 119-121, 124-125, 127

- Parliamentary pensions, 172-173, 202

- Saskatchewan reform, 25, 61, 62, 63, 64-65, 127

Phyllis Sutherland, 219, 222

Political party discipline, 182-185

Belgian Poop Machine, 89-90

Prairie Valley School Division, 133-134

Property taxes, 38-39, 59-60

Public Private Partnerships, 160

Question period, 185-186, 200-201

Ragan, Christopher, 30-31

Rathgeber, Brent, 183

Recall, 193-194

Redford, Alison, 174, 189, 201

Referendums, 97, 191, 193, 194-195, 196

Report cards for politicians, 199-200

Revenue stifling, 147-153

Right to Work Legislation, 127-128

Roosevelt, Franklin, 111-112

Saez, Cesar, 90

Sandy Springs, Georgia, 156-158

Saskatchewan Roughriders, 42-43

Schmidt, Werner, 173

Selinger, Greg, 109, 189

Servus Credit Union Place, 43

Sick leave, 67, 121-123

Simpson, Michelle, 174

Sports subsidies, 81-86, 212-213

Stossel, John, 72-73

Tax Foundation, 88-89

Taxpayer protection acts, 195-196

Teachers contracts, 112-116

Thatcher, Margaret, 204

Tim Hortons, 3-4, 62, 159

Translink, 57

Truth in Politics Act, 197-198

Tufts, Bill, 20, 120-121

U2, 92

Unions

- Government employee pay, 60-63, 118-119, 163-164

- Political donations, 109-111, 128-129

- Labour negotiations, 101-118, 125-126

- Labour-Electoral Complex, 123-125

- Teacher pay contract, 112-116

- Territorial rights, 123

User fees, 169

Vander Zalm, Bill, 192

Voice of Fire, 90-91

Voter turnout, 198, 205

Walkom, Thomas, 80-81

Wall, Brad, 173, 208

Wallin, Pamela, 176

Western Economic Diversification, 75-78

Williamson, John, 202

Wilson, Jim, 125-126
Winnipeg Jets, 82-83, 85
Yellow Pages Test, 49-54
Zombie Spending, 141-142

www.ingramcontent.com/pod-product-compliance
Lightning Source LLC
Chambersburg PA
CBHW050438290526
45786CB00006B/2066